P9-CDX-909

THIS GIRL RAN

TALES OF A PARTY GIRL
TURNED TRIATHLETE

HELEN CROYDON

summersdale

THIS GIRL RAN

Copyright © Helen Croydon, 2018

All rights reserved.

No part of this book may be reproduced by any means, nor transmitted, nor translated into a machine language, without the written permission of the publishers.

Helen Croydon has asserted her right to be identified as the author of this work in accordance with sections 77 and 78 of the Copyright, Designs and Patents Act 1988.

Condition of Sale
This book is sold subject to the condition that it shall not, by way of trade or otherwise, be lent, resold, hired out or otherwise circulated in any form of binding or cover other than that in which it is published and without a similar condition including this condition being imposed on the subsequent purchaser.

An Hachette UK Company
www.hachette.co.uk

Summersdale Publishers Ltd
Part of Octopus Publishing Group Limited
Carmelite House
50 Victoria Embankment
LONDON
EC4Y 0DZ
UK

www.summersdale.com

Printed and bound by CPI Group (UK) Ltd, Croydon, CR0 4YY

ISBN: 978-1-78685-217-5

Substantial discounts on bulk quantities of Summersdale books are available to corporations, professional associations and other organisations. For details contact general enquiries: telephone: +44 (0) 1243 771107 or email: enquiries@summersdale.com.

To everyone I've ever swum, cycled or run with

CONTENTS

SEPTEMBER 2013

I opened my eyes and found the room was still dark. *It must be early*, I thought. I rolled over, trying not to disturb my boyfriend sleeping beside me, and reached for my phone to see the time. Only 5 a.m. I groaned inwardly – I'd gone to bed less than four hours ago, and I'd been up at least three times. First I was thirsty, then I needed the loo, then I was hot – my body a little furnace of burning ethanol. All the symptoms of alcohol-disturbed, restless, unsatisfying sleep.

Ugh. Without moving, I could already tell this would be a groggy day. The self-chastising set in. *Why did I have to drink so much for no reason whatsoever?* I tried to turn off the chatter, willing myself to sleep, but my mind was racing in that all-too-familiar way it does when you've drunk your body weight in cheap white wine – oh yeah, and the cocktails afterwards.

I looked over at my sleeping boyfriend, whose gentle half-snores were emitting eau d'ethanol. That might not sound very nice but it's OK – I probably smelled exactly the same.

I lay there, recalling the previous evening. We'd been to a dinner party. His friends. Well, acquaintances really. Interesting enough people, with interesting jobs. Impressive house in west London. It wasn't a particularly special occasion. It was what I would describe as 'social maintenance' – the sort of occasion where someone finally gets around to inviting those periphery friends over before you fall completely out of touch.

Nevertheless it still turned into a lively affair. After dinner came the Calvadoses, the music got loud, the conversations became more opinionated. It was fun – most nights involving Calvados and new people are fun – but it wasn't spectacular. It wasn't even unusual. I had, this time, managed to steer my boyfriend into leaving just after midnight, which was not usually easy to do.

Lying in bed, I tried to count how many drinks I'd had. It was always the last drinks I regretted most. The ones that you drink way beyond the point of merriment simply because you want to avoid being thought of as boring if you switch to water. They are always the ones I blame for making me feel so awful. My only consolation was how much worse it would have been if we hadn't left when we did. Two sleepless hours later, my boyfriend sprung up – he never seemed to suffer hangovers like me – and began to cook breakfast. His house filled with unhealthily moreish smells.

I got up and opened the curtains to a bright, warm August day. It was the last summer bank holiday of the year. We had no plans.

'I thought we could go for a nice lunch somewhere,' he said cheerfully as he served up a huge breakfast that I didn't really have an appetite for. It didn't feel so long ago that we were feasting on an extravagant dinner.

I forced a half-smile, wondering how to say it. 'I need to head back. I have work to do and things to sort for tomorrow,' I replied awkwardly, guiltily.

I didn't have work to do. I hardly had any work on, which was an altogether separate, but not insignificant, worry. As a freelance journalist, I often fluctuated between busy spells and dry patches. I'd been in one of the latter for months. I couldn't articulate the real reason I didn't want to spend the third day of the long weekend with him. Not even to myself. I just needed to be at home, in my own space, to tidy my flat, do admin, stop eating and drinking all day, and go to the gym.

I rarely dared to confront the thought but it was certainly there bubbling away. The thought that this relationship wasn't making me happy. I wasn't *un*happy, but whenever we were together I couldn't help feeling that we were just spending time for the sake of spending time.

He looked disappointed. Said we could do a lovely walk, one I hadn't done before, said we'd both been invited to someone's BBQ later and they'd feel let down if I didn't go. He obviously knew me well enough to know that I usually respond to guilt, but this time I was adamant. I would head home as soon as the coffee kicked in.

I would have loved a walk. In fact, I wanted nothing more than to be out in that sunshine, but I knew that if we did it together there would be pub and pints involved and, had I been honest with myself, I needed a break from our conversations. It felt like we talked about the same things over and over. I was bored.

Perhaps I sound unappreciative. Here was a wonderful man in my life who loved me. We had been together for more than a year and he was clear he was ready for more. Lots of women my age, 36, would put 'committed, loving man' at the top of their wish list – or so society leads us to believe.

Both of us were freelance, working in the media, so we had far more time, freedom and flexibility to spend time together than many couples. Neither of us came with baggage – no children or recently failed relationships. We had all the ingredients for an idyllic relationship. He loved cooking and good wine; we went away at weekends, staying with friends dotted in faraway places or exploring a new city. When in London we mixed our wide circle of friends. We saw each other at weekends and once in the week. But everything we did together involved drinking – dinners, cocktail bars, media parties. During the first few months it was great fun. We dated, drank lots, stayed up late talking and didn't do any work the next day. But it wasn't sustainable – not if you want to see other friends as well, hold down a career, maintain your health, keep your skin nice and still fit into skinny jeans anyway.

So, over the last few months, I had tried to rein in our nights out. But I had found that we didn't have anything else to do. What do couples do together if they're not cracking open a bottle of wine? Watch TV? Come to think of it, what did I do with anyone that didn't involve carousing?

These were the reasons why I wanted to go home that morning. But when I got home to an empty flat, after an hour's Tube journey to the other side of London, I felt restless. The last of the summer sun was blazing and I wanted to be outside enjoying it. Maybe I should have stayed with him, I thought ditheringly. I was always torn when it came to how much time I allocated to my relationship – ever conflicted between partying and socialising, because that's what we were and it was fun, and retreating from him to keep my life functioning.

I texted a friend and asked if she wanted to meet for a late lunch. I was thinking avocado toast, fruit smoothie, detox tea – al fresco, even a picnic. Not only did I want to be out in that sunshine, doing something, feeling worthwhile, but I also wanted to articulate all these man worries to a good girlfriend. She was busy, doing pre-move prep, as in a few weeks she would start a year's work placement in Miami. I was really going to miss her.

She wasn't the first friend that I'd lost to a tropical American city. Just months earlier, another best friend had moved to Hawaii. I missed her too, but the blow of losing our close friendship had been softened by the fact that I had a boyfriend to fill the socialising slots I used to spend with friends.

I messaged another friend – not a best friend, but one of my regular gossip-over-wine girlfriends – but impromptu invites on bank holiday Mondays rarely get snapped up, as most people make advance plans and stick to them.

… *But let's get a catch-up in the diary soon*, she ended.

I looked at her message, disheartened. I had many friends with whom I was due 'a catch-up in the diary soon'. I knew it wouldn't be soon. It would be a month before we'd find a suitable date, because that's what happens with all your friends once you're over the age of 30.

I so wanted company that afternoon. Despite my lack of sleep and the mild hangover, I was wired. I sat on my balcony looking out on the evening. The deep-blue late-summer sky taunted me. I wanted to be out there enjoying it. It felt like the world was awash with activity and adventure but none of it included me.

It was, I thought, the sort of afternoon to be sitting on a roof terrace somewhere enjoying a drink. I almost laughed at myself – that was exactly the sort of thing I was trying to do less of – but I had energy to burn and I didn't really know any other way to express it than through carefree hedonism.

Instead, I walked to my local park and sat on the grass on a silk sarong in the sun. I tried to read the paper but my hungover brain wouldn't take much in, so I lay down and tried to arrange my thoughts.

I started with the most dominant one of late: what to do about my relationship. I wanted to break free but wasn't that selfish? He would be so devastated it didn't bear thinking about. And what if I was throwing something away that I'd later regret? Then my thoughts wandered to the second-most dominant niggle of late: what my social life would be like if I did go it alone.

My friends were dropping like flies. I used to have a pool of friends I could text or call on any day of the week for a capricious drink. I remember a time, not so long ago, when I had too many friends. Friends' friends became your own friends and vice versa. There'd be a ski holiday every winter, a weekend of drinking games in a country cottage every summer. Sunday afternoons in gastropubs. Email banter. Random dinner parties just for the hell of it in big shared houses with the token pissed-off flatmate appearing at midnight to complain about the noise. What happened to those days?

Friends are everywhere when we're young – we have so much free time, we need people to fill it with. We are all on a mission to collect as many as we can. As we get older, we reach our friendship quotas and suddenly find we no longer bond with random people at three in the morning at a house party 15 postcodes away. People no longer squeal 'we have to have a night out sometime' while tapping your number into their phone. Instead they nod politely and say 'it was nice to meet you', then collect their coat at 10 o'clock because they have kids, a babysitter, a partner, 30 other friends and an important Monday meeting to prepare for.

Not that I wanted kids, a babysitter, a partner or any important meetings to prepare for. I've never really fancied the family life. I split my professional life as a freelance producer in TV news and a writer for newspapers and magazines, pitching my own news and feature stories to different publications. Working in TV news meant an in-house shift in a newsroom. Writing meant working from cafes. I enjoyed the freedom and variety of my working life, and had never felt a need to 'settle' (which I've always thought is an odd term because one can be settled without finding a partner) or have children. But I still felt there had to be something else to life. More than a career or filling my spare time with trendy media parties, partying, regaling funny drinking stories to friends, or collecting new acquaintances at parties who always say 'let's meet up' then never do.

But what else was there? This leaning towards curbing my party lifestyle wasn't preceded by any epiphany. There was no reassessment of life values after waking up with a traffic cone on my head at the end of the Northern Line or anything like that. It was simply a case of physiological necessity. It was becoming increasingly evident that my ability to function on half a bottle of wine and six hours' sleep five times a week was fading with age.

I'd been saying I was going to cut down on drinking for years, maybe even stop drinking one day. Every time I lay in bed with a groggy head, like I had this morning, I imagined a future grown-up Helen, super productive, successful, full of energy, clued up on politics, with flawless skin, because she didn't go out drinking every other night and then spend half the working day watching cute cat videos on Facebook.

But this wasn't going to happen unless I found something new in my life. It wasn't that I couldn't not drink. We're not talking brown paper bags or gin and tonics by lunchtime. When I was on my own I never drank. If I lived in a hut on a mountain I wouldn't think about drinking. The reason it was hard to avoid was because I didn't live in a hut on a mountain and – as with many young professionals – my friends, my work networks, my relationship and even my identity were rooted in a culture of social drinking.

You might be thinking, *No one forces the stuff down your neck, you lush!* And you would have a good point. But you have to admit that most social activities in our culture revolve around the bar… Business dinners. Christmas drinks. Birthday drinks. Catch-up drinks. Leaving drinks. A drink to say thank you. Sunday lunches with wine. Free promo events with flat Prosecco. A date (this definitely needs a drink). Even when I visit family they're disappointed if I announce I need a night off the sauce, as if I've put them second best.

There is an assumption in our culture that we must drink to bond. Getting a bit tiddly together is the initiation test for friendship. Every close friendship that I can recall has started with a memory of some crazy, side-splittingly hilarious drunken antic.

I didn't regret any of those antics, but I was concerned that I didn't seem to have anything else on which to base social activities. To not drink, I felt I had to stay in. Or at the very least, I'd need to excuse myself in advance, informing whoever I was meeting of a reason to not indulge: 'Massive meeting tomorrow/sore throat/on antibiotics. Do you mind if I don't drink?' Do you mind? As if I needed to excuse myself for being sober and less entertaining.

Sometimes I mooted an alternative activity: 'I'm trying not to drink so do you fancy that exhibition at the Tate instead?' How crazy is that? That's basically saying: 'I can't sit with you for three hours and make conversation without either a drink or something arty to look at, even though you're one of my closest friends.' Quite insulting, if you think about it. Especially since I couldn't care less about modern art.

It occurred to me one day that almost every single conversation of any depth was executed under the influence of booze. Aside from a snatched chat in the gym or small talk by the coffee machine in the newsroom, most of my people-facing time was done with tipple in hand.

There were some social occasions when I didn't drink. But you have to admit, going out can often be mind-numbingly boring unless you're at least three times over the legal drink-drive limit. Whenever some annoyingly-dewy-faced teetotaller bounds around proclaiming the most annoying sentence in the world, 'I don't need to drink to have a good time', what they actually mean is that they do things other than hanging out in bars with other drinkers, spraying their words and saying the same thing three times.

And that was exactly what I needed to do, I thought, stirring from my silk sarong. I walked home, my restless thirst for activity no less, but my head a little clearer at least.

When I returned home, my boyfriend texted a photo from the BBQ he'd suggested we go to. It was a merry scene: he amid smiling faces; girls with glossy hair; bottles of lager raised in hands. *You're missing such a good party.* I didn't know whether it was an innocent comment to tell me he missed me, or a deliberate inducement of guilt that I'd chosen not to join him. I had become so consumed and confused about whether I wanted in or out that every little phrase inflicted paranoia. Was I being unloving, or was he too demanding? He would have assumed that I was at home working peacefully, not spending the afternoon craving any other activity than the one he wanted me to do.

I spent the next four weeks agonising, procrastinating and changing my mind until, sadly, I ended our relationship. Then followed the painful extraction process: empty weekends during which I could not for the life of me remember what I used to do when I was last single, 18 months earlier; self-doubt over whether I did the right thing; heartbreaking nostalgia over the private jokes and language that we had created as a unit. It seemed such a desperately sad waste.

The break-up was impeccably timed with my closest friend moving abroad. Just like that, the central pillars of my life caved in. Love gone, and with it affection and security. My career flagging and with it my motivation. My two truest friends lost to sunny American cities. As for the rest of my mates – during the time that I had been in a relationship, all but a handful had got themselves a husband and/or some offspring or two. Arranging so much as lunch seemed to take as much precision planning as a military intervention in Syria.

Those weeks in the autumn of 2013 were some of the most tormented I can remember. Yes, it was my decision to end our relationship, but it still left a gaping hole. I'd spent the last 18 months of weekends doing boyfriend things. Now weekends and weekdays rolled into one. Another Friday would arrive and I would realise I had no plans.

I felt this odd conflict between wanting to get wasted, as had been my fail-safe tonic to get me through the blues in the past, and wanting to turn over a new healthy leaf, now that my life was my own to organise again. On the one hand, I wanted to phone friends, organise get-togethers, go to whatever party I heard about. After any other break-up, even minor ones, I've joined dating sites, gone wild in Ibiza, exposed myself to as much life as possible if only to mask the gap. Sometimes a bit of self-destructive hedonism is the only thing that hits the spot.

But this time I knew I'd been here before. Filling life with nights out that we rarely remember. Having deep-andmeaningfuls with randoms who you never see again when high on party vibes. Drinking because it makes you more gregarious, but at the expense of being extra subdued the next day... I was so sick of it all.

My nerves were fraught – raw with frustration, boredom, guilt and sadness. I had a raging urgency to burn it all somehow, to do something outrageous. I wanted adventures, but not drinking adventures, which were the only ones I knew.

I was a good-time girl who didn't want to party any more. A career type who'd lost faith in work going anywhere. A once-popular socialite whose friends had either moved across the Atlantic or couldn't come out any more because everything clashed with baby yoga.

I couldn't sleep, couldn't concentrate, couldn't motivate myself to work. I was just waiting for each day to end so that another morning could begin and I'd have something to do. My now-ex sent texts trying to persuade me to reconsider. My guilt became so abrasive that I almost considered a U-turn just to assuage it. He was many positive things, on paper: loving, committed, funny. But in my heart I knew these things weren't enough. I knew there had to be something more fulfilling than jollies and drinking, which was all we did.

🌲🌲🌲🌲🌲

The only time my black cloud lifted was when I went jogging. My freelance producer shifts were becoming fewer and so there were many days when a gentle jog, or a visit to the gym, was the only activity that required me leaving my flat. I didn't run far – never for less than 20 minutes, but certainly no more than 30. I went along the river or canal near my home in Limehouse, in east London, and when I got back I felt temporary relief. My little runs were the only time when my cravings for excitement and activity subsided. I loved it most when the sun was out, with my music and thoughts and daydreams. Then I was at peace.

This is not a story of a sedentary couch potato who suddenly defied the habits of a lifetime and got super fit. I did have bad habits, but even in my most hedonistic eras, I always kept reasonably fit. I used the gym twice a week and I jogged or swam once a week. Nothing crazy.

But, let's be honest, it was purely for vanity. It wasn't because I loved the feel of the wind on my skin, or because I loved the sense of absolute, complete exertion, or because I wanted to see what my body and mind were capable of, or because I wanted to see and breathe in some of the world's most stunning and unspoiled places. No, it was so that I could fit into size-eight jeans. Exercise was a necessary antidote to all the bad stuff.

Aside from jogging, I kept all exercise in temperature-controlled environments – an air-conditioned gym, an indoor exercise-class studio with bright lights and disco tunes, a heated swimming pool with pristine changing rooms with fluffy towels and hair straighteners.

Actually, I didn't swim that much because I was afraid chlorine would give me split ends. Mostly I did it when I felt too hungover to use the gym. I didn't see the point in a bike. I was of the belief that once my morning workout was out of the way, it was time to put on a dress and heels and pick up a designer handbag. Tailored coats and sheer denier stockings don't mix well with bicycles.

But that autumn, to fill my empty days, I started to run more and further. I went online and looked for running playlists, and in my research I came across forums about times and distances, then one day I decided to time a run. I'd never done that before. I downloaded an app called MapMyRun, which records distance through a smartphone's GPS signal, and I set out to see how long it would take me to do 5k. I did it in just under 25 minutes.

This made me want to run faster. I wanted to beat my time. I went to the gym more. I wanted to do anything that involved activity because that seemed to be the only thing that calmed my frustration, filled my emptiness and eased my guilt over the break-up.

One day as I ran up the Regent's Canal near Bethnal Green, I passed a large group on bikes, laughing, chatting and politely getting into single file to let me pass. The image stayed with me. That was exactly the sort of thing I wished I was doing with my weekend. Something active, fun, with a group, that didn't involve getting hammered! They were only going slowly – pootling around on an assortment of pushbikes – but to me it looked like a proper expedition.

That group planted a seed. Suddenly I wanted to join bike rides along the canal with sporty, interesting people. Did they get lunch along the way? A well-earned beer perhaps? It wasn't like I didn't want to drink at all – I just didn't want it to be the only focal point.

I started to google local fitness groups. Trail running – what a lovely way to spend a day. Mud runs – there's even a beer tent at the end. Triathlons – I could handle that. I wasn't sure about swimming in a dirty lake though – that can't be good for the complexion, can it? What about a swimming holiday in the Mediterranean, with BBQs every evening? Or trekking the Inca Trail?

I didn't really care what it was. I just liked the idea of filling my weekends with the great outdoors, exercise and a challenge with new people, who hadn't moved to Surrey (where the schools are better apparently), and which didn't end with waking at five the next day from restless alcoholic sleep and vows to never do it again. That's when I came across Victoria Park Harriers, a running club based in Hackney. There were pictures on the website of big groups at all sorts of races. They ran two evening sessions per week, on Tuesdays and Thursdays. On Thursdays, I read, the club bar opens. Well, if a running club had a bar, I was definitely in.

CHAPTER 1
THE BAR

Two Thursdays later, and I was perched on a wobbly wooden stool in a windowless room in an old schoolhouse in Hackney, east London, sipping a beer and eating a ham bagel even though I felt sick and was shivering.

My body had gone into mild shock. I'd just done my first ever 10-mile run. We'd apparently run at a pace of 8.5-minute miles. Whatever that meant. I only knew that because I heard someone say as much as they studied their fancy sports watch when we finally stopped.

Nausea was to become a familiar sensation over the next few months. I now know it's the effect of the body trying to flush away lactic acid, which builds when your heart rate goes higher than you are used to. But I didn't know that then. I was just annoyed because the bar was the bit I had been looking forward to and, now that I was in it, I felt like shit.

I say bar, but it wasn't the sort of swanky bar I was used to. The Victoria Park Harriers club bar was a small room with a well-worn carpet, foldaway tables and plastic chairs, and a few wooden stools at the bar along one side of the room.

On the walls were pictures of skinny runners in the blue and white club vest, holding up trophies. But it did have a very well stocked bar. Bottles of beer or a glass of wine (from a box) cost a bargain £1.50.

On the bar was a stack of bagels with different fillings. They were going for £1 each. Apparently, each week a different member volunteered to prepare dinner and someone else would wash up. Bagels and jacket potatoes were popular but sometimes the chef du jour got adventurous and out came vats of pasta, stews, chillies and even handmade burritos.

During the preceding 10 miles of horror, the thing that kept me going was the thought of this bar. As I ran, I kept saying to myself, *In 40 minutes… in 30 minutes… in 10 minutes, it will all be over and I'll be sitting in a bar, in the warm and dry, with a beer, relaxing, conversing, drinking, meeting new people.* People were what I needed more than anything else.

I didn't have to run 10 miles. There had been two other groups – one doing 6 miles and one running 4 miles. But for some godforsaken reason, I opted for the biggie.

When I arrived at the schoolhouse for the 7 p.m. start, there were at least twenty other people, of all ages, chatting familiarly, in running gear. I didn't have to pay for my first session. The club's website invited new runners to try a few sessions before they committed to joining fees.

I felt out of place in my designer gym kit, which I'd bought far more for its potential to impress the sexy personal trainers than I had for its sweat-wicking potential. My top didn't have sleeves, so I put on a fleece over the top. No one runs in a fleece, by the way. Not proper runners. A fleece is far too warm.

When I ran alone I would usually set out in a fleece and stop to tie it round my waist when I got hot. Little did I know that there would be no stopping on this run.

The runners were grouping together for the three different distances. The furthest I had ever run in my whole life was 10k (6 miles) – and that was only two weeks previously, of which feat I was immensely proud. Maybe it was this pride which made me optimistic enough to join the 10-mile group. Maybe it was because, having made the move to even turn up that night, I was determined to make it count. Or maybe I was just so desperate to be accepted that I wanted to be considered an experienced runner. Whatever, I set off enthusiastically on my suicide mission.

The pace felt easy at first. We ran down the canal towards Limehouse, which is exactly where I'd just come from. No matter. I wasn't here for new scenic routes. I was here to spend time with people and to get out of my deathly silent flat.

At 3 miles, I still felt OK – that was a third of the way already. At 5 miles, we reached Tower Bridge – the turning point. I was hurting by then and I had to do exactly the same distance all over again!

The club has a rule during Thursday-night group runs that no one leaves anyone on their own. All routes go along the Regent's Canal, which can be a scary place once darkness sets in. I didn't want to be the newcomer holding everyone back so I was determined to keep up.

My hamstrings started to hurt and then the balls of my feet. They hurt more and more, until I became convinced I was doing irreparable damage. Sometimes I closed my eyes, trying to forget the pain in the backs of my legs. I'd managed to remove my fleece on the go and now I kept having to tighten the knot around my waist to stop it slipping down.

I can't stop. I can't hold them up, I kept telling myself. *In 40 minutes, I'll be in the bar, and it will all be over.*

'Anyone want to pick the pace up for the return leg?' one of the girls suggested as we turned around at Tower Bridge.

I was filled with horror.

Luckily, a nice, middle-aged man called Dave, who kept telling me in exasperated tones how he could no longer run as fast as he used to, came to my rescue.

'I'm happy to slow down,' he said. Then he added, for the fourth time that night, 'I can't run as fast as I used to.'

Dave was the first person's name I learned.

We dropped back as the others pushed ahead. We continued for another 3 miles, taking it in turns to repeat how I'd never run anywhere near 10 miles before, and how he couldn't run as fast as he used to.

At mile eight, I couldn't go on. Every muscle in my legs and feet ached.

'I'm going to walk now but I know the way back. You go ahead,' I said.

Dave wasn't having that. He slowed with me and encouraged me to go on. Not wanting to rebuff him, I plodded onwards, resigned to the fact that my hamstrings would now be damaged for life. I'd torn them – of that I was convinced.

We carried on with this agonising trot for another mile and a half and only then, when the clubhouse was in sight, did Dave let me walk. He jogged ahead as I limped back, too exhausted and shell-shocked to feel sorry for myself.

I was the last back to the clubhouse and there was no hot water left in the showers. I went into the changing rooms sheepishly, listening to girls chat familiarly. There was a hairdryer on the side. I longed to feel it warm the crown of my head but thought better of it. I was among hardy, outdoorsy types now, and I didn't want to be the prima donna preening herself. No one, I noticed, bothered with make-up, but I sneaked a touch of mascara on to my lashes while I thought no one was looking.

When I reached the bar, I paid close attention to people's sartorial choices. This, I reasoned, must be 'après sports wear' – hoodies and loose jeans or comfortable tracksuits. As for me, I was in skinny jeans and a trendy knit from H&M. That was as close to casual as I got. When I'd packed my bag earlier, I'd changed my mind at least three times about what to wear in the bar. For me, it was more challenging to find a casual outfit than to piece together perfectly matched couture.

Much of my wardrobe was dry-clean only. My version of 'dress down' meant getting one more wear out of last year's fashion before it went into the charity-shop bag. Aside from my running trainers and ballet pumps for walking to the Tube, I didn't own any flat shoes. I owned every imaginable colour of shoe, handbag and matching accessory you can imagine, but I'd never owned a hoodie and I certainly didn't own any thermals – that's what black cabs are for!

Despite my greenness, I was determined to get involved. I saw this as a way out of the great empty void my life seemed to be floating in. On that very first evening, after that nausea-inducing 10-mile run, I set about finding out when and where the next club race would be. I didn't care what it was, I wanted to do it. I didn't have any competitive leaning. To me it would just be a new type of day out. A day out with new people; stimulation to take my mind off the break-up and my friends disappearing. A day out doing something new – something out of my city comfort zone. As it happened, the next race was on Saturday: two days' time. 'What,' I asked someone at random, 'do I need to do so that I can take part?'

All I had to do was navigate my way to a field in Loughton, in Essex (known to me as 'Zone 6 on the Tube map'). It was a 5-mile cross-country race – the first of the winter season. Not that I knew that races were seasonal. I also had to buy a pair of something called 'trail shoes', which apparently have a better grip on muddy terrain.

So that Saturday I set off early, via Sports Direct, the only sports shop I knew, and picked up the cheapest pair I could find. Thirty-six quid, if I remember rightly, which I thought was a bargain compared to how much road trainers cost.

I was wearing my running kit already, with a coat over the top – a gold fashion coat, which was quilted so about the warmest thing in my coat collection. I carried a change of clothes and some toiletry essentials in a bright red Estée Lauder tote bag, which came free with a multibuy beauty offer at Harvey Nicks. I was yet to own a proper sports bag and I certainly wasn't taking a designer handbag to a muddy field.

I stood on the start line amid a montage of bright-coloured club vests. This was a league race, which meant it was only open to club runners, and each club has its own vest. Victoria Park Harriers' is a blue and turquoise diagonal stripe on a white background, in a loose fit for comfort. I was in a neon, racerback, tightly fitted gym top, which I was sure must have screamed out that I didn't belong in this scene. I was also the only one in three-quarter leggings. Everyone, and I mean *everyone*, was in shorts. Shorts are the standard uniform of cross-country even when it's snowing. Only a very sensitive few resort to running leggings. (Which, by the way, are *never* called leggings. They are always called tights. Even when men wear them.)

Everyone else looked like they had done these sorts of races zillions of times. They appeared totally at ease with being in a field on a Saturday afternoon far, far away from a Tube station or civilisation.

I started worrying that I'd be one of the slowest. I knew I could run 5 miles easily enough but I didn't know how fast I would be compared to others. My only benchmark for competitive performance was my school days, and at school I was usually one of the slow ones.

I hated sport at school. It wasn't that I was the slow, unfit kid. Far from it. I loved being active. I spent every free moment helping at my local stables so I could ride horses. I could run fast if it meant running to the fields to catch one of the horses to ride. But when it came to forced PE classes, I deliberately dragged my feet. I resented the militant teachers who yelled at us and made us wear T-shirts even in subzero conditions.

I hated the damp, cold, concrete changing rooms that smelled of industrial bleach, and I hated the sporty, tough girls who mocked me for being scared of catching the netball because it travelled so fast. Most of the time I tried to skive PE by faking illness or hiding in the toilets.

I cannot recall being in a running race since the compulsory sports days at school. Why would I ever travel to somewhere to run on a Saturday, when I could run near home, where a hot shower and hairstyling products await, and then go on to more important things, like lunch out?

When the start whistle blew, everyone hurtled off en masse. It felt good to run in a pack. The course went around a football pitch and then over a small bridge into an open field, along a footpath, into another field, before coming back to the start for another lap. I kept looking back to check how many people were behind me and was surprised to find there were lots. There was a much longer line of runners stretching out ahead of me, however, so I ran faster and pushed harder than I usually would have. I couldn't sustain that pace for 5 whole miles, so I slowed to a walk a couple of times to get my breath back.

People ran past crying out words of encouragement: 'Keep going', 'Don't stop' and 'You're nearly there'. It was a pleasant surprise to discover such a warm display of sporting camaraderie.

Walking in the middle of a race was another dead giveaway of my inexperience. Proper runners don't walk. If you can't sustain the pace, you should go slower. Afterwards people asked me: 'Were you OK?', 'Did you go off too quick?' and 'Did you have a stitch?'

But no, I walked simply because walking was what I did when I got out of puff.

I finished the 4.8-mile course in just under 38 minutes, which was somewhere in the middle – not near the front, but, thank the Lord, not near the back!

I had nothing to worry about in this department though. Thankfully local running clubs shed themselves of performance snobbery years ago and all levels are welcomed and encouraged. Just 20 years ago, recreational sports clubs were only accessible to the athletically gifted or socially privileged. Some of the veteran members of my club have told me that as young men or women, they had to apply to join a club and were asked to produce evidence of their Personal Best times (PBs) for a series of distances. Some said if they couldn't do 1 mile in less than 5 minutes or didn't attend a school with a strong sports reputation, they couldn't join the club. Imagine that: a whole social scene closed to previous generations. No wonder the pub has become the choice activity of the masses.

Fortunately for me, my Loughton debut was relatively painless in comparison to the more typically muddy, hilly and rainy cross-country experience. That autumn was unseasonably warm and it hadn't rained that year since about June, so I escaped the mess. In retrospect this was very fortuitous. Had my introduction to cross-country been as testing as later experiences proved to be, I may well have been so traumatised as to never return to running club again.

After the race, I hung around trying to chat to people. I was expecting a post-race outing to a local pub, but people started to head home. *Is that it?* I thought. *I've travelled all the way to*

Zone 6 and got my Estée Lauder tote bag dirty, only to travel back again in sweaty clothes?

My spirits sank. Somehow I'd expected that joining a running club and going to my first weekend race would immediately make me part of a new gang. I'd thought I'd be drinking and joking with new chums by teatime. It was clear that one club outing was not going to be an overnight fix. It takes time to become accepted into a new group and I obviously had to do a lot more to ingratiate myself into this new circle than one run around a flat field on a mild autumn day.

Pub or not, I returned home glowing. The race may only have taken 38 minutes but it had been a whole afternoon out. I'd been in the fresh air, talking to new people, learning new things, visiting a place I'd never seen before (even if it was only Loughton). It hadn't involved a single drop of alcohol and I hadn't thought about the break-up, the guilt and the emptiness all day. *This*, I thought, *is how weekends are supposed to be spent*. And not, as I had hitherto believed, chasing the high life.

CHAPTER 2

FAKING IT

When I realised that I neither froze to death nor developed some incurable skin condition from the lack of immediate access to a shower, the great outdoors no longer seemed so barbaric. I didn't have to stick to a temperature-controlled gym or a quick run near home so that I could get on with my day; I could make fresh air and exercise the main feature of my day.

I made it my prerogative to go to run club every Thursday. There were sessions on other nights too, but Thursdays were when the bar opened.

First, I had to sort out how to get there. My first expedition had involved two buses and a long walk. The most direct route to travel the 3 miles to the schoolhouse was up the Regent's Canal and through Victoria Park, and the quickest way to do that was by bike. It was time to get that six-month-old puncture fixed.

My bike, I should explain, was a battered burgundy Dutch shopping bike with a wicker basket on the front. I'd bought it two years ago, after moving to the Limehouse area. Surrounded by canals, river paths and docklands, it had seemed a romantic idea to go cafe-hopping by bicycle with my laptop in the basket. Roads were scary and I only considered two wheels because in this area of London I could access lots of places by river or canal.

After three journeys, the base of the wicker basket started falling away because my laptop was too heavy. Then the brakes started to get stuck every couple of miles. I had no idea how to fix them so I'd get off and give them a twiddle so they'd work OK for another mile or so.

The furthest I'd ever ridden was 10 miles up the canal with the now-ex the previous July, and another 10 miles back. We had considered this an epic adventure. We'd made a whole day of it, stopping at lots of pubs for a break. Afterwards we pored over Google Maps, exclaiming what intrepid pioneers we must be to venture so far.

But now my bike had a real purpose: to get me to a destination and back. When I rode it to running club the following Thursday, it looked distinctly out of place amid the lithe road bikes locked to the bike stands. I tried to slot it into a gap but the huge basket kept getting caught on all the other handlebars. Even my lights looked pathetic against all the other aerodynamic, USB-turbocharging laser beams. Mine took AA batteries, sealed in with Sellotape, and emitted about as many lumens as a glow-worm.

As winter set in, I remained dedicated to my mission. Each Thursday night I cycled to the club, feeling like a bold adventurer every time I scooped up my bike lights and helmet along with my keys as I left home.

We would gather in the hall and split into groups according to pace and distance. I always joined the 10-mile run, which went along the canal to Limehouse and then through Shadwell and Wapping to Tower Bridge and back. For the first few weeks this feat still left me shivering and nauseous, but the blow was slightly less each time.

Whenever I felt like staying at home in the warm instead of cycling 3 miles up a canal in the dark and drizzle, I'd simply recall those evenings at home just a few weeks earlier – bored, unsettled, heartbroken and alone. I was on a new adventure. I didn't know where this path would lead but I knew I had to follow it.

After a few weeks, I developed a bike inferiority complex and invested in a respectable one, without a basket on the front. My vintage burgundy Dutch friend got put up for sale on Gumtree. It was becoming embarrassing locking it up next to the slick carbon machines on the bike stands. Besides, since I rode predominantly along canals and rivers, because I was scared of traffic, it meant I had to regularly carry it up steps to cross bridges and over cobbled stretches of towpath; it was heavy and cumbersome.

So when I invested in a white £300 hybrid bike, it quickly became my best friend. I was mesmerised at the difference. Not only was it lighter and easier to ride, but it was shorter in length, which meant I could fit it in the lift in my block of flats without having to tilt the front wheel into a wheelie position and balance the frame on my thigh to get down to the basement bike storage.

I still didn't own anything in the way of waterproofs for a long time though. The first Thursday it rained, I looked out of the window not knowing what to do. It doesn't matter running in the rain because you stay warm, but cycling in it would mean my clothes for the bar afterwards would get wet. Then I remembered. *I have a ski suit!* It was on top of a wardrobe, where it had laid untouched for years. I got out the stepladders and retrieved my salopettes and ski jacket. I put them on over my running gear and off I wobbled up the canal to Victoria Park. I arrived very hot but dry as a bone, and I praised myself on my ingenuity.

I always stayed in the bar until the last people left and then I cycled home, sometimes as late as 1 a.m., in the damp winter mist along the canal. My chest would be tingling from being out of breath and my legs were sore and heavy. To me this was the stuff of superheroes. Every night on my way home I would proudly reflect on what a tough chick I had become: *I do 10-mile runs and then drink beer and then cycle home* in winter!

I was growing used to the sensation of permanently but subtly sore legs as my muscles developed. This began even before I joined running club, when I upped my leisurely 20-minute riverside jogs to 10k for the first time. I'd increased my running and gym-ing ever since, so mild aches had become part of my day-to-day physiology. I noticed how much harder it felt to do simple things like walk up escalators on the Tube.

On Saturdays I turned up to whatever cross-country race was on the agenda. It didn't matter where it was, whether it was a scenic course or uninspiring loops around Wormwood Scrubs, which was once the case. It didn't matter if it was a friendly local league race or a national championship. I had no idea about the point-scoring system or whether my participation even contributed to club points. I just ran as fast as I could sustain for that particular distance and afterwards talked to as many people as I could.

At my second race it soon became clear that cross-countries weren't always going to be as sanguine as my Loughton debut. This one was in Stevenage, a 45-minute train journey out of London. It was a rainy, windy, autumnal day. At the bottom of the first hill a big quagmire of black, muddy, stagnant water loomed. I remember this milestone well. Carried along with the pack of bare-armed, bare-legged runners, I hurtled straight for it. There was no time to squirm and no place to wince. There certainly seemed to be no sign of concerns from anyone else about having wet feet for the rest of the afternoon. I closed my eyes and sloshed straight through it, sending mud splattering up my legs on to my chin.

That one puddle splattered more mud on my bare skin than it had seen in the last 15 years. But guess what? It didn't hurt. I didn't die. I didn't get spots. It didn't even ruin my pedicure. I remained in my mud-splattered skin for the rest of the afternoon – in the pub, on the train back – and still nothing bad happened. When I got home, the mud got cleaned up. Another barrier had been crossed.

By my third cross-country race, I'd bought the white and blue club vest. A shapeless and unflattering thing – definitely not something I'd wear among the fashion-conscious clientele of my expensive gym – but it was the club running uniform. Most of the cross-countries were part of a series of London league events, which meant they were rarely outside the Tube network. So no matter how cold, wet, muddy, exhausted, dehydrated, chapped lipped or dirty I got, I could always console myself that I was within reach of a warm Underground network that could magic me back to sanitary conditions. This was not exactly polar exploration. But still, to a city girl like me, stripping down to shorts and vest in a windy field in Stevenage before running through puddles was as good as going into combat in Helmand.

There could be anywhere between ten or fifty club members at any one race. Members were encouraged to sport the club's blue and white stripes at as many events as they could, no matter what their running ability. There were always extra supporters too – people who were injured and couldn't run or members' partners. There were a few long-term members – I presumed, because they seemed familiar with everyone – who felt comfortable enough to hand their young children and even the odd baby to one of the support crew to look after while they raced. I loved the positive community spirit, and the inclusiveness of all ages and backgrounds.

The races were only short – between 5 and 8 kilometres (3–5 miles) – but they wiped me out for the afternoon. The race atmosphere made me run faster and because I wasn't used to pushing my body so hard, I think it went into shutdown. That's my theory, because I could go for a 10k (6-mile) run on my own (I did at least one other run a week in addition to the club sessions, or on weekends when there wasn't a race) and not feel half as tired. But after a cross-country, my core temperature would plummet and in the evenings I'd always lie motionless on my sofa, feeling how I imagine it feels to be concussed. Yet strangely I liked being incapacitated with fatigue. There was something satisfying about knowing that

I'd used my body to its limit. A stark contrast to feeling incapacitated because I'd drunk too much or stayed up all night having repeat conversations. Knocking myself out with fresh air and running had a purpose at least. It was getting me fitter and stronger and tougher. After my melancholy of recent weeks, a new purpose was exactly what I needed.

In some leagues, the women raced separately to the men, so after the women finished, we would stand around in our damp, muddy clothes to cheer the men. On those occasions I'd get cold beyond the point of return. No matter how many clothes I put on, by the time we got to the pub, I'd be shivering uncontrollably. I remember several times when my jaw was so numb that I couldn't articulate words.

On the day of an event at Alexandra Palace, in north London, it rained and rained all day. I walked from the train station to the park, dreading having to strip down to my shorts and vest when I got there. *You don't have to do this*, said the voice inside my head. But the nearer I got to the event base, the harder it became to turn around and go home.

The entrance to the park was waterlogged and I squelched my way through to find the Victoria Park Harriers flag. *There go my dry shoes for later*, I thought.

There was not a patch of dry ground on which to place our backpacks so they were simply piled up atop a mud swamp. Wincing with the cold, I stripped down to my club vest. Then I squinted my way through the pelting rain with 50 other shivering runners to the start. We waited, hugging ourselves and jumping up and down. Our only consolation was that within a few minutes of running we would be warm.

The whistle went. I made it 500 metres to the end of the first field before I tripped over uneven ground and fell hard on my shoulder on to the soggy grass. I'd been running for exactly 2 minutes 40 seconds – not even long enough to stop shivering. Instinctively I picked myself up and carried on running, but after 100 metres was forced to stop. The pain from any movement in my arm was unbearable. A marshal intercepted me as I walked back to base clutching my armpit. He ordered me to the St John Ambulance. They gave me a sling, which relieved the weight of my arm but they took their time putting it on and I was getting colder and colder by the second.

The rain was now pelting sideways. I made my way to the club's patch and the pile of backpacks. Mine had sunk deep into the mud with the weight of the other bags on top. All my dry clothes inside were soaked. The shoes I had arrived in were soaked. The shoes I had started running in were soaked.

Not that I could put anything on anyway because my arm was in a sling. I pulled my gold quilted coat over my shoulders, once more vowing that I needed to get a proper waterproof coat for days like these (I still didn't really know what to look for or where to get one). Then I watched the women run by for their third lap of the course. My chin was quaking. I wasn't sure if it was from the cold or from holding back tears of pain and frustration. I had been so tempted to stay in the warm and dry instead of coming here. I'd scraped the depths of my soul for the willpower to turn up and this was the reward I got. It seemed so unfair.

The men were nearby getting their trainers on. They were due to start as soon as the women finished. I still didn't know many people's names and I asked one guy at random to help zip my coat up.

By the time the men finished, I was so cold I couldn't speak. Our team captain, Sim, spotted me shivering. My blue complexion must have said it all because without even asking he arranged for someone to give me a lift home. A nice Australian called Paul let me and three other sodden, muddy bodies into his car.

We got stuck in traffic for two hours. Three of us were squeezed in tightly in the back, wet backpacks on our laps, the smell of damp filling the air, but I didn't care. I was under a roof and my shoulder didn't have to move. This was the height of luxury.

Paul had come in the top three in the men's race, not that he mentioned it – he just chatted away about the rain like the rest of us. I had no reason not to assume he was another recreational weekend runner like us. I later learned that he's a semi-pro marathon runner and holds course records for marathons and half-marathons several times over and is the UK 100k world champion. I didn't even know it was humanly possible to run 100k!

The injured arm turned out to be a pulled pec muscle – at least, that's where I felt it when the pain settled. I didn't get it seen to but just let it heal on its own. I'd had pulled muscles before from the gym and I knew that most minor injuries heal best with one simple thing: rest. I couldn't run or use the gym for three weeks though. I tried after a week and turned back before I got to the pedestrian crossing 100 metres down the road.

Despite the mishap, the thing I took away from that race was not the horrible memory of the cold and the fall but the lesson that, in future, when it rains I need to put my dry clothes in plastic carrier bags.

I learned a new survival tip at each race. By the end of the season, I had kit essentials nailed: a small towel to wipe off the excess mud, dry socks, dry shoes, clean bra, clean knickers. This was not for cleanliness but for warmth. I soon learned that to prevent my core temperature plummeting I had to remove *all* damp items as soon as I finished the race, including sports bra and knickers. The moisture against your skin takes away your body heat because, when moisture tries to evaporate, it takes away heat from its surface. This fact I learned from June, one of the older and wiser runners after a cross-country. Not only was I learning about running but I was relearning physics.

Removing damp clothes usually meant stripping down to nothing behind a bush but I didn't care. Staying warm was a bigger priority than modesty. Then, once in the pub, I'd splash my face, comb my hair and apply toiletry essentials – moisturiser, BB cream (the more natural version of foundation, and an absolute must if you're thinking of taking up outdoor sport and care remotely about your appearance), mascara and a dash of lip gloss if I could get away with it.

That Christmas I asked for proper walking boots for getting around muddy fields before and after races. My mum nearly choked. But what a revelation they were. I had become so resigned to my feet being wet and freezing for the entire day of a cross-country event that when I first used the boots and went to the pub with feeling in my feet, I could not stop wiggling my toes in wonderment.

One weekend in January, I volunteered to marshal at one of the club races. The club encouraged members to help occasionally as well as just turn up for races. Keen as ever to get involved as much as I could in my new social sphere, I put myself forward. The forecast was wind and heavy rain, so I finally forked out for a proper, warm, waterproof coat and even some waterproof trousers, which I had never before owned in my life.

Another trick I learned that winter, through a ruthless trial-and-error process, was taking bin bags to put the walking boots in while I was running so they stayed dry, and more carrier bags for any waterproof layers I travelled in. And to fold said waterproofs in such a way that the outer layers don't get the inner layers wet. It is a delicate and complicated science but I was a quick learner.

When I got home from every soggy, freezing, Saturday cross-country race, it became my ritual to run a bath. I never used to like baths but for some reason I developed a specific craving for just that! As I panted in pain around the course, my feet freezing and squelching, my calves aching from pulling through thick mud, I would think to myself, *Soon this hell will be over and I'll be warm and breathing in Epsom salts*. I always honoured this promise to myself. I'd lie in piping hot water, with a zillion lotions and exfoliating potions around me, cleaning mud out of my toenails, with piles of muddy clothes resting on plastic bags queuing up for the washing machine, my mud-drenched spiked shoes floating in the kitchen sink, and I'd think with an overwhelming feeling of satisfaction what a super-tough cookie I'd become.

It was easy to let my new running social life replace the rest of my social life because there was simply more going on in it. It wasn't that I suddenly ditched my friends in favour of something new. It was more that until I joined running club, I had been the one making all the effort with my other friends. The break-up, my two regular drinking buddies leaving the country and a dearth in work meant *I* was the one needy of company. It was easy to be part of a club because the agenda was ready-made. I knew, for instance, that every Thursday there was a bar I could go where I was welcome. Each time there would be different people but it was a guaranteed night out without endless emails about babysitters.

I did still see old friends, of course, and I did still go to parties and birthdays and Sunday lunches in the pub like I used to. But the fact that I had extra activities, more people, more choice patched up the gaps and sense of loss that I'd felt just a few months ago.

When I did go out with friends, I didn't drink anywhere near as much because I relished feeling fresh. I used to joke to friends that I didn't have an 'off' button when it came to boozing, but now I could find my 'off' button very easily. It no longer felt like a dearth of excitement having five alcohol-free days in a row because those days were filled with something else. Something that made me feel so, so much more spritely.

The extra busyness made the break-up less significant too. The empty weekends, the blurring of a Friday into a Saturday because I had no plans, were gone. I hadn't just found a replacement – I'd found an alternative. I had been catapulted into a lifestyle as far removed as could be to the one I shared with the ex, which was exactly what I needed.

CHAPTER 3

FASTER

It wasn't long before I wanted to get faster. What with everyone talking about paces and PBs, it was contagious. The popular people seemed to be the fast people and I wanted to be part of it.

I'd never pushed myself when it came to physical exercise before. Sure, I made myself get up on cold dark mornings to get to the gym and I made myself go for a run even when I was hungover, but I'd never pushed myself so that I was gasping for air, counting down every metre. There'd been no need.

I started to go to a track session on Tuesday evenings at Mile End Athletics Stadium. I had often jogged past this athletics track, located just off the Regent's Canal less than a kilometre from my home. I used to think to myself, *Why would anyone want to run round and round in circles on a track when there are so many lovely river paths, canals and docklands around here?* But now here I was, handing over £3 to run round and round in circles because it was, I'd heard, a structured session designed to make you faster.

My first visit, on a cold December evening in 2013, was intimidating. I'd stepped out on to the salmon-pink asphalt track, looking down at the criss-crosses of white lines at my feet, wondering what they all meant, when someone bellowed, 'TRAAAAAACK!'

I looked up to find a sprinter hurtling towards me, head tilted back, arms powering through the air, face grimacing. I jumped out of his lane just in time and watched him disappear around the curve and pelt down the next 100-metre straight.

'Watch the track!' snapped a woman nearby, dressed in about fifteen layers of clothes with a whistle around her neck – presumably someone's coach.

The track was bustling with people and there were different groups doing different sessions – junior athletics clubs, corporate sports teams and other running clubs. Each group seemed to claim a different corner of the track, from where they started their sets. I didn't know which one I was supposed to join. Eventually, after I'd asked enough people, someone said I should 'look out for a man called Peter, with long grey hair, who looks like an eighties ex-rock star'. This was apparently the popular 'speed session', open to all recreational runners and not affiliated to any club.

I spotted Peter among a large gathering of mostly male runners in black running tights (yes, I'd even started to call them tights, not leggings).

'Tonight's session,' he was saying, 'is twelve hundred metres at ten-k pace. Eight hundred metres at five-k pace. Followed by four hundred metres at three-k pace. Three sets of each, with sixty seconds' recovery. We'll finish with four laps of straights 'n' bends. Anyone who's racing at the weekend, stop after the second set.'

I had absolutely no idea what he was talking about and I didn't want to ask. This group looked serious. I just joined them on the start line and hightailed it as hard as I could to keep up, for as long as I could, until I heard the whistle, which meant it was time for the 60-second 'recovery'.

If you've ever considered masochism, this session would be a good starting point. My first track session made that first 10-mile run feel like a spa day. The distances are short, but the intensity is off the scale. Nothing compares to the pain of a track session. That evening I only completed half the session because it hurt so much. But I started to go every Tuesday and gradually built up to the full one-hour session.

A session like these is known as 'interval training'. At higher intensities your heart rate goes up into what's called the 'anaerobic zone' (80–90 per cent of its maximum working capacity). At this heart rate your body cannot produce enough oxygen to meet its energy needs – that's why you get uncomfortably out of breath. Usually your body burns a mixture of body fat and glycogen (the stored form of carbohydrates) as fuel. When oxygen becomes unavailable, the body burns mainly glycogen. The by-product of the body switching to this anaerobic energy system is lactic acid. Lactic acid is what makes your muscles burn and what makes you feel sick, if you haven't built up a tolerance to it.

Repeating high-intensity bursts followed by a short rest or 'recovery' teaches the body to tolerate lactic acid. It also trains the body to process oxygen more efficiently (a measurement known as 'VO$_2$ max'). As your lactic acid threshold increases, you can sustain a higher heart rate for longer and thus maintain a faster speed for longer. Interval training hurts like hell but gets you fitter.

The other reason that a track session helps with speed is simply that running with fast people makes you go faster. I didn't own a fancy GPS watch or anything like that back then so all I had for pace judgement was how out of breath I was when the whistle blew at the end of each rep. What I knew was that running had never hurt like this before.

Afterwards I would be well and truly annihilated. I felt dizzy and sick, and my lungs felt as though they had been burned with a red-hot poker.

An hour after getting home, I could do nothing more than stagger around my flat like a drunk. I soon learned to get ready for bed and do anything practical like getting stuff ready for work the next day straight away because after an hour I lost the physical or mental energy to even compose a text.

I dreaded those sessions all day, and still do. At five o'clock my stomach would go topsy-turvy with nerves at the thought of how much pain I would be in in three hours from then. How I actually persuaded myself to put my running kit on and get out of my cosy flat to jog down the dark canal for an hour of torture still amazes me. But my motivation remained as strong as ever: to fill my time with a worthy cause and connect with people. Goals are what keep us all going. Improving how fast I could run a race in a field in the rural outskirts of London may not seem like a grave goal but, given that I'd grown despondent with my career, had no relationship to nurture and felt removed from all my friends as they were absorbed in families and kids, it was little wonder that I seized on what was novel in my life for my focus.

And track sessions worked. Each week my lap times were a second or so quicker and I felt less broken afterwards. Perhaps without the challenge to get faster or fitter, the novelty of running itself may have faded quickly.

I adopted coping mechanisms to get myself through the pain of a track session. These are the same things which get me through races today. The simplest one is to tell myself that soon I'll be at home with my feet up/in the bath/under the duvet and all this will be a mere memory. This works because I find that when I really am back home, lying with my feet up/in the bath/under the duvet, detached from all the pain, I'll look back on a training session and think, *I should have pushed a bit harder*. In other words, the pain is easily forgotten and only hurts for the time you are doing it.

Another trick I used was focusing hard on the back of someone's head. *Keep your eye on them and think of nothing*, I'd tell myself. *Push ahead, look ahead, don't think*. Sometimes I'd fix my gaze so rigidly that the white lines of the track would blur until I couldn't see them. I started to make this into a game of 'make the white lines disappear', which seemed to make each hyperventilating lap come around quicker. Not such a great strategy for cross-country, when looking at the ground is critical to not falling over in the mud again.

I was always near the back at track sessions but I didn't have a complex about this. Quite the opposite. These sessions attracted some of the fastest runners in London as well as mediocre ones, like me, who just wanted to improve their 10k time. Our coach Peter McHugh runs an elite athlete management agency called Run-Fast and many of his athletes have competed in Commonwealth Games, Olympic trials and hold UK and world records for various cross-country courses. Some weeks, a group of elite Kenyan runners joined us as part of their overseas training programme. The fact that I was training with this group at all was pretty darn awesome to me.

With the group being predominantly male, I could grant myself extra leniency. From my fast-growing running trivia I had learned that men are naturally faster runners because they have a higher muscle mass, narrower hips (which make for a more economical running style), a higher VO_2 max and a greater red blood cell count. Take the gender handicap into account and I wasn't faring too badly.

Gradually, my body adapted and the sessions left me feeling less and less like I had OD'd on Valium in the hours that followed. I grew to love the two hours between crawling home from the track and bed. I could bathe in the relief that all the hyperventilating agony and biting cold were over. There was a certain buzz about post-track evenings – knowing that I had pushed my body to a level it hadn't been to before, done something virtuous and ticked off another night that hadn't involved drinking.

It didn't take long to feel like an established regular at the track. I started to recognise faces – some from my running club and some from other clubs who I'd seen at races. I loved the running chat as we hung around waiting for Peter to arrive. It made me feel part of a new community. It wasn't that I wanted to become best friends with everyone. It was simply the comfort in knowing that I was part of something new. I was opening doors and leaving a stale period of my life behind.

I had, through my own efforts, found a whole new social circle and culture that just weeks ago I had not known existed. These people had been intimidating strangers wearing wicking tops and heart-rate monitors, talking about tempo runs and tapering. Now I was part of it.

A tempo run was just one term in my growing vocab. It means 'fast'. 'Threshold pace' was another one, which refers to the point at which your heart rate goes from aerobic to anaerobic. Put simply, it's the effort at which you are on the very edge of what you can stand. 'Marathon pace' means 'easy', 'tapering' means toning down training before a race so your muscles are not fatigued and there is even such a thing as a 'recovery run'.

I experienced a few cultural revelations too. Like, it's OK to spit when you run. All runners, I had noticed, did this without embarrassment or apology. There are no looks of disapproval (though do give a half-glance behind before you spittle in case the wind is about to carry it into someone's face). I had also observed that among runners it is perfectly acceptable to get out a flapjack and eat it no matter what the setting. It doesn't matter if you are mid-conversation, on a bike at traffic lights, in a cafe that prohibits your own food or if someone has just cooked you dinner. Producing a half-chewed energy bar at any time, from any pocket, is de rigeur in the world of endurance sport.

Aside from spitting and snacking, there was something very honest about this social environment. These were people brought together by a shared love of the outdoors, an interest in well-being, a sense of purpose and dedication to training. There was a notable absence of materialism. Of course, all of these people also had lives outside running. Maybe they too had jobs or friends or indulgences which were incongruous with the running world. But within this hub things like social status and physical appearance didn't seem to count like they did elsewhere.

Many of them were life-long fitness enthusiasts and outdoor adventurers. I would listen to their sporting quests, past and present, with awe and enthusiasm. A marathon around Lake Geneva. A triathlon in Biarritz. A swim trek around the Dalmatian Coast. Mountain biking through the Peak District. Cycling from London to the southern tip of Italy...

My repertoire of holidays, on the other hand, has featured: rocking up to Koh Samui airport for a flight with just one shoe after raving all night at a full moon party; being picked up drunk from the floor of a petrol station on a coach trip to a ski resort; and tripping on hallucinogenic drugs on the water chute at Disneyland. Not proud.

Hearing their pursuits, my Saturday cross-country races at the end of the Central Line no longer seemed quite so grandiose, yet rather than being intimidated by the fitness and competence of these people, it gave me confidence. They were evidence that it is perfectly humanly possible to do strenuous things with your body. Braver now, I aspired to more challenging things – longer runs like a half-marathon or even a triathlon when the summer came around. I still loved the idea of long bike rides but I would have to get over my fear of cycling in traffic first. A whole new range of activities and holidays was suddenly revealed to me.

One evening in January 2014, I marked my calendar with all the events that had piqued my interest. Things I'd heard about through the crowd at the track or run club. Then, I entered them all. It didn't occur to me that I might be too tired to do two triathlons, a half-marathon and a fell race on four consecutive weekends. Now that I'd survived getting wet and muddy for cross-country, I felt invincible. I was confident that a sports bag containing thermals, dry underwear, dry shampoo, waterproof mascara and BB cream could get me through everything.

There were so many events I wanted to try that a weekend with nothing on seemed a dreadful waste. As I clicked my way through online entry forms, my credit card company temporarily blocked my card then called to check they were my transactions. This spending pattern clearly constituted a radical change in behaviour!

CHAPTER 4

LETTING GO

My graduation from club cross-country to a more hardcore challenge came the next month, with a 10-mile trail race in Epping Forest in Essex called the Mercury Ten. It was hosted by a local running club, Orion Harriers.

I was nervous when I got on a train at Bethnal Green station to travel to Chingford, where the race would begin. Ten-mile runs with the club on Thursdays were one thing but this was off-road and over hills.

I spotted Martha on the train, a Spanish girl from the club, also new to running. She was even more nervous than me. 'I had pasta for breakfast,' she laughed, 'to make sure I have energy.'

Instantly I felt better. I had a buddy, and we reassured ourselves that we could run-walk our way round.

The start was in the middle of a puddle – literally. *Bit unnecessary*, I thought. But no one else seemed to even notice it. Sixty runners and I stood obediently, ankle deep in murky water, listening to a 5-minute briefing about following a trail of sawdust.

The whistle blew and 60 pairs of feet splashed through the puddle, joyfully showering everyone with speckles of mud. I barely flinched over mud any more.

We ascended a hill straight away. Big tree roots protruded from the forest track, threatening to trip us up, but I weaved between them safely. Despite it being February, the weather was glorious. It was so mild that I took off my gloves and stuffed them up my sleeves.

The sky was a deep shade of blue and the winter sunshine, low in the sky, dazzled us as we ran. Less than a mile in, we reached the crest of the first hill and I could see the city of London glistening white in the sunlight beneath me.

This is why I run, I thought. *For this*. Feel-good endorphins spilled through me. The view. The feel of the first rays of sunshine on my skin after midwinter. The promise of summer. The energy of other runners around me. I couldn't think of anything else I'd rather be doing with my Saturday. For the next two hours there was nothing else to think or worry about – not even my wet feet bothered me.

I now had a proper running watch and after it recorded 1 mile, I thought, *That's 10 per cent already. Only 9 more of what I've just done. Easy!*

I always break the distance down in fractions like this. Quantifying it in manageable chunks helps me cope psychologically. My three main markers are: *I'm a quarter of the way through*, *I'm a third of the way through* and *I'm halfway through*. I visualise the fraction as a slice on a pie chart, so I can comprehend how much has passed and how much there is to go. Then to pass more time, I think of the fraction in as many different ways as I can. *One third means I've got two again of what I've just done* or I think things like, *Half again of what I've just done will mean I'm halfway through the whole thing* (because a third plus a half of a third equals one half). By the time I've worked out one set of fractions, another fraction has gone by so I can think of new equations all over again. The more exerted I am, the harder it is to do maths, which is a good thing because the longer the calculations take, the quicker the time goes by.

I picked up speed as I headed down the hill, making sure I took in the view as I did. I felt great until mile three, at which point I told myself as good as a third has passed. Then the mud became thick like cement. A narrow path along a golf course forced everyone into single file and we had to grab the wire fencing to pull our legs through the mud. We were forced to slower than a walking pace as we pulled one sinking ankle after the other out of black sludge.

There were no water stations on this race. It always makes me smile when at large commercial events – like half-marathons, triathlons or mass 10ks – there are officials in fluorescent jackets handing out water everywhere you look. Organisers give health and safety briefings highlighting the importance of staying hydrated. Within running clubs things are less formal. For a mere 10 miles and a £2 entry fee, water stations are not considered necessary.

But the unseasonably warm weather and the undulating terrain gave me a thirst so, when I spotted a pub at around 5 miles, I dived into it in the hope of getting a glass of water. No one batted an eyelid at this red-faced, mud-splattered blonde with a number pinned to her running vest standing at the bar. In fact, I was having trouble getting served so, after a while, I butted into someone's order: 'Really sorry but I'm in the middle of a race. Could I get a glass of water?'

The bar boy was most obliging. 'Ice and lemon?' he replied cheerfully.

I downed a whole pint and then trotted back into the race.

I passed runners who I had overtaken once already. Ten minutes later I had to stop in a bush to pee, and 5 minutes later I passed the same runners for a third time.

One girl kept passing me, then I ran past her, then we'd do it again. She spurred me on when she saw me slow down, and I spurred her on when she slowed down. I'd never seen her before but that's the spirit in running. Everyone jostles each other. We're kindred spirits and we feel the same aches and the same sense of exertion.

By mile eight, my legs were smarting. The hills and the mud had taken everything out of them. I slowed to a walk.

'You can't walk now!' cried my new friend. 'There's less than two miles and the hills are all over.'

It was only because of her words that I picked up again into a slow jog.

At the finish, we high-fived.

She looked like an experienced club runner so I was pleased that I'd almost kept up with her – until she added, 'I did Parkrun this morning. God, I regret that.'

Here was me doing what I considered a breakthrough event and she'd done a 5k race as a warm-up!

Still, I tried not to compare myself to other runners. I was a newcomer and every fixture I did was an accomplishment, not just the activity itself but the resourcefulness it required: getting there, owning and packing the right apparel, not caring that I was wearing a clashing combo of pink, purple and fluorescent green or that my hair was sticking up on end. I liked that I was no longer precious about these things.

I sat on the grass at the finish, drinking cup after plastic cup of water, and watched the remaining runners come in. I observed the looks of relief on their faces as they rounded the corner and saw the finish. I had finished ahead of every single one of these runners coming in now. Not coming near last always surprised me at every event I did because I'd never believed myself to be a sportswoman.

The great thing about exercise is that once it's over, the memory of pain goes away instantly. Your heart rate returns to normal within a minute, your breathing recovers in seconds, your legs stop hurting (at least until you stand up again anyway). Other than feeling a bit sticky, you're fine.

Memory is selective but particularly so when it comes to the pain of exercise. At the end of a race when someone asks how it went I genuinely can't ever think of anything bad to say. I forget that – in this particular case – I spent the entire 1 hour 41 minutes doing fractions to coax myself through, that I gasped my way up every hill, promising myself I'd have a walking break at the crest, that mud splattered in my eye and it stung, that my nose was running and I wiped it so much that it got sore, that I was thirsty and my legs hurt. When they ask, 'How did you find that?', I forget all of this and all I can recall is the gorgeous scenery and the life force flooding through my veins. 'Fine!' I reply.

I felt so good about finishing the Mercury Ten that I braved the Orion Fifteen two weeks later. Hosted by the same running club from the same location, this one was longer, hillier and busier. Until now I had considered it out of my league, but if I'd completed the 10-mile route, what was another five? I could run-walk it. The memories of sunshine, the view of London from the first hilltop and running across unmarked forest were fresh in my mind. There was much talk about the Orion Fifteen in the clubhouse bar on the preceding Thursday and that confirmed my decision. I didn't want to miss out on a big club outing.

But winter returned, delivering a freezing, windy day with rain and hail. Great big crystal stones pelted down on my bare arms. Bare arms was not something I would have chosen had I learned at that point to always check the weather forecast when selecting kit. I still had lots to learn.

I stood next to Dave on the start line. Dave, who had dragged me through that first 10-mile run. He had become the closest thing to a real friend in the club. He would be an unlikely friend in any other environment because of the age gap – he was nearly 60 – but I almost always ended up talking to him at the bar, or sitting by him on the minibus to a race, or running at the same pace during long runs.

As we waited for the briefing about following trails of sawdust, I told him and anyone else who'd listen how I'd never run further than 10 miles in my life. Dave assured me it wasn't a race and that if I walked up all the hills to save my energy I'd be fine. Then he added that he was also going slowly because 'he wasn't as fast as he used to be'.

I felt nervous but told myself, as I had with the 10-mile version of this course, that I could just run-walk my way around. I was shivering already, which added to my sense of dread. I'd deposited my outer layers in the Orion clubhouse changing rooms a whole 20 minutes ago. How I regretted not bringing a long-sleeved top to wear under my club vest. This run would be much longer than the cross-countries I was used to so I would be going slower and wouldn't generate as much heat.

I set off at an easy pace, placing one foot in front of the other, without any effort at all. My pace seemed to synchronise with Dave's and we ran alongside each other mostly in silence, with the odd benign observation about the scenery or a puddle. This happens with group running. You enjoy a silent connection for a while, as if forging a bond with the patter of your feet. Then, just as naturally as you came together, you start to drift away. It is neither rude to ease on ahead nor intrusive to find yourself running at someone's shoulder if that's the pace your legs decide to turn over.

I ran with Dave for half of the race. Sometimes he got ahead and sometimes I did, but we held roughly the same speed. I lost him around mile eight when I popped into the bushes to pee (I really must stop drinking so much green tea before long runs).

He remained ahead for the rest of the race but I could just about see him a couple of hundred metres ahead and I used his green top as my pace marker.

The mud had dried significantly from two weeks ago, which made it easier, but we now had wind to contend with. Then after my pee stop it started to hail. It pelted my bare arms and I saw goosebumps emerge.

Still, I felt strong. I passed the 10-mile mark with purpose. Every stride beyond this point was officially the furthest I had ever run. My legs seemed happy to continue. Buoyed by the fact that I had surpassed 10 miles and felt fine, I caught up with a few runners who had passed me earlier. I overtook, giving a few standard words of encouragement as I had noted runners always do. Before I knew it, I passed a sign for 13 miles. I did a double take. I was expecting to be walking by that distance, or breaking down the race into fractions so complex it would keep Einstein preoccupied, but I was still going strong.

Then 5 minutes later, on the next hill, I started to struggle. My legs were getting wearier and wearier and now they were burning. I wasn't out of breath but my energy dipped and my whole body was telling me to stop. I could just about see Dave in front. I didn't want to get too far behind because we'd got this far together and so his position had become my benchmark.

My core temperature was warm from running but my arms smarted from the wind and the intermittent hail, and my clothes were uncomfortably cold and wet against my skin.

I passed the final marshal. 'Just five hundred metres to go,' they encouraged, which was a lie because it was more like a kilometre.

I kept expecting the finish to appear around every corner but it didn't. The last 6 minutes seemed to last an age.

I finished 5 minutes behind Dave. He gave me a gentle squeeze. Already I'd forgotten the struggle and I was beaming. Fifteen miles!

I didn't hang around on the grass at the finish line this time. It was too cold. I headed swiftly to the changing rooms, had a rinse in the crowded lukewarm showers and then joined the congregation in the Orion Harriers clubhouse hall for tea and cake.

Cake features big in the world of club running. Members bake, give or sell their creations after races. I never used to eat cake. Mostly because, having battled with eczema my whole life, there is a whole load of food groups I don't go near – dairy being one of them. And also because I considered cake 'bad'. In my old life – pre-10-mile runs and track sessions – I was a typical, weight-conscious carb dodger. I wouldn't say I had an unhealthy obsession with weight, but, like many women, I was always in 'restrict' mode. I followed the fad at the time to base meals around protein and vegetables. No white pasta. Don't even think about reaching for the bread basket when eating out. Avoid cake like the plague, unless it's low-fat, low GI, sugar free – in which case it isn't actually a cake.

But this was changing. I was discovering, through my new friends and by reading around my new hobby, that carbs are the elixir for runners.

Carbs get a bashing in the media – especially the sugary, starchy, 'white' carbs – but it isn't strictly true that they're bad for you. Carbohydrate is the body's first choice of fuel. Your body stores it in your muscles as glycogen. If your glycogen stores are full and you eat more carbs than your muscles can store, your body can store it as fat. The advice to limit your carbs is all well and good if you have a desk job, drive to work and your hobbies are watching soap operas.

Most people can store enough glycogen in their muscles to fuel moderate exercise of around ninety minutes. So while an hour in the gym or a 30-minute run around the park is great, unfortunately it does not mean you can eat a box of doughnuts afterwards without any unwanted consequences. But should you go galloping through Epping Forest for 15 miles in a hailstorm, it's safe to assume your body will have used up all its glycogen stores.

The sooner you can refuel with carbohydrate after exercise lasting longer than 90 minutes, the better. The body is more receptive to nutrients in the first 20 minutes after exercise and its ability to restore glycogen to the muscles is heightened. This is when, for once, fast-release, high-GI, white, refined, 'bad' carbohydrates are good!

This makes cake, which also contains a small amount of protein, not a bad recovery food at all. It was with this science in mind that I sank into a slice of lemon polenta cake, followed by a hearty slice of carrot cake.

An hour later, we piled on to a train back to east London, cluttering up the carriage with our bikes. Almost everyone in running club owned a bike. Being a runner seemed to be part of a wider fitness lifestyle. I too found I used my bike more and the Tube less, but still only for journeys which didn't involve roads.

The train stopped at Clapton, which I knew to be near to the River Lea. I remembered this from when my ex and I did our day-long bike ride the previous summer (the one which was just 20 miles but which we considered to be a mammoth adventure). Because of that ride I knew that the River Lea ran into the Limehouse Cut, which ended right by my home. I'd had no reason to revisit that river path. Until now.

It was approaching 4 p.m. so I had just enough time before dusk at around five. The rain had stopped, even though it was bitterly cold. I was full of triumphant energy. I'd completed a 15-mile trail run yet I felt fine. I was ever fascinated with my body's ability to adapt to whatever I threw at it. There seemed to be no limit to its increasing fitness.

I was wrapped up warm in dry, clean, sensible clothes and adequately refuelled thanks to carrot cake. So, on a whim, I got off the train with my bike at Clapton and followed a sign for the river.

It wasn't far – about seven miles home – but those 7 miles were deeply symbolic. Retracing this route signified how much things had moved on since my break-up. This route had once seemed epic, and I was now making it into a leisurely commute home after a 15-mile run in a forest with new friends who had taught me so many things.

I took a few wrong turns from the station, one of which took me down the steepest hill I've ever cycled down, and I had to turn around and walk back up it. But once I found the river path I recognised it. As I pedalled south towards Limehouse, I recalled that day nine months ago.

It had been a hot sunny day then and I was riding my clunky Dutch shopping bike with the broken basket and the dodgy brakes. It should have been the recipe for a perfect day out with a man who loved me, yet I was agitated and bored and consumed by the thought that I wanted to break free.

Now, I had a different bike and my life was totally different. The hail resumed and low black clouds darkened the sky but I laughed because, despite the gloomy weather, I felt happier, freer, fitter and more resilient than I could have imagined on that sunny day.

As I pedalled on into the wind, the memories of that day continued to play back. I passed a pub overlooking the water and I recalled how we had stopped for a respite drink. The benches where we had sat in the sunshine were now deserted and soaking wet. I remember sipping my pint with a sense of self-loathing. I remember thinking that it was such a waste to have a lovely activity to focus on yet we were dulling it with drinking. I remember feeling frustrated that we never did anything that didn't involve drinking (of course, there were other incompatible things about us). And I remember sitting there feeling resentful because I knew that I wanted to spend my days doing more fulfilling things, though I didn't know what.

But as I cycled now, I started to feel tenderness towards him. It hadn't been his fault that I'd been so frustrated. It was me who had wanted to seek new things, me who had grown tired of our routine. I'd expected him to mirror me.

It occurred to me that perhaps some of my drive for this new active lifestyle was my way of distancing myself as much as I could from this previous way of life, justifying to myself that it had been the right thing to get out of what I was part of before.

I also felt my guilt ease. Since we had broken up, he had put pressure on me to change my mind, which had created uncertainty at first, then guilt, and then irritation because I wanted to get on with my life but he wouldn't let me.

As I turned over events and our relationship in my mind, I felt all my exasperation thaw and my sadness over the finality of it dissipate. I forgave him for everything that he wasn't and for the guilt he had inflicted. If it hadn't been for him, I wouldn't have felt compelled to go seeking the thing I had found now.

I was approaching Three Mills, near Mile End. I was soaked through – the hail had become stronger. It was hitting my head through the gaps in my helmet and whipping my cheeks. I knew my legs were going to ache like hell when I got home. Yet I felt nothing but joy. I was going home to an empty flat with no plans on a Saturday night but that was exactly what I wanted. My weekend had been full enough. Those days of frustration and craving and guilt were over. I had found what I set out to seek and there was so much ahead to look forward to.

CHAPTER 5

LOST IN FRANCE

Spring arrived and my ambitious calendar of endurance challenges would soon begin. So far, I'd signed up to a 100k bike ride through the night around London, a mud race, two half-marathons, a fell-running weekend, a 5k ocean swim in Greece and not one but four triathlons!

I didn't wait to see if I enjoyed my first triathlon. I was certain I would.

I fully intended to do all of them on my hybrid bike. I knew from listening to conversations in the club bar that the proper way to do a triathlon was on a road bike, but I certainly wasn't going to upgrade again. A bike's a bike. How much faster can curly handlebars make it go?

But before I had to worry about that, I was off on a week-long triathlon training holiday in south-east France with 20 others from run club. It was with a mix of excitement and nerves that I went on this excursion in a particularly chilly week of May. The trip was organised before I joined the club – the deposits paid, the email banter established, the room-sharing plan agreed. I was a late addition after a dropout and so I was more conscious than ever about my non-sporty heritage. I was afraid that my true past as the Clarins-loving, creature-comfort-seeking city girl would be exposed.

This brought on major packing anxiety. What, for instance, would I wear in the evenings? My jeans were too trendy, my tops too fitted. My only sunnies were Gucci. As for footwear, the only options in my non-heeled range were trainers, the walking boots that nearly made my mum faint or gold flip-flops with giant sequins. Would it be very wrong to take a hairdryer? This was not so much to do with style as it was to do with warmth. I get cold when I sit around with wet hair.

What luggage would I take? My only suitcase was a Louis Vuitton wheelie. I had recurring nightmares about turning up at the airport to see everyone in tracksuits, hoisting weathered sports holdalls and me, immaculately dressed, towing a giant case on wheels with a bikini spilling out of a Prada handbag.

Most importantly, what if my fitness wasn't up to the others'? There was a core group of established club members on this trip and I desperately didn't want to be the one struggling at the back, or worse, the one holding people back.

So I stepped things up in the weeks before. Essentially I trained for a training holiday. My first Olympic-distance triathlon would be six weeks after I returned, so I had to prepare for that anyway.

I didn't download a training plan or consult a coach or anything organised like that. I just used common sense. I didn't need to do anything extra for running since I did lots of that. Swimming would need some work. I needed to be comfortable with 1,500 metres of continuous front crawl.

I could swim but I'd never had any lessons on technique. My swim sessions had generally been a relaxed routine of breaststroke, backstroke and a self-taught version of crawl. This cycle was repeated at a leisurely pace until the clock said I'd done 30 minutes.

One day, I went to my gym's heated 20-metre pool and set about doing my first ever all-front-crawl session. Fifteen hundred metres would be 75 lengths. The first few times I attempted this, I could only manage 10 lengths at a time before the sides of my upper back ached and I needed a few breaststroke lengths for a break. The whole time, I thought about my impending triathlon at the end of June. Not only did I have to swim 1,500 metres but I had to swim it effortlessly because immediately afterwards I'd have to cycle 40k and run 10k. This spurred me on to go every week, building up my crawl-breaststroke mix each time with more crawl, less breaststroke. Within a month, I could manage the full 75 lengths of continuous front crawl in about half an hour. By the end, as I tired, I could feel my arms flopping down on the water surface. But who cares about style? It was all about the numbers.

Then there was cycling. I was still too scared of traffic to cycle on roads – the triathlons I'd entered were all on closed roads. For short journeys I was happy to dodge tourists on canal towpaths. To build stamina for the 40k bike leg of a triathlon, I took up spin classes.

These made my legs ache, a lot. I thought my legs were strong from running and gym workouts. But this was a different type of ache from different muscles. The classes were intense too and for the first few weeks I experienced the same unpleasant cardio chest burn as when I first started going to the track. I was doing the extra swimming and spinning in addition to Thursday long club runs, Tuesday track sessions and one or two gym sessions. Cross-country season was now over so there were only occasional road races with the club on weekends. Like everything else, after a few weeks, spin classes felt easier and soon I was even doing a swim before spin, though I had to have a lie-down afterwards if I did that.

I love to look back on those milestones in my fitness journey because in a matter of weeks I forget how hard it first felt. I now try to see other people's achievements through their eyes. For someone who never exercises, running a mile is a lot for the body to cope with. It's pushing the limits that is commendable, not the distance or speed or any other measurable variable. Forgetting how hard things used to feel is perhaps why fitness is so addictive. Unlike work goals or relationship goals, where results depend on uncontrollable factors, fitness is a biological reaction. If you train you get results.

It wasn't until I arrived at Les Stables training retreat in the Dordogne that I got my taste of 'real' cycling on a road bike. I hired a bike. Some of my environmentally conscious run club friends brought their own, having driven through France instead of flying. I remember watching in awe as two friends, Mick and Ben, unloaded their bikes from a roof rack and effortlessly put the wheels back on. I silently prayed that my triathlon journey would never require me to do that! It looked so complicated. I would never trust myself to put a wheel back on to a bike in case it fell off at high speed.

Six of us flew to Bordeaux airport. As it happened, my reality was not that much different from my recurring nightmare. I did indeed have the biggest bag and I was indeed the only one with a designer wheelie bag. The others had sporty holdalls and one girl even took everything – including cycle shoes, running shoes and toiletries – as hand luggage. *I could never do that*, I thought. I need not have been so self-conscious about these things, though I didn't realise it at the time. There are plenty of other runners and triathletes like me who enjoy a bit of glamour and sophistication. In fact, one of the first female marathon runners, back in 1967, Kathrine Switzer, famously wore lipstick. (Quite how she managed not to smudge it all around her mouth as it mixed with sweat and dribble is another question.) Whenever I thought of sporty people, I'd think back to the domineering girls at school who played hockey in shorts and T-shirts and didn't feel the cold and who would pick stones out of open knee wounds without even flinching.

Les Stables is set in the secluded countryside of the Dordogne. They have six apartment blocks, converted from stables, which accommodate four or six. Large fields lined the long drive. There was a running track on one side and an outdoor swimming pool on the other.

I shared a room with Dave. There was an odd number of males and females and, with me being the newest member, I was always going to be the one sharing with a bloke. I was relieved it was Dave. He was the one I knew best among what seemed like an already established group of sporty friends and, given our familiarity, I imagined he would be the most forgiving of my ridiculously non-minimalist packing and my toiletries that took over the bathroom.

A couple of times I found myself wondering if there was something more in our friendship, but in the same thought, my voice of reason would cry, *Don't be ridiculous – he's 60!* Besides, the thing I found most cathartic about my new outdoorsy lifestyle was the very fact that it was so far removed from the romantic dramas which I used to court in my old life. Drinking, dating (before the boyfriend) and socialising had all been par for the course of keeping busy, peppering my life with excitement for the sake of it. I was enjoying not doing that.

If there were any faint feeling of attraction, any danger of it growing was promptly put to rest as we were preparing our bikes for our first ride.

I was waiting for someone to help with my cycling cleats. As instructed, I had dutifully bought a pair of special cycling shoes, with so-called 'cleats' to clip into special pedals. Thing is, cleats don't come ready-attached to the shoes. You have to screw them on yourself. That had looked complicated and I figured there would be someone at my destination who could do a much better job at aligning them than me. So I turned up to our first cycle session clutching my cleats in their plastic wrapper.

'You haven't even got your cleats attached. Jesus Christ!' said Mark, the no-nonsense owner of Les Stables. 'Can you at least put your pedals on your bike?'

'I can have a go.' Until last week, I hadn't even known pedals could be removed from a bike.

'Philippe, sort her out,' sighed Mark.

I looked over to see whom Mark was addressing and there walked forth this beautiful, tall, strapping man with a delicious French accent. He smiled and took the shoes and plastic-wrapped cleats from my hands and got to work with a spanner as I stood by, not daring to say a word.

Once assembled, I rode around the driveway, practising the seemingly impossible art of clipping my special shoes in and out of special pedals. I fell off a few times. This apparently is a rite of passage for budding road cyclists, just like falling over when learning to ski.

I could feel Philippe watching me, chuckling.

The purpose of cleats, since you may rationally ask, is to enable you to pull up on each pedal stroke as well as push down. It is a more efficient way of using energy because you utilise hamstring muscles as well as quad muscles, hence you can go faster for longer. And yes, you may reasonably ask, it does make cycling in traffic more dangerous because you can't always unclip when braking suddenly. But, as I was soon to learn, in the world of cycling and triathlons a little bit of danger is nothing if it means gaining a few seconds.

Once I'd managed to stop and start three times in a row without toppling sideways, Mark and his similarly no-nonsense girlfriend, Sibbs, split us into three groups. Both ex-triathletes themselves, they'd moved from Britain to France to set up Les Stables.

'If you've never been on a road bike before I'd recommend you stay with the slow group,' Sibbs warned, looking at me dubiously as I took various layers of clothing on and off, undecided whether I would be hot or cold – a giveaway of inexperience.

'But I'm very fit,' I insisted. I'd been training hard for this trip and I wanted to get everything I could out of it. I had grown to crave that glorious mix of exertion and satisfaction when you've pushed your body just beyond its limits.

'You do know how to change gears on a road bike, right?' Sibbs asked, maintaining her dubious look.

'Oh yes,' I said confidently. I'd ridden scores of bikes in my life and there's usually a switch on the handlebars to change gears. Why would this be any more difficult?

Before Sibbs could say anything else, I wheeled my bike over to the 'middle' group, which included the fast girls plus Dave. Most of the boys were in the fast group. In the slow group were mostly wives and girlfriends, here to enjoy the holiday.

I was adamant about being in the middle group. All the girls who were regular club members were in this group and I wanted to be part of that gang. Strangely, I feel more comfortable being behind people and busting a gut to keep up than being at the front of a group I find easy. This had been my default setting when I first started running with the club. From that inaugural 10-mile run, desperate not to be the one slowing everyone down, to track sessions with rabid runners, it has become my norm to bust a gut to keep up. I'm most familiar with this dynamic and somehow it's even become a comfort – it's like I've found my place in a pack and that's what I want to stick to.

However, that day in France I got a bigger challenge than I bargained for. I set off with the middle-level group but then got confused and followed the wrong set of Lycra. It happened so quickly. Everyone looks the same in a helmet and logoed T-shirt.

Before I realised my error, I was swept along in a terrifyingly fast line of cyclists, sweeping the hills of the Dordogne, taking corners at such speed I clung on to the handlebars for dear life, my jaw locked in terror. I desperately tried to stay with them, panting and sweating. All this, as I was still figuring out how to change gears. There are two levers on the top of the handlebars. Nudging the right lever to one side changes the big chain up (so the pedalling gets stiffer). But how to change it down again is not so obvious – there's a small lever buried within the main lever which you press with your index finger. Conversely, on the left side of the handlebars is the lever for the big chainring at the front, and for that one the main lever changes it down and the hidden small lever up – the opposite way around.

I managed to stay with my group for 5 minutes before they started to pull away. I pushed and pushed to keep up but, to my despair, the distance between us increased. Their shapes began to shrink. Every couple of minutes, it looked like I was gaining ground. The dots looked like they were getting closer, millimetre by agonising millimetre, but if I eased off a fraction they become distant again. Every cyclist will be familiar with this experience – it's called 'being dropped'. That might sound mean but dropping someone isn't always deliberate. When a rider falls behind, the others don't always notice. If they're your friends, or if it's a sociable 'no-drop' ride, they'll stop and wait when they realise. But the serious Lycra brigade operates on the policy of cafe-only stops.

I was hot, I was thirsty, I needed to wipe my sunglasses and blow my nose and take a sip of water, but there was no way I could take a hand off the handlebar. One second of hesitation and I lost even more ground.

Breathe deeply, I told myself as I hyperventilated up a hill. *Get some oxygen going around your body.* This was a tip I'd learned from runners at cross-countries. When you're out of puff, the best thing is not to pant with short, desperate breaths but to inhale deeply into your diaphragm so you take in more oxygen.

But I needed a lot more than fresh air. I needed a miracle. They rounded a corner and I couldn't see them at all. I felt totally alone in the alien French countryside. Only then did it dawn on me that I'd followed the wrong group. I didn't know if the group I was supposed to be in would take the same route. If they were, I could wait for them, but maybe they were taking a shorter route?

It was too much of a risk to wait. My best hope now was to carry on and keep the dots on the horizon in my vision as much as possible while we went around bends. If I lost them I had no idea how to get back to Les Stables. As I was thinking of a plan, which involved Google Maps and an expensive data-roaming bill, I noticed one of the dots on the horizon had come to a halt. The dot looked like it was looking back at me. The dot was waiting for me! I pushed on, fuelled by relief. The dot became clearer until I could make out the blue and white logo of Les Stables on its T-shirt. It was Philippe.

'Are you OK?' he asked in that lovely French accent.

'I followed the wrong group!' I panted. Then I added, 'I've never been on a road bike before.' I didn't want him thinking I was this hopeless for no good reason.

'You are doing well,' he purred. 'These guys are fast.'

I was pleased to hear that the middle group was doing the same route as this one and would soon be pedalling past at a more sustainable speed so I could join them. Rather than wait here, Philippe informed me there was an official stop in 10 kilometres, where both groups could use toilets, fill up water bottles and eat flapjacks. We headed there together.

'You are on the wrong ring,' he pointed out as we cycled side by side.

'Wrong ring?'

'You are on the small chainring. This one is for climbing.' I love how the French emphasise all the wrong words. 'This *one* is for climb*ing*.'

'I've been trying to change it,' I replied, 'but it's stuck.'

It wasn't stuck. Philippe pointed out calmly that I was flicking the gear lever the wrong way. I was still trying to compute that the two gear levers for the front and back chainrings work in opposite ways.

Stupid system, I thought.

Once we got the subject of rings out of the way, we talked about triathlons and training. He told me he worked for Mark and Sibbs in the summer, rescuing English girls like me who get lost in the French hills. In the winter he worked in Paris, organising the Castle Triathlon series of races.

'You are strong,' said Philippe when there was nothing else to say.

Clearly I was not a strong cyclist. This was the first time I'd ever ridden a bike properly on the open road. There was no other explanation – he was flirting!

Once we reached the water stop and I rejoined the appropriate group, things were more enjoyable. The pace was challenging – enough to push myself, but not so much that I couldn't keep up. We covered 70k that day with two breaks, and it took 3.5 hours. Not bad, I thought, considering I hadn't been on a road bike before. (Did I mention that?)

The next day my lower back ached. Sibbs told me knowingly that this is a classic symptom of doing too many miles too soon. Whatever. I was still glad I'd joined the group I did, and not the slow one, which only covered half the distance.

We went for a long ride every other morning. Riding in a peloton was exhilarating. A 'peloton' is not a type of road crossing, as I had initially thought. A peloton is a group of cyclists, who ride close enough to each other's wheels to get the benefit of a draft from the one in front, which pulls them along. I was petrified at cycling so close to the wheel in front of me, but I didn't have much choice because every time I let a tiny gap open, Mark would shout, 'Get on her fucking wheel. Save your fucking energy!'

And so began a new learning curve into the world of road biking. There is a lot more to the sport than simply cycling. There is a whole etiquette, dress code and lingo. Much of this I learned from Brenda, a long-established member of running club and also an active cycling club member. She imparted much wisdom that trip.

For instance, if you 'ride on someone's wheel', as it's known, it's polite to take the front occasionally so that the one at the front doesn't do all the hard work. Drafting can reduce your effort by as much as 20 per cent on a windy day. If you do take the front you need to make sure you can sustain the pace or the others will end up slowing down. Brenda also told me about arm-warmers and leg-warmers, which are not only slicker but more aerodynamic than a jacket or a baggy running top, which I was using.

The importance of fuelling for long rides was hammered into us. Mark virtually force-fed us energy gels and tipped powdered energy drinks into our water bottles.

'Even if you want to lose weight, it's counterproductive to restrict your calories because you'll run out of power and you'll slow the whole group down,' he told us.

I knew about the 90-minute rule (your body can store enough glycogen for 90 minutes of training) so I brought dried figs and dates with me. I avoid anything processed or acidic, like energy gels or powered sports drinks, because I'm prone to indigestion and eczema flare-ups. Even today, my fuel of choice for a long-distance event or double training sessions is dried fruit and nuts.

Then there are all the shouty commands, which I found to be wonderfully cathartic. When the peloton is about to turn left, the one at the front yells, 'LEEEEEFT!' The one behind them yells, 'LEEEEEFT!', and the one behind them, and so on until it's heard at the back. But even if it's blindingly obvious that everyone heard 'LEEEEFT' the first time, everyone still shouts it just because it's so much damn fun. When else do you get to yell at the top of your voice as an adult?

When there's a car ahead or behind, we yell, 'CAR UP!' or 'CAR DOWN!' respectively. Some people use 'CAR FRONT' and 'CAR BACK' – cycling dialects, if you will, and it can be confusing. I find though, that the moment I see a car, there's no time to compute whether it's car up, car back, car front, or whether it's a great big truck. I simply shout 'CARRR!' in exactly the same tone as my nephew did when he was three.

The other command every cyclist needs to know is 'CLEAR!' when going through a junction to let the person behind know that the road they're turning into is safe. Sometimes it's obvious the junction is clear because everyone can see it on the approach, but we all shout it anyway, just because.

It is also pertinent to warn riders behind of things in the road. You can be riding along quietly, and suddenly someone will yell: 'POTHOLE!' or 'SPEED BUMP' or 'ROADKILL!' or 'BRANCH IN THE MIDDLE OF THE ROAD!'

Occasionally on our morning rides the sun came out and, when it did, I remember thinking that this was all I wanted to do. Here I was in a foreign country, on a weekday, all my work on hold, laughing with new friends and yelling 'CAR!' at the top of my voice. Nothing in the world seemed to matter except moving the pedals and breathing in the fresh air of the Dronne Valley.

CHAPTER 6
DIZZY

Despite me having the biggest suitcase out of everyone on that trip, I still had nothing suitably warm for the evenings. I was used to holidays in warm climes or dressy resorts where the focal point of packing was style. It was hard to break the habit of a lifetime. This was France in early May and the evenings were cool. We spent many of them sitting outside and my cropped black faux-leather jacket didn't quite cut it. I was forced to buy my first ever hoodie.

A hoodie is something I had never really considered to be of enough use to buy my own. Before I got involved in outdoor sports, there were occasions when I needed one. Like visiting my sister in the country, which is always 4 degrees colder than London. Or a freak outdoor event, like when a friend hired a canal boat for a birthday party and it was absolutely freezing (I really thought she had gone mad). But I always borrowed one. In my mind hoodies were something you borrowed – a bit like borrowing a baggy T-shirt to sleep in when you unexpectedly stay over. So when I purchased my very own 'Les Stables' branded, blue cosy hoodie it was a big moment.

All those clothes I'd brought with me. All that planning, working out how I could go casual while still looking good. And guess what I wore every day for the remainder of the holiday? Yep, my hoodie. I loved that hoodie. It was fleecy on the inside, and baggy and comfortable to move around in. Plus, I noted, the bluey-grey hues went perfectly with jeans.

I was particularly grateful for it when walking between the on-site pool and the apartments. Each afternoon at Les Stables we had swim coaching. The water wasn't heated and given the time of year it was bracing. We weren't allowed wetsuits because Sibbs needed to inspect our body positions in the water.

Until now, I had never seen the point in learning to swim 'efficiently'. Before I became enlightened by running club and my new fitness lifestyle, my main objective of exercising had been to burn calories. Being more efficient was the opposite of what I had wanted to achieve. But now my objectives were all about being faster, being good at something, controlling my body. I was starting to tune in to competitive vibes.

We each had a video 'diagnosis' and Sibbs gave us tailored drills designed to help with our biggest flaws. For me, this was a drill called 'catch-up' to lengthen my stroke. To swim most efficiently the hand in front should glide out in front for a fraction of a second before you start the next stroke. That way you cover a greater distance for each stroke, hence you use less energy, which means you can go for longer, or you can go faster.

A drill is an exaggerated motion of the part of the stroke you are trying to correct. Doing a drill over and over again is supposed to ingrain the motion into your neuromuscular system and it should become second nature. It's a subconscious process of learning that is supposed to take several weeks. But, naturally, I wanted it to be ingrained immediately, so I stayed in the pool going over and over the same catch-up drill. I swam and I swam and I swam until my arms felt like they weren't attached to my body any more.

Up and down I went, concentrating on nothing but the position of my arms when I started and ended each stroke. I lost track of time and body temperature. I was so absorbed in my catch-up drill that I didn't look up at the end of the lane. Had I looked up, I would have realised that everyone else had left the pool except Brenda and Dave, who were looking down at me with concern. Eventually, at the end of one of my lengths, I felt a tap on my shoulder. It was Dave.

'Helen, I think you'd better get out. You're going to get freezing.'

'Just a couple more,' I panted, and off I went again.

When I returned to the end of the pool again, it was the wise Brenda who tapped me. 'You've been practising that thing for an hour and we can tell you're tired because you're swimming totally differently to how you were swimming thirty minutes ago.'

Now they mentioned it, yes, I was quite tired. And cold. Now that I had stopped to talk, I noticed I felt a bit dizzy. I lifted myself out, tried to stand up and *boom*! I stumbled and half fell, half sat on the floor, paralysed with dizziness. I didn't know what was happening. I was a bit cold, but not that cold. I was a bit tired, but not that tired. Everything was spinning, which in a strange way felt quite nice.

I tried to stand up and fell down immediately. Every muscle felt like jelly.

'Lie down, lie down.' Sibbs, who was nearby clearing up, came striding over, seeing the commotion. She pushed my head gently towards the ground. 'Lie flat for a minute and let the blood re-pool. You've got swimmers' spins.'

'Swimmers' spins', I was informed, is common after swimming in cold water. When it's cold, our bodies – clever little things that they are – concentrate the blood flow to our vital organs to keep them warm. When we suddenly go upright after being horizontal for a long time, the blood re-pools around the body, flowing away from the brain, which causes dizziness. The longer you are horizontal and the colder the water, the worse it is.

I was escorted back to our apartment by Brenda and Dave. There I stood under a scalding shower for an amount of time that I would not care to take a guess on. Maybe it was 10 minutes. Maybe it was an hour. My mind was not in focus.

Two hours later, I was still shivering and totally vacant. It was only when I'd consumed a plate of pasta and two glasses of red Bordeaux that I started to feel normal again.

The dizzy spell at the pool was nothing compared to our first real open-water swim on our penultimate day. This was a 1,500-metre swim down the River Dordogne. The water was 12°C that day. To put this into perspective, a typical indoor public swimming pool is heated to 28°C. Most people wear wetsuits at anything below 22 degrees and the swim gets cancelled if the water goes below 12.5°C. Not an ideal introductory open-water swim.

It was 9 a.m., and the air was cool and damp as we gathered on the riverbank, listening to Sibbs's tips on handling cold water. I wore my gold, sequined flip-flops, which Mark had a good old laugh about.

'When you first enter the water, pull the neck of the wetsuit away so the top part of the suit fills with water, then get out and allow your body temperature to warm the layer of water next to your skin,' said Sibbs.

The fact that we needed a safety briefing about how to deal with the cold was worrying.

'Put your face in the water a few times before you swim. This prepares your body for the shock of the cold. And, finally, keep moving! Tread water until everyone is in and we're ready to swim.'

These were all good tips, but did absolutely nothing to make the water feel any less glacial.

It was so cold it smarted my cheeks. I got an ice-cream headache without the ice cream. We'd only been going for a few seconds when I was overcome by breathlessness. I had trained myself to breathe every three strokes, but I couldn't keep my head in the water for even one stroke because I was so short of breath. I was gasping and spluttering and then I began to panic. *Why can't I breathe?! I swim a mile in my gym pool without so much as a pant.* I wondered if my lungs had shrunk in the cold.

In less than 4 minutes, my fingers and feet were numb. I couldn't see. My goggles were tinted anyway and now they were foggy. The cold on my head felt like a pressure cooker. Every bit of my body was thrashing, fighting, panicking. I was so breathless I worried I might pass out in the water. I reverted to breaststroke in order to breathe. *I have to keep going,* I thought desperately. *I have to stay with the group!*

I tried to calm myself. There were still plenty of people behind me so I could breaststroke a bit before there was any danger of getting left behind. With my head out of the water now, my breathing eased and I tried a few strokes of front crawl. I started breathing every two strokes, instead of the usual three, so as to get more air. Eventually, my breathing calmed and I could swim normally. I say 'normally', but the new technique that I'd diligently practised that week was washed away. I defaulted right back to the old ways. This was pure survival. And besides, it's hard to concentrate on your hand position when you don't even know if your hands are still on the ends of your arms.

I endured this smarting, breathless ice bath for 30 minutes. Then, at last, I could see the white swim hats ahead of me veer over to the bank and pull themselves out of the water. The end! I couldn't swim to the bank fast enough.

But when I got out and tried to stand up, I instantly fell over. Everything was spinning again. It was three times as intense as it had been a few days ago by the pool. I was confused, dazed, and all I could say was: 'I'm so dizzy. God, I'm so dizzy.' I tried to sit up but I couldn't even do that.

Philippe came to my rescue. 'Lie flat and keep still,' he instructed.

Mild panic overcame me. I wanted to get up but I had no control over my muscles. Philippe stood over me for 2 minutes, while my blood re-pooled. Then he led me by the hand to where the others were drying off cheerfully by the pile of backpacks, which had magically arrived by jeep. My holiday companions had clearly built up a lifetime of resilience to cold, exertion and shock. The closest yours truly had ever been to open-water immersion was a hot tub at a spa.

I couldn't feel or move my limbs. I've felt my feet go numb hundreds of times, but I've never, ever felt my whole leg go numb.

It took intense mental focus to locate my bag. I sat on the ground next to it and tried to get my wetsuit off but my hands were unable to grip anything. Inside my bag were my usual staples: towel, dry underwear, warm clothes, recovery snacks, BB cream, mascara and a big comb (nothing feels better than the untangling of wet, matted locks). But a fat lot of good any of it was because I couldn't even undo the zip.

'I'm shivering so much,' I kept repeating, to no one in particular.

I stood like an electrified scarecrow, shivering and trying not to cry, as various people helped me dress. I couldn't even pull my sensibly packed thermal base layer over my head because I couldn't move my arms without help. Tying laces was out of the question, as was fastening the zip on my jeans so I just had to hope they wouldn't fall down.

Dave tied my shoelaces, and Philippe zipped my fleece over my damp swimsuit and then rubbed my back to generate some heat. 'You've got no fat on you – that's why.'

I could hear other voices of concern: 'She looks a bit blue.'

I was beyond responding.

I vaguely remember us walking to the local cafe at the top of a hill, Philippe holding my hand to guide me. Then we sat *outdoors*! It was a chilly morning and my uncombed hair was still drenched. This was not the time to enjoy al fresco croissants.

Philippe asked what I wanted to drink.

'*Chaud*,' I replied. I meant 'hot water'. Where that French vocabulary came from I have no idea. I don't remember a word of French from my school days but out of the depths of my unconscious I managed to produce the word for 'hot'. Survival instinct had kicked in.

Philippe understood what I meant and I drank endless cups of *eau chaud*, hoping it would warm me, but all it did was make me need the loo, which was a disaster, because how in my state was I going to pull my jeans down and then up again?

You would think blue lips and being unable to dress myself would put a dampener on any flirtation between Philippe and me, but apparently not. He stood behind my stool and continued to rub my shoulders and back through my fleece for the entire 45 minutes that we sat outside the cafe. A more coherent me would have moved away, conscious of the spectacle, not to mention friction burns, but at that stage pride was a distant objective.

When we got back to the apartments, I planted myself under another scalding shower for what seemed like time immemorial. Then I climbed into bed wearing every clean item of clothing in my suitcase. I curled into a ball under the duvet and slept for an hour.

When I awoke, sweating, Philippe was sitting in the kitchen of our apartment.

'I have come to see if you are OK, Hélène,' he said in that lovely accent.

It was time for our next session – running on the track.

Given that I was on the brink of hypothermia just three hours previously, I didn't do too badly. It was a speed session with sets of 200 metres. Mark went through running technique and gave us each feedback. I'd never been taught anything about the mechanics of running before. I just ran. According to Mark though, there were lots of improvements to be made: knees, feet, posture, arm movements, the way my foot landed. I had a lot of homework to do.

After the track session, we had two hours to refuel and rest and then it was out on the bikes for a hill session. By then I was raring to go again. We were supposed to do three reps of a big 3-kilometre hill. I did four. I had to. It was becoming a compulsion to max out every training session I did. I may not have been the fastest, nor the most naturally gifted athlete, but I was certainly the most tenacious.

On the way home, we stopped at a bar and sat outside again. It seemed that every bar and cafe in the whole of the Dordogne was outdoors!

Before I'd finished my first large glass of beer, any body heat that I had generated from cycling cooled and I was chilly again. Maybe that's why I drank more, the lukewarm beer numbing the cold. I have no idea how many I drank but, all of a sudden, I noticed it was dark and I was now inside the pub with Dave, Philippe and two other guys from our group. We were all dancing to a live band in our cycle cleats. The rest of the gang were nowhere to be seen. They had sensibly gone back to the warmth and tranquillity of the apartments.

It must have been 9 p.m. and we hadn't eaten. I had a lucid moment in which I thought of two things. First, our bikes were still propped up outside, unlocked. Second, we had no lights.

I expressed these concerns to Philippe.

He shrugged and said, 'Don't worry, Hélène. I will get you home.'

Philippe led me outside, but as we were lingering, trying to remember where we had left our bikes, Dave and the two other stragglers stumbled out of the bar, having also just realised that it had got dark. And so we all cycled back together.

Philippe looked visibly annoyed that his plan to gallantly escort me home in the dark had been shamelessly gatecrashed by three drunk, middle-aged men.

We giggled our way up the steep hill back to Les Stables. It was pitch-dark. If a car had appeared, we'd have been flattened. We opened the door to our apartment to find a party going on. There were pasta dishes and salads and bean stews in the middle of the table and lots of wine. While we had carried on drinking in the bar, the others had used leftovers from all four apartments to create a feast – a final show of team spirit to end the holiday.

When the dancing stopped and everyone went to bed, Philippe finally seized his opportunity to kiss me. It didn't seem to worry him that I was caked in six-hour-old sweat and stale beer and was still wearing my padded cycling shorts, which had soaked up all the water from the wet chairs outside the bar. I savoured our brief shared moment but soon sent him on his way, conscious I was sharing a room with Dave.

The next day, the two of us took mountain bikes into the woods and I missed my afternoon swim lesson. We talked and we kissed, and on a whim we arranged for him to come to visit me in London in the coming weeks. By a stroke of luck, he was doing one of the same triathlons as me later in the year at Hever Castle. How exciting it would be to have a lover at a triathlon.

CHAPTER 7
MUD RUNNING

Days after returning from France, I met some (non-running) friends for lunch on London's South Bank. I cycled there. The holiday had left me considering myself even more of an adventurer. It was a sunny day and with the route being all river paths I could not justify getting the Tube. My friends thought it was hilarious when I turned up in a stylish outfit, kitten heels and all, topped with a bike helmet. I shrugged – I liked wearing a bit of my new lifestyle, as if broadcasting my new sense of practicality over glamour. A helmet meant I did things, rather than just looked good.

Cycling there was the finale to my exercise quota that day. I'd already done a long run in the morning. Topping it off with a ride as part of my commute gave me both satisfaction and a huge appetite for food and wine. One of my new favourite things was doing loads of training then meeting friends to drink. There was something extra rewarding about it. It felt like I'd earned it, rather than doing it because it was the default way to entertain myself.

I told my friends about my trip to France. They weren't interested in my cycling the French hills but they were very interested in Philippe, and I delighted in telling them how he'd had to dress me after getting out of the river because I was so cold. Here I was regaling tales of mischief over wine just like I used to, only this time it was with the backdrop of triathlon. Perhaps some traits – like my propensity to get drawn into mischief – will never change.

Having trained twice a day in France, I wanted to keep it all up when I returned. My old training routine no longer felt challenging enough. I kept up cycling with extra spin classes. Swimming was no longer just swimming up and down. One week of lessons and I considered myself a pro, so I made up speed sessions, hammering out sets of 100-metre and 200-metre sprints.

Training can be very much like getting hooked on a new drug. Each time I crossed a new fitness barrier I got a new high. Every breakthrough distance widened my perspective on what I believed my body capable of. With that came a desire to push more, test more limits, feel more exertion, endure more testing conditions. With every ache, I felt my muscles getting stronger. With every laboured breath on the track, I felt I was getting faster. With every shiver riding my bike home late from training sessions, I felt I was becoming hardier.

Part of the allure was witnessing my body change. Not just how it looked – though I loved that I was becoming more athletic – but how it coped. Every time I thought I'd reached my peak, and that at my age this was it – I probably couldn't get any fitter – I'd amaze myself by doing more. Or doing the same activity but finding it easy. Me, the waif-like, glamorous, central-heating-worshipping follower of fashion was doing all this tough stuff!

It got me thinking just how little of our physical capacity we utilise with modern, sedentary lifestyles. I used to think my three-times-a-week gym routine was a lot. I thought it unnecessary, obsessive or even detrimental to health to do more. Undemanding daily life gives us self-limiting beliefs. Now that I was surrounded by people striving for sub three-hour marathons, who cycled to Cambridge on a Sunday just for something to do, nothing seemed excessive.

The lovely Philippe, with whom I remained in regular contact after returning from France, would tell me how he'd just got back from a 25-kilometre (15-mile) run before breakfast and was planning a 5-kilometre swim session for the afternoon. Sim, our passionate running club team captain, was training for the gruelling Comrades ultramarathon. He'd talk of 30-mile training runs as if they were a game of tennis.

I wasn't training for anything specifically. I had such a variety of events on my calendar for the upcoming summer – half-marathons, wild swims, triathlons, a two-day fell race – that I approached the whole thing like an experiment. How fit can I get?

There are many similarities between endurance sport and other forms of excess. When I was a teenager and I tried to be cool by getting into the clubbing scene, there were always recognisable characters on a mission to push limits. How many pills can they take? How many nights could they stay up for without sleeping? How many war stories do they have? The people you will find running ultramarathons, swimming the Channel or trekking the Himalayas are similarly seeking to experience the extreme. Endurance junkies want to push, see and feel more and more, just like some people want to push the limits with drink, drugs or other substances. The effects on your body may be less destructive but the drive behind it is the same.

In his book *Running with the Kenyans*, Adharanand Finn quotes a race competitor comparing running to substance addiction in reverse. He said that partying and drinking give you a high then pain. Running and sport give you pain then the high.

If fitness can be an addiction then perhaps, like with drugs and alcohol, some people are more predisposed to getting hooked than others. I find it intriguing how some people love punishing their bodies with killer training sessions while others detest it. Sometimes I would look around at the people at running club and think, *Every single person here shares a common trait in that we all derive some sort of reward from the discomfort and exhilaration and the dread and the desire to run.* It's a mystifying thought because none of us knows what that common trait might be, but whatever it is it bonds us.

The idea that some of us are born with a greater drive to exercise than others was a popular hypothesis among sports scientists in the noughties. There have been many studies to investigate whether genes can be linked to the amount of exercise people do, with mixed results. One study in 2006 found that our likelihood to take up sport is 62 per cent linked to genes. In 2009 another study found as many as 37 DNA regions linked to exercise. Their conclusion? It's impossible to link our drive to exercise to any genes because the combination of the DNA involved is just too complicated.

Still, endurance sport has never been so popular. There are now more than 800,000 running events in the UK every year. Apparently 100,000 people a year take part in cycle events and there are 140,000 active triathletes. Not bad for a country which only has about two months of warm weather a year. Browse your Facebook friends' photos and it won't take you long before you find a profile picture of someone on a finish line at a half-marathon, at their first triathlon or on the peak of a mountain they've climbed for a charity challenge.

Maybe the trend for extreme exercise is because we've run out of options for other extremes. Twenty years ago when people had a mid-life crisis, they bought a Harley-Davidson or had an affair. But my generation (that is, ahem, the ones approaching middle age) are partied out. We took cocaine, popped pills and slept around in our twenties and thirties. Now we're chasing the exact opposite because that in itself is a rebellion against the old ways.

🌲🌲🌲🌲🌲

I may well have been getting a bit obsessed with training and club events but how could I possibly see this as a bad thing when it was opening so many new doors – not only into new social spheres but back into old ones too?

One evening, browsing Facebook, I saw a photo of an old school friend covered in mud, smiling, with a medal around her neck. She'd completed a so-called obstacle run.

These events, the most famous of which is Tough Mudder, are becoming hugely popular and typically involve a long run while navigating swamps, high walls, tunnels, mud slides, rope swings, monkey bars and various uses of electric fencing and/ or barbed wire.

A year ago there would have been about as much chance of me signing up to that as going to live on a settlement in Mars. But now I was excitedly demanding to know more about it. A few messages later and we'd arranged to become willing participants in Xrunner later that month in Staffordshire, near to where she lives and I grew up. I hadn't seen my school friend for years. She's in the married-with-kids category and lives outside London. I suppose, if I'm honest, I'd had little reason to connect with her in recent years. Visiting friends with kids in the country always seemed a bit too far away from the hustle and bustle of city life for my liking.

I made a weekend of it, staying with my mum the night before the race and with my friend the following night. It felt lovely to involve my mum and her partner, Tony, in my weekend plans. Living far away from London, a visit had always meant a whole weekend stay, which required more organisation. I'd only been there a few weeks earlier so, had it not been for this event, I may not have gone again for several weeks. This was another unexpected bonus of my new hobby, which I went on to notice several times over the coming months. I could combine a cycle with popping in to see a friend, or plan a race in another part of the country and visit a friend on the way back. Previously, I used to think life revolved around London and that planning to visit someone was a big investment.

Mum stocked up on my favourite foods. She and Tony got up early to ferry me the one-hour drive to the race and then hung around for three hours in the cold until we were done.

An obstacle race is as much a test of mental endeavour as a physical one. It requires the willpower to plunge into cold water (head first down a water chute), squeeze through a long, dark, narrow pipe filled with sludge, jump over flames and then do it all again on the second lap when you know just how cold the water at the end of the chute is going to be.

It's a test of body strength as well as running fitness, with walls and hay bales to hoist yourself over. It is a test of agility, with obstacles to crawl under and over and balance on. Not to mention a test of your pain threshold. We had to wade through a swamp full of thorny weeds that scratched and cut my poor aching legs.

The biggest challenge was a mile-long stretch of thick, thigh-deep mud. People were losing shoes everywhere I looked. Quite what happened to those poor souls whose shoes disappeared into the black, I do not know. There would have been no hope of finding them in a quagmire so they would have walked several miles back to base in socks.

I kept my toes firmly flexed. It kept my shoes on but it didn't help my propulsion and I got stuck. Right leg in front of the left, I was frozen mid-stride as if in a game of musical statues. I would have to be tugged out by two competitors.

'There are three outcomes to this,' one of them chirped. 'A dislocated shoulder, two dislocated shoulders or you lose your trainers.'

Luckily it was none of the above. They rescued my legs, my arms remained in their sockets and I was freed from the swamp to go on to another lap.

At the finish, I was delighted to find hosepipes and tanks of water so we could rinse the mud off. Compared to cross-country races, where you just pull on your jeans over mud-caked legs and head to the pub, this was luxury indeed.

I also had my mum as a personal dresser. She held up a towel while I peeled off the saturated garments and pulled on dry ones. No more trying to remove a sports bra while crouching under a coat. She could unzip my bag and reach for things which my own numb hands couldn't grasp. No more struggling to turn clothes from inside out to the right way round or to squeeze cream from tubes. After cross-country races I usually have to ask someone to zip up my coat because my frozen fingers just can't do it, but today everything was handed to me.

My mum was impressed by the functional items of après-race kit coming out of my bag: dry leggings, socks, thermal base layer and my beloved hoodie. Months ago I probably would have brought a pair of skinny jeans and a furry poncho. Maybe not even that. Arriving by car, I might just have relied on her having something warm going spare in the boot. *Now look at me*, I thought. *I'm basically Bear Grylls in female form.*

That night I stayed with my friend, her husband and two children. We had barely seen each other in five years but a joint activity involving exertion, triumph and the raw elements reunited us. We launched into conversations about how high those walls were, how deep that mud was, how much of the brown lake water we swallowed after plunging in head first, how slippery the timber climbing frame was. It didn't matter that she was a mum of two and lived at the other end of the country in a rural village far removed from the bright lights of London. It didn't matter that we hadn't kept up with each other's key life events and professions and lifestyles. We went right back to communicating as we had done as kids – laughing over a shared experience.

I reflected on this in the days that followed. In recent years there had been little in my life with which I could connect to family and old friends. There had been no room for fresh air, exercise and national parks. Over the last five years, I could barely remember going for a walk with a friend or having a day out where we did something active or challenging. The closest to an outdoor activity was a picnic in the park with a bottle of fizz. Socialising went hand in hand with excess. If I wasn't drinking with friends, I'd be networking, always focused on achieving or impressing. I don't know when I had stopped appreciating simplicity. As a teenager and young adult I wasn't afraid of the outdoors. Hanging out hadn't always required fancy restaurants or some sort of entertainment. Yet somewhere along the way I'd been caught up in a rat race and by the relentless demands, temptations and torments of our materialistic world.

My former lifestyle, I reflected, had been restrictive. It had excluded a whole group of people and activities. I was always busy, but I wasn't fulfilled. Maybe it wasn't so much a case of me losing all my friends to marriage and kids and moving abroad. Maybe it was that they had diversified and I had not.

The next day was a Monday, but I wasn't in a hurry to get back to London. Before, I'd have been itching to get back to the energy of city life. Back to the gym, back to work, back to my social calendar. Now I didn't need to. I'd done my exercise as part of my socialising. I no longer had an empty craving for bright lights and activity like I used to. I got the local train back to my mum's house and spent another day hanging out, not necessarily talking about anything groundbreaking but just being there. I felt like I was becoming a more approachable, patient and overall warmer person.

CHAPTER 8

PEACE WITH CARBS

Every time I passed a new level of fitness it came with its own set of unique symptoms, which I found as fascinating as exhausting.

First there had been the permanently sore legs. Then there was the nausea, after Tuesday night track sessions or weekend cross-countries, because I wasn't used to so-called 'anaerobic training', when your heart rate goes sky-high. Then I'd experienced the zombified stagger-around-like-a-drunk-unable-to-get-off-the sofa phase.

Now came the good side effects. Non-stop munchies without putting on weight. Though even that isn't as good as it sounds – my hunger never felt quite sated no matter how many extra snacks I introduced. Then there was the sleeping phase. I've always been a light sleeper but now I was sleeping deeper and longer than ever. When I awoke in the morning I was disorientated from such deep sleep. If I got up in the night to go to the loo, I'd stumble there as though I were drugged. I started to love and appreciate sleep like I never had before. I started to look forward to going to bed knowing that refreshing deep sleep was ahead.

Fitness is nothing short of a medical miracle. Put simply, it is the result of our bodies overcompensating for the damage caused by exercise. That might not sound very healthy, but essentially you have to weaken your body to make it stronger. Coaches and sports scientists call it 'training overload', or use nifty equations like: Fitness = Stress + Rest. Immediately after training you're less fit than you were when you started. It is the recovery process over the next day or two which makes you stronger, not the training itself.

This applies both to muscle strength and aerobic capacity. When you get out of breath, you deprive your body of oxygen. Over time, our marvellous, clever bodies will start to produce more blood plasma, more capillaries and a greater concentration of red blood cells so they can transport higher volumes of oxygen to cope with the extra energy expenditure.

When you stress your muscles – lifting something heavier than you're used to, or running further than you're used to – your muscle filaments get stretched to their limits. Your body sends cells to clear out the damaged tissue and other cells for the rebuilding process. The weakest links are effectively weeded out in this repair process, so gradually you get left with only the strongest links. The outer membranes of the muscles get damaged in this process. This allows fluid in, which causes swelling and the release of something called 'nerve growth factor' – and that's what causes the sensitivity and pain. So the good news is that when your muscles ache the day after exercise (known as Delayed-Onset Muscle Soreness or DOMS), you know that the repair process has begun and you're already getting stronger. Our clever bodies do most of this repair work during our sleep, when we produce growth hormones. This is why you hear of elite athletes spending 12 hours a night in bed, plus naps.

The body is the most sophisticated, intelligent, regenerative, phenomenal machine. Anyone – with the exception of those with an injury, disability or medical condition – can become fitter and stronger. There are some people in my run club who couldn't run a mile when they first joined and in as little as six months they completed a half-marathon. The more I discover about how the human body works, the more I want to look after it and the more I want to see what it can do.

But while the human body is capable of more than we might think, it does need looking after. Something happened a few weeks after returning from France which served as an awakener. I was no longer an average fitness fan going to the gym a few times a week. My body was taking a serious toll and I needed to get clued up on some science and nutrition.

It first happened after the Windsor Half-marathon in June. This was the first in my long list of summer events that I had entered with gusto back in January. I'd signed up independently of running club, a sure sign my motivation was changing from the social opportunities to the sport itself.

As I walked with my backpack from the train station to registration, I felt surprisingly nervous. This wouldn't be anything like the informal cross-countries I was used to, where everyone gathers around the club flag in the middle of a field, dumps a bag in a soggy pile and has a last-minute scrabble for safety pins to fix numbers on vests. This would be official, with microchip timing, a ticketed bag-drop and marshals checking you run outside the markers when going round a corner. I'd never done a commercial race like this before and once more I felt like I must be the only one new to it all. When I got there, I missed the familiarity of club members around me. I felt I was an inexperienced outsider again.

The course ran along the river, one side out and the other side back. It was a beautifully sunny day, which always makes me run better because sunshine is so uplifting. My legs ached after 10 miles but I resorted to my usual game of fractions: *I'm ten-thirteenths of the way, which means there's only the equivalent of a third of what I've just done to go. Actually, a bit less than that.* I had no expectations of my time because I'd never timed myself over the precise 13.1-mile distance. I finished in 1 hour 45 minutes, an average of 8-minute miles, and I was delighted.

I waited at the finish, stretching and getting my breath back. Then I thought, *What am I waiting for? There is no one to wait for.* I didn't know whether I should go home or carry on absorbing the atmosphere. I thought fondly of the last cross-country race I'd done with run club, when we descended on a local pub, shedding half of Hampstead Heath all over the toilet floors as we removed muddy clothes and then taking over every radiator in the building, drying out hats and gloves. It suddenly seemed a bit pointless to have come all the way to Windsor for a run.

I couldn't recall visiting Windsor before, so I washed my hands and face in the public loos, put on a dry top and then walked around the town for two hours, doing nothing, buying nothing – just walking and observing. Despite the absence of the club chatter, I enjoyed the solitude. Eight months ago, a vacant Saturday afternoon would have highlighted that my social life was no longer what it used to be. But that day I enjoyed it. My run, a new town to explore and the race atmosphere had all been fulfilling enough.

I would have stayed longer drinking tea and watching the world go by but I had to get back because that night I was supposed to have a date. (Yes, Philippe was still due to visit, but this was another one and had been booked for a while.) My date had arranged to meet somewhere swish. It was an occasion to wear a dress and to be excited, but I didn't really care for it. I was happy to relax at home and recover. Looking after my body was becoming a meaningful project in itself.

Somewhat reluctantly, I got the train home, showered, ate my third snack since finishing the race, stretched, pedicured my poor battered feet and headed into town to the Garden Lounge at the Corinthia Hotel.

That's when it hit me: a wave of dizziness. One minute, I was fine, upbeat from post-exercise endorphins. The next minute, the room was spinning and I needed to hold on to my seat. I didn't say anything – it was a first date. I nodded along to the conversation. There was a tray of nuts, olives and rice crackers in front of us – the sort that you get 'free' in expensive bars. Absently, I consumed the lot. The dizziness subsided, then came back, then subsided, then came back.

I was eager to go to dinner. Once there, I simply could not stop eating. I didn't necessarily feel hungry but my body took over. I devoured the bread basket before the starters arrived – I think I left one piece for him. It was the sort of upmarket restaurant where plates are artfully presented and the portions are barely bigger than the base of a wine glass. My starter was gone in less than 30 seconds. My date, who I read to be a well-mannered type, left a pool of purified parsnip 'reduction' on his plate. I'm afraid I did the unthinkable and took the last remaining crust and mopped it up from his plate.

My main course was presented. A delicate fan of sea bass presented on a succulent pile of pak choi. But where were the carbs? I'd say it took less time to eat what was on my plate than it took to run the first third of a mile.

My date had steak and fries. I willed him to leave some. He did, and I polished them off, excusing myself.

'I did do a half-marathon this morning.' I laughed.

Blank expression from my date. This meant nothing to him. He had no comprehension of that great sequence of depletion, elation and appetite that follows from endurance sport. He was wrapped up in the decorum of fine wines and dining, as I once was.

This was not the end of the dizziness (but it was the end of my date).

The next morning when I awoke, I was dizzy again, with aching, heavy legs too. I ate breakfast as normal and by mid-morning I was seeing stars again.

Over the next few weeks, as my ardour for training and my weekend fixtures continued, I had several dizzy spells. I had increased the amount I ate to account for the extra activity but it didn't seem to make any difference.

When the dizziness got so bad I couldn't concentrate on my work, I went to see my GP. I googled 'brain tumour symptoms' so many times it's probably a top-10 search term now. I also looked at other possible causes. Maybe I was doing too much high-intensity training, like sprints or bursts of speed in the pool?

The doctor was attentive. He had me lying on a couch as he performed all sorts of tests, tilting my head this way and that to establish whether I could have symptoms of an inner ear infection.

'Is it any worse now?' he asked, jarring my neck to the right.

'No.'

'What about now?' And my neck would be yanked to the left.

'No.'

There was much humming and sighing but no sign of an inner ear infection. So he ordered blood tests. I had tests for everything imaginable: iron, calcium, cholesterol, thyroid, liver function, fasting glucose, red and white blood cell counts and more.

All the results came back healthy – except for my red blood cells being huge, which apparently is common in athletes, because the cells grow to carry more oxygen around the body. The next plan of action, if the dizziness persisted, was to go for neurological tests.

The obvious explanation was that I wasn't eating enough for my training, but often I felt dizzy even after eating. And besides, it felt like I was permanently eating because I was permanently hungry. I hadn't lost weight, though this was deceptive because I was putting on muscle. My tummy was getting flatter, my shoulders broader, but my weight remained the same.

Around the same time, my periods got lighter and one month I missed one completely. I took to Google again and it didn't take me long to deduce that I was not getting enough carbs.

Many women experience a lightening or temporary pause in their periods if they up their exercise dramatically. While it may be convenient, it means they have stopped ovulating and that means they have stopped producing oestrogen. Oestrogen is what keeps bones healthy so it puts them in danger of osteoporosis. It also begs the question that if the body is under so much strain that it shuts off one of its non-essential functions, what else has it stopped?

I invested in a good book on sports nutrition – and what a revelation that was. I thought I knew all about healthy eating. Thanks to a lifetime managing eczema and IBS, I've always had an interest in clean eating, but this has been from the point of view of keeping my skin clear and trying to keep a flat tummy. It turned out I knew nothing at all about the primary role of nutrition: fuel.

I was well versed on the benefits of cranberry juice cleaning your kidneys after a night out, brazil nuts helping brain function, cider vinegar flushing out toxins or that everything green is good for free radicals. I thought nutrition was all about sprinkling goji berries on my porridge and eating organic purple sprouting broccoli.

I've done many of the things that the consumer media tell us are 'healthy': choosing salads, avoiding white bread, snacking on nuts and seeds. I ate a high-protein breakfast (eggs or smoked salmon) on the advice of trainers in the gym, who told me that replacing carbs for protein is the way to a lean physique and washboard abs.

The trouble with mainstream dietary advice is that it is geared towards weight loss, probably because most people don't use their bodies enough to match the amount of calorie-dense foods that are pushed at us all the time. What populist health advice does not teach us is the roles of the different food groups and how we can use those to make informed choices about what is right for our own bodies and varying needs.

Re-educating myself, I learned that all calories come from three so-called 'macronutrients': carbohydrate, protein and fat. All food contains one or more of these macronutrients in different quantities. There are 4 calories in every gram of carbohydrate, 4 calories in every gram of protein and 9 calories in every gram of fat. (Foods can contain fibre and water too but these have no calorific value.)

Someone who does little exercise needs around 4 g of carbohydrate per kilogram of body weight per day and 0.8 g of protein per kilogram of body weight per day. A recreational athlete like me can need up to twice that much.

The reason people are so phobic about carbs is because they can end up being stored as fat if you don't use them up for energy. Carbohydrate converts to glycogen and then gets stored in our muscles and liver for energy. The body can only convert 25–35 g of carbs per hour from food into glycogen. If you eat too much, your body can't use it. But if you don't eat enough, your energy, performance and recovery will be impaired. Worse, if your body can't get glycogen from muscle stores, it will turn to glycogen stores in the liver. Glycogen in the liver regulates blood sugar so if you disrupt that, guess what? You might feel dizzy.

Armed with this information, I set about logging my macronutrients for a week (there are many apps to help you do this). At the end of each day you can see the grams of protein, carbs and fats consumed. Many apps list well-known brands of pre-packaged foods so you don't have to decipher the ingredients of everything.

Be warned: it is both time-consuming and fascinating! I lost hours calculating the protein-to-carb ratio of a tin of chickpeas or the amount of vitamins in a melon. Even weighing things was enlightening because I'd never considered food weights before. Who'd have thought that half a broccoli head weighing a whopping 400 g has only 5 g of carbohydrate, whereas just 100 g of potatoes has 20 g of carbohydrate? And did you know that one large brazil nut weighing 5 g has 30 calories, most of which come from fat?

By tracking my diet, I found my calorie intake was roughly 3,000–3,500 per day. But surprisingly, the highest calories were not from the things I considered 'bad' like rice or pasta or bread, but from the nuts and seeds and oily fish. My diet was high in 'good' fats and protein and therefore high in calories, but I wasn't getting anywhere near the amount of carbs needed for my level of activity.

I had to change years' worth of dietary habits. I added all sorts of new things to my weekly shopping list, including an old favourite – freshly baked doughy bread. Hooray! I prepared big bowls of couscous, brown rice and sweet potatoes for snacks. I stopped the protein-based breakfasts and went back to porridge. Lo and behold, my dizzy spells disappeared and I stopped craving sweet things. Maybe it was my imagination, but Tuesday track felt easier. I did put on weight but none of it went to flab. It allowed my muscles to grow as they should have been and soon I noticed a markedly more muscular frame.

As I read around sports nutrition online, no end of articles popped up telling me which foods to avoid (mostly carbs). This frustrated me because this was the very advice that I needed to *unfollow*. Even some of the apps with which I tried to log my nutritional intake were geared towards calorie restriction rather than calorie management. Most asked for a 'goal weight' before I could even begin and one, clearly horrified at how many calories I was consuming, flashed a warning in red letters: *If you eat this many calories every day, you will put on 3 kg in 3 months*. In fact, the opposite was true. If I didn't eat that many calories a day, I'd be back at the GP with a dizzy spell.

What also struck me is the conflicting messages about food in our culture. On the one hand, we have the consumer press playing carb police. On the other hand, marketeers make indulgence sexy. Chocolate is a sophisticated delicacy. Baking cakes make us likeable. Food is pushed at us wherever we go. At a business meeting there are biscuits. We travel on a plane and we get handed pretzels. We pay for petrol and are asked if we want a half-price giant bar of Dairy Milk. Most of us mindlessly munch whatever is presented to us, regardless of whether we're hungry or even care that much for it. It's no wonder many people struggle to control their health.

After all my research and the rude awakening of my dizzy spells, my attitude to food changed completely. Instead of thinking about weight, I adopted a healthier concern for my nutritional needs. I used to worry that I may be eating too much; now I worry whether I have eaten enough for optimal recovery. I used to go to a restaurant and look for the lightest option; now I look for the most substantial. I love the feeling that my body is solid, strong, fuelled, healthy and ready for anything I'm going to put it through.

CHAPTER 9

NIGHTRIDER

A couple of weeks later, I put my new fuelling strategy to the test with my next challenge, a 100-kilometre bike ride around London through the night.

Nightrider, as the name suggests, starts at midnight and takes in the highlights of and around London. My dear, old friend Kath, who has absolutely nothing to do with my new sporty life, suggested it to me and three other friends. This in itself was a buck of trend. I was much more used to sitting in a bar all night with this particular group of friends than on a bicycle saddle all night. Clearly I was not the only one looking for a more diverse use of leisure time. I couldn't help noticing that now I was open to doing new things, new things came to me, not just from new friends but from old.

As the emails bounced around our group in the weeks leading up to Nightrider, I realised what an asset my fitness was. Although I hadn't ever cycled 100 kilometres in one go, it didn't seem a big deal to me. After the 70-kilometre rides in France and other victorious milestones, I had acquired a new confidence. I knew my body and my mind would cope, as they had coped with other unprecedented challenges. I revelled in this feeling. I loved knowing that underneath my clothes is a body that can fire up on request. It can run half-marathons; it can swim in 12-degree waters. It can lift and squat heavy weights in the gym. It knows that no matter how much everything hurts, it will be OK when it ends.

The others, however, were noticeably nervous. There were jokes about cramming in last-minute training and self-deprecating humour about how unfit they were. It's common in our culture to proclaim a lack of fitness: 'I'm so unfit I couldn't run for the bus the other day, ha ha!' It's as if we want to advertise that our life is too full with fun to make time for anything boring like running. I actually find these jokes a little sad. I wish I could share just some of the joy I've found in growing fit and strong and agile with people who have negative associations with exercise. There are many reasons people avoid it – lifelong habit, perceived inability, fear of pain, fear of what they look like, aversion to the cold. It doesn't help when there's cultural kudos for being unfit.

In 2016 a survey by the British Heart Foundation found that one in five adults can't run further than 100 metres. In the same year Public Health England estimated that 83 per cent of middle-aged people are either overweight, don't exercise enough or drink too much. When you think that we lived as hunter-gatherers for almost two million years before the agricultural revolution – walking, scavenging, killing and preparing everything that passed our lips – it makes today's ready availability of food seem obscene.

There is a well-established theory called the 'endurance-running hypothesis' that suggests humans developed a propensity for long-distance running to aid our survival as a species. It theorises that the most successful hunters were the men and women who managed to catch prey even though most prey could run faster than them. They did it by walking, running and tracking a prey until it dropped dead with exhaustion. Our ancestors who managed to do this were more likely to survive (because they got to eat), so eventually the gene for endurance became embedded in our DNA. It is a tragedy that we've let our engines rot away because of our pursuit of convenience and allegedly more fulfilling lives.

But back to our night cycle. The preceding week, I got my bike serviced and invested in proper lights at last. This was a learning experience in itself. Every time I made a visit to a bike shop I left thinking that cyclists must be born with a knowledge base of bike accessories. Asking for advice on a product seems to require a PhD in physics to understand the answer.

When I asked for a good pair of lights, for instance, it transpired that there is no universal system for displaying brightness. Some manufacturers use lumens, some use candle power, some use watts. Some lights are designed to enable you to see the road; others are designed for *you* to be seen. Some lights are perfectly visible from the front but not from the side. Some are cheap but use batteries that are expensive to replace. Some are expensive but can be recharged via a USB.

I left the shop armed with several other items I hadn't gone in for: a saddlebag for a spare inner tube, not that I would use it as I hadn't a clue how to fit an inner tube; flashing, reflective armbands; a high-vis jacket, which I didn't need because we got free ones on the night; and a multitool.

In the days before Nightrider, two of the four dropped out. Convenient excuses were found. So it was just me and Kath. We met before midnight at Alexandra Palace in north-west London.

Neither of us had any idea how long 100 kilometres would take but Kath's husband is a keen cyclist so we made an optimistic guess.

'Nick does a hundred k in around three hours,' she chirped. 'So I reckon about four.'

I nodded.

I didn't own proper cycling kit. I had the padded shorts, which I bought for the riding in France, but on my upper half I just had on a long-sleeved running top and my new high-vis jacket. The difference between a cycling top and a running top is that a cycling top is tighter for aerodynamics and has three huge, stretchy, back pockets which you can carry all your belongings in for the day. Because I had no pockets I wore a bumbag around my waist. Most of the space was taken up by dried figs and dates.

Three thousand cyclists took to the streets that night, starting in waves 5 minutes apart. I was pleased to find that they didn't look like serious cyclists, clad in skin-tight Lycra to match their bikes. Most wore simple outdoor clothes, carried rucksacks and rode hybrid or mountain bikes.

We set off down the steep hill from Alexandra Palace, down through Hampstead, passing over the top of Belsize Park, which was where our friendship was formed when we were flatmates 15 years ago. Then we went around the perimeter of Regent's Park and on to Baker Street. Now we were among central London traffic and I was petrified.

When I first heard about Nightrider, I had assumed the roads would be closed. When I learned they weren't it was too late. I assured myself that there would be thousands of other cyclists on the road, which would provide safety in numbers.

My fear of cycling in traffic did not come from a bad experience, but the knowledge of how deadly cars can be. Part of the problem was that I didn't know how to navigate junctions. I thought bikes should stay tucked into the left-hand side of the road. That's what most of us who grew up in the eighties were taught when we did our Cycling Proficiency test. But if I was supposed to always stay left, how did I turn right? Where should I wait if I was turning right at a T-junction? Still in the left lane? I didn't know so I always got off my bike at junctions and walked it across the road.

(Shortly after completing Nightrider, I signed up for one of the government-funded Bikeability courses. They are totally free and I got an instructor all to myself, who even met me near my home. The single most useful rule I learned was to position yourself like a car at a junction. Think as a car and use the whole lane. If there isn't room for a car to overtake, don't let it. Don't squeeze alongside a car, but stay behind it in the middle of the lane, to avoid being squashed when it turns. The trouble is that many drivers today also did their Cycling Proficiency test in the eighties and still think cyclists should be tucked into the kerb. I've encountered many angry drivers who use colourful adjectives when I take the middle of the lane.

I'll take the abuse – the official advice says that's the safest place to be.)

Despite it being one in the morning, the traffic on Baker Street was as solid and as aggressive as ever. I tucked in behind Kath, trying to copy her. But when we got to another busy junction at Westminster, it was too much. A big noisy bus behind scared me and I resorted to what I always do when I think death is imminent – I veered on to the pavement and watched it pass in wide-eyed terror.

That was the worst of the central London traffic and, soon after, we pedalled along the north bank of the River Thames until we crossed Chelsea Bridge. Then we were in the leafy south-west neighbourhoods of Clapham, Wandsworth and Wimbledon. The cars thinned and we rode side by side. It was another overdue opportunity to catch up with a friend who I rarely get to see any more.

Doing an activity together takes the intensity out of conversation. If we hadn't been on bikes we never would have sat down sober and talked for six hours. Tonight we dipped in and out of chatting. We were hanging out without an agenda, sharing an experience in a real environment. It made for a very different interaction to the constructed backdrop of a bar, which was what I was more used to.

Not that we talked much after 3 a.m. Tiredness hit us simultaneously. I used to work night shifts when I worked full-time in a newsroom and 3 a.m. seems to be the point when it hits everyone. It was as if someone sprinkled sleeping dust across the office every night at precisely the same time.

We were passing through Crystal Palace when the sleeping dust hit, right at the bottom of the great big hill to climb, which would take us to Crystal Palace Park, the halfway point. We passed a sign saying, *Feed station ahead*.

'Makes it sound like we're horses,' said Kath, and I found myself in a fit of giggles. An unexpected witty remark cut through the silence and the darkness to perk us up and help us up the hill.

We were not in a hurry to leave the feed station at Crystal Palace. We used everything on offer – tea, toilets, water and people to chat to.

'Let's not delay the inevitable,' I said to Kath, and reluctantly we set off again.

From here it was back into London. We headed north-east towards the City and Canary Wharf. We reached Tower Bridge, 70 kilometres in, just as the sun started to rise. The dark sky lifted to silver, the lights of central London became dimmer and slowly our surroundings became more visible.

There was another feed station at Tower Bridge and we stopped to take photos of the dawn sky, feeling energised again. It is amazing how daylight can trick the body into wakefulness. Everything seems OK again in daylight.

The route led us along the cobbled streets of Wapping and then – painfully – within twenty yards of my flat.

As we rode away from Limehouse and towards Canary Wharf, we saw a girl, who looked in her twenties, sitting on the side of the road alone, crying, her bike lying on the ground beside her.

Kath and I looked at each other.

'Should we stop?'

We hesitated. Classic bystander apathy. But then we turned around and approached the girl. Kath got off her bike and crouched next to her.

'I'm just so, so tired,' the girl sobbed.

'There really isn't much further to go,' Kath encouraged. 'Have you eaten enough?' The girl nodded and sobbed again.

'Do you want us to call someone for you?' I asked after a few moments.

She shook her head.

'Do you want a fig?' I tried, and she shook her head. They are an acquired taste, I suppose.

We stayed a few minutes more, and as she came to her senses she looked embarrassed and insisted she was OK.

'I just need to sit for a while and then I'll start again,' she said.

When we still didn't move, she urged us to 'press on', so we did.

One thing I had noticed about group-participation sports events is how much fellow competitors offer emotional support to each other, like when I was given words of encouragement in my first cross-country race in Loughton when I slowed to a walk. Most races and events that I've taken part in – that is to say, at a recreational level – are friendly affairs with mixed abilities. The achievement is in finishing, not being placed highly. They are nowhere near as intimidating as I once thought they would be.

The miles passed more and more slowly after that incident. I looked at my GPS watch more and more. We were on

85 kilometres as we passed Stoke Newington. *Just 15 kilometres to go. That's less than 10 miles. That's like cycling to running club, cycling back and cycling there again*, I told myself, as usual playing tricks with my mind to help me through.

We arrived back at Alexandra Palace at 6 a.m., collected our medals and bags, and then sat on the steps of Alexandra Palace and ate bacon rolls, which were handed out for free at the finish.

There was once a time when I wouldn't have dreamed of eating such a thing – white bread and streaky bacon. But after my recent schooling in nutrition, bread was no longer bad, but a good source of fast-release carbohydrate to replace depleted glycogen stores. Bacon was no longer on the naughty list, but a good source of protein, best eaten immediately after you finish exercise.

'I think if my husband has a bike that can do this in three hours, and mine takes six, that seriously justifies an expensive pair of shoes!' said Kath.

I laughed, warmed by my friend's wit, even at six in the morning after no sleep. A snippet of humour that bridged my two worlds. Shoes and bikes – perhaps they weren't so far apart after all.

CHAPTER 10

TRIATHLON

Philippe was due to visit the weekend after Nightrider. He'd booked his flights and I had planned a romantic weekend of running and touring London. Days before he was due, he cancelled. He had got back with his ex-girlfriend. It had been a whimsical decision in France. Since then I'd done mud runs and night bike rides and half-marathons. I realised that I wasn't particularly bothered – a sign perhaps that I had been looking forward to his visit more because it was another source of excitement for a weekend rather than because there was any substance between us.

It left me with a weekend of no plans and so I did what I was in the habit of doing. I made efforts to find some sort of group sporting activity to fill it.

A couple from my run club, David and Susan, who were always arranging fun things and including other club members, announced they were going to Stubbers Lake in Essex for an open-water session. I joined them.

It was the first time I had dared to tackle open water since my near-hypothermic experience in France and I was nervous about tackling open-water swimming again. The last experience was traumatic enough to produce a Pavlovian response of fear when I stood lakeside. When I immersed myself, the temperature was nowhere near as bracing as it had been in France. Still cold and it still made me more breathless than normal, but I was spared the ice-cream headache, smarting cheeks and disorientation.

Instead of just getting in and swimming though, I joined an open-water skills class that was taking place in the lake. We learned how to 'sight', a skill to help you swim in a straight line – without the black lines of a swimming pool floor, this is not easy. Sighting involves spotting a buoy (or a tree on the horizon if there aren't any) and lifting your head out of the water occasionally to fixate on it.

When I got out, I started to shiver and felt a little dizzy again. It was only a fraction as severe as it had been after swimming in the Dordogne but still, it was enough for me to recognise a pattern. My body had a lot of adapting to do before it could cope with swimming in cold water.

This opportunity turned out to be very fortuitous because the following weekend I had my first triathlon. Had Philippe not cancelled his trip, I would never have learned to swim in a straight line in time for this event.

I hadn't realised how excited I was about my first triathlon until the week leading up to it. I could think of nothing else. I couldn't say exactly why triathlon had, and still has, such a personal appeal. Maybe because triathlon is a test of all-round fitness. I know I'll never be a super-fast runner – not compared to some of the impossibly speedy people in my running club who knock out a 5k in 19 minutes as a 'recovery run'.

Triathlon, on the other hand, requires speed, endurance, strength, skill and mental perseverance. It is a fairer competition for those without supergenes.

Or maybe the particular appeal is that triathlon requires a more varied training regime than just running. Three disciplines means more opportunities for more events and training circles. It means hello to open-water swimming, long-distance cycling, trail runs, aquathlons (running and swimming), duathlons (cycling and running) and more.

There were deeper, personal reasons that triathlon resonated with me too. Triathlon required me to confront things I've shielded myself against: getting cold, swimming in dirty water, forgoing my hundred-step beauty regime until I get home, sitting in the pub with goggle rings and other ungainly things like that.

My first triathlon was at Cholmondeley Castle in Cheshire. I'd selected it because I could combine it with another visit to my mum. I hit the 'enter' button without checking the logistics. Same county – it couldn't be that far. I didn't check the exact location, the start time, nor ask if she'd be on holiday that day.

The most terrifying thing about the trip was getting my bike to Euston station. I dodged central London with a lengthy, roundabout Tube journey using the lines which allow bikes. It did not occur to me how I would get both a bike and luggage on to the train until that morning. I had to rush out and buy a rucksack. My last-minute options were limited and I ended up with an ugly, bright-orange thing. The sort I had as a student and never imagined I'd need again – I had a matching set of Louis Vuitton cases, thank you very much.

On my way to the station, as I wheeled and rode my bike between Tube stations, orange backpack bulging behind me, I felt very enterprising. The only shoes I carried were the trainers I needed for the race and the cycling shoes I was wearing. The only clothing I carried was my race gear and the outfit I was wearing.

I passed normal people, in fashionable clothes, with handbags and designer sunglasses, walking dogs, holding hands with boyfriends, sitting in restaurants, drinking wine, and I felt a sense of superiority to be unaffected by it all. No need for all that superficial stuff. My weekend endeavours required a wetsuit and practical gear for doing and not for being seen.

That night, before my race, I carefully rearranged my bags in my bedroom at my mum's house. This was more daunting than my first club cross-country race because there was no one from my club to watch, copy or ask what to wear, what to expect or what the atmosphere would be. What did I put in the 'transition area' for instance? Where did you attach your number? I had learned from the triathlon holiday in France that triathletes wear an all-in-one 'tri-suit' for all three disciplines. It goes under your wetsuit, so after the swim you peel off your wetsuit and you're ready for the bike. It has light padding in the groin area to make sitting on a saddle for 40 kilometres more comfortable, but isn't as thick as cycling shorts because you have to run in it too.

But this didn't explain what I should do with my race number. Should I attach it to my tri-suit before the swim and put my wetsuit over it? Wouldn't it get damaged while swimming? Or should I attach it after I took the wetsuit off? But wouldn't that take up loads of valuable time in transition?

Also, wouldn't I be cold in nothing but a sleeveless tri-suit on the bike? Was it permissible to leave an extra layer in transition? Cycling is a lower intensity activity than running so you don't stay as warm. It was predicted to be 14°C that morning with wind. So, if I did use an extra layer, did I then need another number to pin on it?

I spent ages pondering these things. I used my own bag for the items I would leave in transition, and borrowed another smaller one for things I'd need after the race, like warm clothes and food. I decided to leave my fleece (the bobbly, worn old thing that I used to jog in) in transition to wear on the bike leg. I stuffed everything I imagined I might need into the pockets of that fleece: dried figs for fuel; spare contact lens (only one because it would be really unlucky to lose two); lip balm (quite how I'd take the lid off with my hands pinned to my handlebars hadn't crossed my mind); my running watch to show speed and distance (I couldn't put it on my wrist because I had to swim first and I didn't know if it was waterproof); and a spare inner tube in case of a puncture. My seemingly bottomless pockets would have made Mary Poppins proud.

On race morning, my mum and her partner, Tony, sportingly got up at the crack of dawn to ferry me and my bike there. Luckily, they had a car big enough so I didn't have to do anything scary, like take wheels off, to fit it in.

It turned out to be an hour's drive but we got there in good time and, after picking up my number at registration, I waited by the lake for the start in my constricting wetsuit and bare feet because the only shoes I'd brought with me were the ones I needed to run in. *Mental note to bring flip-flops for my next triathlon.*

I'd heard all sorts of intimidating things about triathlon swims ('People kick you in the face deliberately' and 'Don't start near the front because the fast swimmers will swim over you'), so I lingered near the back. I didn't have much of a benchmark for my swimming ability because the only time I'd ever swum continuously with others was in France.

A horn sounded and we were off: 1,500-metre swim, 40k cycle, 10k run. The Olympic distance.

Within 10 strokes I was totally breathless. *What's wrong with me?* I thought in a panic. I swam plenty more than 1,500 metres in my gym pool – often followed by a spin class. Why was I gasping after 30 seconds? I was both alarmed and confused. I wondered if it's possible for a body to spontaneously lose fitness overnight.

The breathlessness did not subside after 5 minutes. *I'm going to have to stop*, I thought. I'd have to raise my hand out of the water like they told us in the safety briefing and get rescued. Then I remembered how breathless I had felt in the River Dordogne and at Stubbers Lake. *There must be something about cold water which affects my lungs.* I didn't know what, or how, but now that I could see there might be a potential scientific explanation, it didn't seem so drastic.

Swim slowly, I told myself. *Don't worry about your time.* I reverted to breaststroke for a few minutes and my breathing slowed. People swam past but I tried not to care. Breathing was a bigger priority. When I was sufficiently calm, I tried crawl once more but my breathing went haywire again, so I tried to front crawl with my head out of the water, which made me thrash around like a drowning monkey. Another 200 metres though and I felt comfortable enough to put my head back in the water and breathe on every stroke. Another 400 metres and my breathing was controlled enough to breathe on every second stroke. By 600 metres, I was into my normal rhythm and started to pass people. One, two, breeeeeeathe. One, two, breeeeeathe. By 800 metres I was even enjoying it. The sun was emerging – I could see it every time I breathed to the right. One, two, breeeeeathe. One, two, breeeeeathe. I was passing loads of people now. I was enjoying it so much I didn't want the swim to end. I looked behind and was amazed to find there was a swathe of swimmers. I was easily in the first quartile.

I've since spoken to experienced open-water swimmers and breathlessness in cold water is common. It's caused by a rise in adrenalin. Race nerves are likely to exasperate adrenalin, so a race in cold open water is the perfect cocktail for hyperventilation.

Any advantage I made on the swim I quickly lost in transition. If ever I need to remind myself how far I've advanced in triathlon, I just have to think back to this day. My wetsuit came off easily enough with a little hopping, but what I did next probably took longer than a makeover for a cover shoot of *Vogue*. I picked up my towel and gave my hair a good rub. Then I applied sun cream to my arms and legs. *Oh, don't forget the nape of my neck.* It wasn't even that sunny but I was more concerned my skin would feel dry after coming out of the water.

Not wanting to put the cheap stuff on my face, I whipped out the Decléor anti-ageing hypoallergenic SPF 50 protector for my face. *Just need to find it in my bottomless fleece pocket... There it is. Better put the lid back on properly – it's very expensive.*

People were grabbing their bikes and legging it out of transition as I was gently massaging facial contours. I put on my fleece, but on noticing that no one else was putting on extra layers I took it off again. Then I remembered that I had all that stuff in my pockets so I put it on again. Then I put on cycling gloves (the pressure on your palms pushing down on the handlebars can be quite painful after an hour from what I remember from France). Only then did I unhook my saddle from the rack and wheel it out of transition to the 'mount line'.

I counted only three other hybrid bikes like mine. Rider after rider sailed past me, hunched over the handlebars in their calculated, aerodynamic positions on skinny road bikes or time-trial bikes. Some had blocked-out wheels, designed for wind resistance, that made a terrifying whirring noise as they passed me.

I did not see one other rider in a fleece.

I reached for my figs but I couldn't get at them. Diligently I'd put them in a polythene bag. I hadn't contemplated how I'd pierce a hole in a bag with one hand on the handlebars while being overtaken from all angles. That was another mental note for my next race.

My spare contact lens proved useful though. My left one came out 30 kilometres into the 40-kilometre course. I tried to ignore it at first but soon discovered that one-eyed vision impedes the ability to estimate distances. So the pothole in the road that looks like it's 2 metres away turns out to be… ouch… right there!

I spotted a parked car in a lay-by and took my opportunity. 'Can I use your wing mirror?'

Before the shocked driver could answer, I leaned in so my head was virtually pressing against his window and inserted a lens.

'Thank you!' I cried and pedalled off again.

I made another mental note: to learn to do that without a mirror.

The second transition, from bike to run, was an improvement. I took off cycle shoes and put on running shoes, took off my helmet and dumped the fleece. Other people had elastic laces in their trainers so they could pull them on without stopping to tie them. Another mental note…

The run was beautiful. It followed a path around the stately grounds and passed in front of Cholmondeley Castle itself. It was at this point that I needed to pee. While cross-country races had taught me the art of peeing outdoors, I'd never done it in a one-piece tri-suit. I found bushes, rolled up the leg as high as I could and tried to pee through the gap. It was not the most successful operation. Another mental note to find out whether there was such a thing as a two-piece tri-suit. I couldn't imagine ever doing a race lasting more than two hours without a toilet break.

I finished that race in just over three hours, which for a first attempt on a hilly course, with a hybrid bike and a makeover in transition, wasn't bad. It was a luxury to get straight into a car and be driven home to a warm shower. No changing into dry clothes in the middle of a field, no trekking to public transport or waiting in the cold.

We had lunch in a pub later that afternoon. I devoured my own plate and finished my mum's roast potatoes. Eating others' leftovers was becoming an occupational hazard, especially when in polite company. I'd always been a salad orderer. Now I was in competition with Tony over who got the leftover spuds.

Dave texted me that day and asked how it went. I was touched because he was the only friend who did and it struck a chord. My first triathlon was more significant to me than other things I'd done so far. It was something I had chosen myself, without running club. My other friends wouldn't have known that. I had been so busy over the last few weeks, filling my weekends with sporty events, that I hadn't seen any of them to talk in depth about my endurance challenges. They may have seen the proud pictures on Facebook but they wouldn't have known that this event meant more than the others. To them it was just Helen doing another one of those crazy sporty things. The only reason Dave would have known more than them was because I saw him most weeks at the club.

When we returned home, I hosed my wetsuit in the garden and my mum washed my kit. I got a flashback to my teenage years. Between the ages of 12 and 16, I spent every waking hour at my local stables, trying to get a free ride in exchange for mucking out. I cycled 3 miles each way after school and sometimes before school. When I got to the stables I'd run to the fields to bring in some of the riding school ponies one at a time. The more I got done, the more chance there would be for a free ride.

I begged to have my own horse but it wasn't until I was 14 and had proven my dedication that I got my ultimate dream. Her name was Willow. She was young and barely broken in. I spent every hour of my free time training her. I read every book and magazine I could about the science behind feeding and training and found out about all the local horse shows.

My dad (rest his soul) got heartily involved. He converted an old transit van from work into a horsebox. At weekends we travelled together to local shows, getting up at the crack of dawn. When we got back, my mum would make me strip all the smelly clothes off before I was allowed into the house and they would be quickly bundled in the washing machine for decontamination.

Now, as I washed my wetsuit with my mum in the garden, it was like going back in time. The similarities were striking: preparing kit the night before, getting an early night for an early start, putting up with wet weather, the muckiness, the exhilaration of speed, the kinship with others involved in the sport, the jargon, the seasons for different types of competitions, the training, the nutrition, the inevitability of injuries. The only difference was that now I was training myself, not a horse.

During summer holidays I'd take Willow for a ride for a whole day. I'd explore new routes and steer her on the narrowest of canal towpaths where no one else dared take their equine friends. People would worry where I was and I'd return late, tired and hungry but glowing after an adventure. It is exactly what I'm like now with running and cycling.

In a way, riding was a form of rebellion for me. I wasn't brought up in an outdoor family. Getting muddy to my mum's chagrin and disappearing for hours alone on my horse was a way of asserting my independence. I grew out of horses when I discovered boys and parties and, although it broke my heart, we sold Willow to a good home when I was 17. There had been nothing to replace that affinity with nature, until now.

What happens to our raw, wild spirit as we get older? As a 14-year-old out riding, I didn't feel the cold, I didn't worry about my skin getting dry and weather-damaged, my clothes smelling or having 'helmet hair'. Do we get lazy? Neurotic? Or do we become desensitised to the simple rewards of nature? The adventurous, resilient side of me has always been there. I just lost it for a couple of decades. It is probably still there in all of us, waiting to be rediscovered.

CHAPTER 11

YES WOMAN

With summer well under way, my fervour for competing only grew. Summer was a doddle in comparison to the harsh nights when I first started cycling to run club. Just getting myself anywhere in winter was a complicated task requiring great mental effort. I had to gather up lights, reflective gear, two sets of hats and gloves (one for running and a thicker version for cycling home afterwards), over-trousers to keep jeans dry on a flooded towpath. The list goes on. It is said that the hardest part of a training session is getting out of the door and that is never truer than in the winter.

But with the light, dry evenings, there was no stopping me. I must have tried, at least once, every training session going in my area. On Saturday mornings a small group from the track met for hill training in Hampstead or Greenwich, so I joined. There was always coffee afterwards. Everything I did was to sate my prevailing drive to make new friends and make my weekends feel as full as possible. I became a yes woman. Every training session, race or trip away I heard about I said yes.

On Sunday mornings I dared more open-water swimming sessions. The local London Fields Triathlon Club ran one at the West Reservoir in Stoke Newington – a 6-mile cycle away. I got up at 6 a.m. to make the early session. The water was much warmer now but it was after I got out when I suffered because my core temperature would plummet. Then I had to cycle home with wet hair. Every time it had the same effect: head spins when I first got out and shivers for hours afterwards. I took so many layers with me that I'd pedal home looking like a roly-poly, passing people in shorts.

One cool summer evening, I turned up to my first 'brick session' at the Olympic Park. A brick session alternates between cycling and running in order to train your legs to be able to run after jumping off a bike, like you have to in triathlon. Having done a triathlon and four-hour bike rides in the rolling hills of the Dordogne, I didn't imagine a couple of hours going around a 1-mile loop would be that exerting, so I had even gone for a swim that morning. Everyone else turned up on road bikes – I was the only one on a hybrid. Desperate to be taken seriously, I pedalled like mad to try to keep up. I hadn't taken into account that the session was two full hours, and I had to cycle there and back in the wind and the rain.

When I returned home, shivering in my wet clothes, I felt exactly the same as I used to when I first started doing track sessions – burned out but buzzing. My chest was tingling from catching my breath, my legs were seizing up, my limbs were heavy, my cheeks were smarting from the wind. Yet as I lay incapacitated on the sofa, I thought how much I loved this feeling. I hadn't felt like this for a few weeks because my body was ever adapting to cope with the increased training load I inflicted on it, but I'd obviously crossed a new line today. *This* was the feeling that I was always trying to chase.

I was never happier than when I finally made it home in a dazed state of mild exhaustion, extra gratified that another day or weekend had been completed in sobriety. You would be amazed at how appreciative you can be of your base level hierarchy of needs when you've been battered by the elements. There would be many times over the next few years when I would welcome the sight of home, starving after long marathon-training runs in the frost; near-hypothermic after open-water swimming; filthy and freezing after a long winter ride, covered in mud, sweat, bike oil, snot or whatever I'd picked up while trying to change out of wet clothes in a public loo. On each of those occasions I would be desperate to stand under a hot shower, eat and then sprawl on the sofa. For the remainder of the day it would feel like pure ecstasy simply to be clean, dry, warm and not moving.

My sources of pleasure had become so much simpler now that life was no longer a high-octane, boozy, party-centric quest for good times. Deep sleep, a feeling of well-being, the smell of fresh air, the sight of ducks on the canal while running. I used to be on an endless pursuit of ephemeral highs – quaffing cocktails, flitting between social circles, shopping for sparkly things. None of it delivered any lasting benefits. Already I could see that what I had discovered recently promised a lifetime's source of satisfaction and serenity.

One other opportunistic event I said yes to was the Hackney Half-marathon. It was the inaugural year of this now hugely popular event. Being my running club's stomping ground, loads of members had entered. Entries were full when I tried, but the night before the race I saw that someone had dropped out and I snapped up their offer of a place.

It didn't matter that I'd done the gruelling hill-running session the morning before, a double spin class the day before that, or the club 10-miler the day before that. Everything I did that year was for experience rather than performance. To top it off, I went to a friend's birthday drinks the night before the race.

Serious runners would never dream of going out before a race but I wasn't doing the race to get a brilliant time – I was doing it because it was something sociable and healthy to do with my Saturday. And secondly, organised dos among my old friends were getting rarer and rarer due to their family commitments, so I wasn't going to miss it. I didn't drink much and I left to get the last Tube – very out of character for the Helen of old. It didn't go unnoticed and as I walked away, towards King's Cross, I felt like I was letting them down. I was torn between wanting to stay out all night with my old friends and feel one of them again, but also wanting to remain dedicated to my new lifestyle, which overall made me feel more alive and content.

It was not the first time I had felt a tug of war between old life and new. Old friendships were where I had the history but I rarely saw them. Club friendships were where I had all the fun and activity and weekends away – a ready-made social scene without any effort. It was more wholesome but also more superficial because it was all about big groups and banter and there was rarely opportunity for the sort of one-on-one confessional conversations I had with older friends.

Predictably, I overslept – not drastically enough to miss the race, but enough to turn up flustered, breakfast half digested, tight muscles unstretched and my number a screwed-up mess. I cycled the 4 miles to Hackney Marshes along the Limehouse Cut. In the winter there had been a cross-country race at the same venue so I vaguely knew where to go. The Limehouse Cut was the same route which I'd cycled through the hailstorm after the Orion Fifteen in the winter, and with my ex a year previously.

I pedalled speedily along the gravelly path, praying I wouldn't get a puncture. I still had no idea how to remove a tyre. I had to dismount several times as the towpath turned to cobbles, went over a bridge at Three Mills and up steps at Hackney Wick. I cursed each time. Race start time was looming and I still had to lock my bike, discard my bag and go to the loo.

I don't remember all this! I thought as I passed under and over yet more bridges. I knew the way – I just didn't remember it being quite so far. I was getting hot in my hoodie over my running gear but there was no time to stop. When I turned into the path which leads to Hackney Marshes with 6 minutes to spare, there was a bike chained to every single post, fence, railing, tree or drainpipe. The fences were decorated with bikes. The scene could have passed for an exhibit of modern art.

I searched for a gap to squeeze in my little white hybrid, becoming ever more determined to slide it into one of the narrow gaps, but it was no use. There was no space which allowed me to get my D-lock close enough to anything solid. I ended up lifting the bike high in the air, balancing it precariously and locking the frame to a lamp post. I left it suspended four feet up, directly above another bike. How I'd get it down again later I did not know, but now was not the time to worry about that.

When I emerged from the cluster of trees, the sight on the main field took my breath away. A sea of runners opened up before me. I'd never been part of an event this big and it was exhilarating. There were 12,000 people in that race – 12,000 people with different lives all joined together by running.

The sea of runners was flowing to the start line but there were so many of them, no one was going anywhere fast. I was going to make the start after all.

I spotted several Victoria Park Harriers vests. I loved the sense of belonging from being part of a big running club. I knew I could approach anyone wearing the blue and white stripes, even if I'd never seen them before. I saw Ben from triathlon camp in France at the bag-drop and then, as I made my way to my start pen, I bumped into Helen, who was also on that trip. We walked together. I abandoned looking for the correct pen for my target finish time, preferring to wait and chat with Helen instead.

For a moment, as we stood sandwiched among the chattering crowds, I felt like I was in an entirely different life to my old one. How much my social sphere had changed.

What would I have been doing, had I not ventured to run club the previous October? Would I be awake yet? Maybe I'd be in bed, feeling lethargic, my skin dull, my eyes puffy, regretting how much I'd drank yet unable to find any activities to break the pattern. Instead I was standing in full sunshine in a big green open space, only 20 minutes from home, which I didn't even know about before. I was surrounded by smiling, healthy, welcoming faces. All had different reasons for choosing to run a half-marathon on a Sunday morning. Some were experienced runners. Some would be first-timers. But all had at some point pushed past boundaries – physical or mental ones – to be able to run this distance.

The start gun fired but there were so many people it was a whole 10 minutes of walking slowly forward before Helen and I reached the start line and our timing microchips were activated. I wished her luck and ran on.

The first thing I noticed was the overwhelming thud of runners' feet hitting tarmac. If the average runner's cadence rate (how quickly your legs hit the ground) is anything to go by, those thousands of pairs of trainers would each be producing 170 patters a minute. That sound, in between shouts of support from spectators, bolstered my spirits. It brought to light the scale of the event and the sense of unity between all these strangers, each with their own struggle and objective.

Occasionally I'd hear, 'Come on, Victoria Park.' Wearing a team vest automatically gave me a network of supporters, who didn't even know my name.

There were so many runners, I had to step up on pavements to pass them. The course weaved through Hackney, Homerton, Haggerston, Hoxton, Victoria Park and Stratford. I knew this area by jigsaw from all my involvement with run club and the course helped me piece it together. Every mile or so I would see a familiar place that I had run or cycled through or a cafe where we'd gathered after training.

It was 28°C that day and some struggled in the heat. I like heat (which is perhaps why open-water swimming leaves me one step away from being cryogenically frozen), but today the heat affected me. My lack of rest in the preceding days was evident. It felt harder than anything I'd ever done. It wasn't just my legs which ached, but my neck and shoulders. I had no acceleration, no power – everything felt a slog. My motor was quite simply out of gas.

I told myself that even if I had to walk the last 3 miles, it would still be a decent performance. That would make it the equivalent of a Thursday night 10-mile run. I always tell myself things like this to make it more manageable, though to date I've never actually quit a race so it's just a sales tactic. It's like the rational part of my brain, which I can control, tries to tame the unruly defeatist part of my brain, which I can't control. Often, when I'm dreading a training session (usually the track), I say to myself, *Just do half*. When I get to half, I urge myself, *Just do three-quarters*. Then after three-quarters, I always think, *I may as well finish*. Without these mind games, I'm sure I wouldn't do half the training nor complete half the events that I have.

The mile between twelve and thirteen felt like the longest mile in the world. Most of it was a long straight stretch of tarmac in the blazing sun, which turned around at a traffic cone and came back the same way. These bits are known as an 'out-and-back' and are usually stuck on to a course to make up distance. I find them particularly excruciating because with every step, you know that you have to do the same again the other way.

Being the penultimate mile, it felt extra long because I was anticipating the end. From running in this area, I knew exactly the fastest route from that tarmac stretch in the Olympic Park to the finish in Hackney Marshes. But torturously the route wound around a few streets to make up the distance. If it were socially acceptable to curl up in a ball and sleep by the side of the course, I would have done so. This wasn't just muscle fatigue – this was whole body and spirit fatigue.

When I eventually turned into Hackney Marshes and through the much-welcomed sight of the finish posts, my finish time was 1 hour 47 minutes and something – almost 3 minutes slower than the Windsor Half-marathon. That doesn't sound much but 3 minutes was a big deal in my circles. Well, in a race situation anyway. The idea of a race, I had learned, is that you run to your maximum potential. So while a training run can easily vary by a few minutes depending on how tired/in the mood/hormonal/hungover you are, your race pace should reflect you at your rested, fuelled, fittest best. But I didn't care. My eye was on the bigger picture – getting as fit as I could and being ready for whatever challenge I happened to be signed up to next.

I found the gathering of VPH vests near the finish. Almost everyone had a sub 1'40" time, including the women. This seemed desperately impossible to me. I could not imagine ever running that fast for such a sustained period of time. I also could not see how I could train any more than I already was in order to get that fast. What I didn't realise at the time was that most people would focus on a particular distance in their training. Longer medium-fast intervals before a half-marathon.

Shorter fast-fast intervals before a 5k. Runners wouldn't cycle in the weeks before a key running event because that would detract from their running. And vice versa. Nor would runners or cyclists waste their energy swimming or pumping their upper body in the gym. I had been doing a bit of everything, because I loved – and still love – the sensation of overall fitness, but I couldn't expect to perfect one activity if I wasn't focusing on it completely.

This dawning didn't make any difference though. I continued doing a bit of everything. Each of my training sessions had a different crowd (faces at the track were different to run club, which were different to hill sessions, which were different to the triathletes swimming at the West Reservoir or the brick sessions). Each thing was a joyous gem of discovery and if that came at a price of a few minutes on my run times, I really wasn't that bothered.

We went to a pub that afternoon. I was glad that I didn't have to rush back for a date to somewhere swish, like I had to after my last half-marathon. Instead I could simply hang out in running kit, drink cider by the canal and talk about the gaps between the mile markers that went on for ever.

CHAPTER 12

BIG KNICKERS AND BACKPACKS

I did something very stupid two days after the Hackney Half-marathon. I gave myself Monday off but on Tuesday I was back at the track. I knew the drill about recovery. Fitness = Training + Rest. A race requires higher effort than training over the same distance so a couple of days' rest minimum is recommended after a half-marathon. I always gave myself at least one day's rest a week but I just couldn't bring myself to miss track on Tuesday. I had seen only progress so far, and my body seemed to cope with everything so I didn't feel I needed extra rest.

But all day I felt a strong sense of dread, as if every fibre in my body was resisting. I struggled through the session. My lap times were several seconds slower than usual, my breathing more elevated, my heart rate higher and it generally felt more tedious.

The body is an intelligent device and it has ways of telling you when it needs rest. It isn't just the micro tears in your muscles that need time to repair – your nervous system needs to recover and stress hormones like cortisol, enzymes, iron levels and acidity levels in the muscles all need time to regulate.

I've since learned to listen to my body, but not so then. I was not focused on the session. All I could think about was what I'd do when I got out of there. Work I had to finish, a phone call I had to make, the online Tesco shop. Instead of heeding my body's cries, I carried on, but my mind was absent.

When I stopped, I felt pain in my right foot. I ignored it. The next day I swam. On Thursday it was still niggling but I was still game for run club's monthly 5-mile friendly race.

The next day, Friday, I could not put my weight on my foot. Two of my toes were swollen. This was my first proper running injury. It is no coincidence that this coincided with fatigue. This was my body's sophisticated damage limitation system – it knew it was on the way to injury before my stubborn conscious mind did. It has taken years and several injuries to learn this. Now I never train if I'm rundown, sore or have an overwhelming feeling of ennui.

I was convinced it was a stress fracture. After a few googles I'd diagnosed myself with an acute metatarsal fracture. Gradual build-up of pain. Tender on the top of the third toe. Caused by increasing miles too quickly. I had all the signs. No question. According to Google this meant six weeks' rest: my summer was done for!

However, a few (expensive) visits to a physio revealed it was not so severe. The tendons on the top of my toes were strained because they had been overcompensating for an injury further up my leg. Sometime over the last few weeks I'd been putting too much strain on my peroneus longus. That's a muscle that runs down the side of the lower leg to the foot. I had a lump on the side of my lower calf to show for it, which tingled with numbness sometimes. I had noticed it. It erupted after exercise but would always go down again so I had ignored it. Doing a half-marathon without tapering and then bounding back to the track two days later had pushed it over the edge.

Here began another learning curve on sports injuries. Overcompensation injuries are common. You don't always feel an injury at the point it is damaged. Often, as in my case, the injured or overused muscles 'switch off' and the surrounding ones step in to take the extra strain. It all sounded very complicated and involved lots of Latin names but the upshot was that I needed a big dose of the most effective but unpopular remedy administered to athletes – rest!

My injury wasn't serious in the grand scheme of sporting afflictions but if you'd heard me go on about it, you'd have thought I'd never run again. I was fitter than I had ever been, and having to stop training for a month was like watching myself decay. More tormentingly, it was summer and there was so much more to miss out on. On Thursday nights at the club, the bar moved outside and there were BBQs. The light evenings meant more varied routes. Instead of the repetitive 10-mile run along the canal to Tower Bridge we could go north to Hackney Marshes or along the River Lea for hill reps in Springfield Park. There were bike rides on weekends and even at the track there were novel taster sessions for field athletics. I'd been dying to have a go at hurdles and long jump, because why not?

I still went to the clubhouse bar a couple of times during my month of rest but I felt a fraud for not having taken part in the preceding activities. A cold beer and a BBQ don't quite taste the same when you haven't done a 10-mile run. There were many things that I missed about not training and one of them was my voracious appetite.

On Tuesdays I practically had to lock myself in to prevent temptation to join the track. At 7.30 p.m. I pictured everyone gathering by the shelter by the fence and desperately wished I was part of it.

It is an anomaly that fitness can become so addictive despite the fact it can hurt so much and make you look so dreadful immediately afterwards. The endorphin hit from exercise might be one factor. But for me it was also because I had little else to do without it.

My career, for instance, as a freelance journalist was still not moving anywhere. Sadly, modern times have not been good to journalism. Papers are shrinking because advertisers have cut back. There are fewer pages to fill and more freelancers pitching to fill them. Editors are more stretched and pitches go unanswered. As for freelancing in TV news, I was becoming increasingly disillusioned with the antisocial shift patterns and the intensity of a newsroom shift that did not pay well. I had been trying to break into reporting from producing for years and I could see no way it was going to happen quickly, so I lost my drive and then felt resentful when work interfered with track or any other of the assortment of evening sessions.

Other professional projects outside journalism seemed equally fruitless. A TV gig which 'nearly' happened. A radio show I 'nearly' got. A TV deal on one of my books which 'nearly' materialised.

Instead of tackling this mini career crisis, I buried myself in training because I seemed to achieve exactly the same whether I sat at my desk sending proposals all day or was out on my bike in France. I couldn't control who replied to my emails, who commissioned a story, who booked me for a producer or reporter shift in a newsroom. But when it came to my sporting performance, I could set a goal, train and achieve it.

Then there was my personal life. Since my two closest friends had moved away, I suppose I'd been looking for a replacement for that easy company and frequency of contact. I had lots of other circles of friends. There were the settled ones who'd partnered up and had kids and seemed permanently unavailable. And there were the single ones, like me, who were available but we'd already set the precedent on the sorts of activities we did together. I had lost interest in our former favourite pastime of sitting in waiter-serviced members' bars and making my way through the cocktail menu. If I'm honest, I had lost interest in it years ago but through lack of an alternative, I'd continued, under a shadow of self-loathing for doing so.

I felt like an inbetweener. Not fully established in my new sporty social circles, yet drifting away from my old ones. While my new outdoor pursuits had brought great people, fun, energy and laughter into my life, they were just a sticking plaster. I still hadn't made solid friends in running club, other than Dave. If I were to examine things closely, I would see that some of the emptiness from the beginning of my fitness journey was still there. Whenever I couldn't train for some reason, because of work or illness or that pulled pec muscle, it brought these realisations to the fore.

Like now. The one thing that made me feel alive was the thing which was forbidden because of my foot. My project, which gave me purpose, was on hold. The dampener on my mood from not being able to run made me question whether I was becoming too absorbed in my new hobby. If I could so easily feel desolate without it, perhaps this was not the easy answer to fulfilment after all?

There were, however, a few good things that came from not training. Not least that I no longer had a permanent clothes horse stuck in my bedroom drying the constant turnaround of kit. I tuned in again to professional work, instead of sitting down to work every day at noon because I'd spent the morning training, stretching, foam rolling then eating. But more groundbreakingly, I made peace with flat shoes.

The only shoes which didn't squash my swollen toes were flip-flops. So I wore them with everything. Jeans, dresses, suits, party wear. Leaving the house became a simple task. No decisions. No kicking all the other shoes out of the way to get to the shoe cupboard. No wearing flats to the Tube and carrying heels in a bag. No trying on two different pairs in front of the mirror to decide which make my legs more shapely. Just slip on and flip-flop out. I went on holiday later that summer for a friend's hen do and I didn't pack *any* shoes. I didn't even need to take them off to go through airport security.

Then a funny thing happened. I went all feminist about it. My injury and the consequent visits to a physio enlightened me on the musculoskeletal intricacies of our feet, legs and backs. It wasn't difficult to conclude that walking and dancing in such an artificial pose is not good for you, especially for runners, whose legs and feet are likely fatigued already. So I stopped wearing heels altogether, long after my injury went. A lifetime love affair dropped, just like that. On the rare occasion I did wear them, I felt unnaturally dressed up.

Once I'd ditched the shoes, pragmatism took hold. I then developed a disdain for handbags. Now that I had a hybrid bike, sans wicker basket, my laptop had to go into a backpack. Why had I not tried this before? Backpacks, I discovered, make life easier. Manoeuvres like running for a bus, going shopping or carrying a bottle of wine no longer resulted in aching shoulders or spilling possessions on to the pavement. Out went the Gucci and Prada, and to hell with colour coordination.

Next went fiddly, lacy lingerie, thanks to the discovery of anti-chafing cycling knickers. This epiphany originated from a discussion in the run club bar among keen female cyclists about the perils of a long bike ride on a rainy day. Not that I'd ever encountered such problems but I thought I'd better be prepared for my future feats, so I bought a pair. If you've never tried such fine sartorial specimens may I suggest you do.

Anti-chafing cycling knickers are made from feather-light, silky-smooth, quick-drying synthetic fabric which feels like a cushion of air against your skin. There are no hems, no elastic, no bits which can rub on newly waxed areas and they are totally wedgie-proof. I started using them for spin classes, then they became the go-to underwear for running and the gym. Then, I conceded, why wear any other type of pants ever?!

I also stopped going into town so much. I used to pack my laptop and work from trendy members' clubs or other shared work spaces with entrepreneurial types game for a glass of wine at the end of a day. But now I had better things to do. I no longer craved the hubbub of the city and was happy working from local cafes.

Instead of putting on a dress and heels and getting the Tube, I put on jeans and boots and set off on two wheels up the canal. I loved discovering east London's eclectic coffee shops, with their sprouted rye bread sandwiches and dairy-free brownies. I nearly always passed someone from running club out cycling or running wherever I went, which added to the charm.

All this made me question ideals of feminine beauty. By society's existing standards, many things that make women beautiful, sexy or alluring are things which are restrictive, uncomfortable or potentially harmful. Throughout history women have had to endure corsets, foot-binding and in some African tribal cultures heavy weighted jewellery to lengthen their necks. Stifling women appears to make them more attractive to men. Even the seemingly harmless cocktail dress is an injustice if the air con is cranked up or someone has the bright idea of hosting a party in a marquee during a British summer. Men, meanwhile, remain toasty in their woven dress shirts and jackets.

I started to see high-maintenance hairstyles, formal dress codes, painful waxing regimes, time-consuming manicures in a whole new light. Female sex appeal is juxtaposed with functionality. Not so for men. A man can roll out of bed, unshaven, uncombed, pull on a faded T-shirt and he's rugged. The equivalent female is 'rough'. A man can go out with black fingernails and casually put it down to the puncture he had to fix that morning. On a woman it's 10 times as unseemly. Men can get away with wearing Scooby-Doo socks with a suit, whereas a woman needs every type of hosiery with differing grades of denier depending on the shoes she's wearing, which in turn depend on whether her jeans are cut-off, long, skinny, boot leg or if she's in a skirt. And don't get me started on coats.

What does it say about a society that encourages women to be primped and preened to such a standard that it impedes her agility and discourages her from becoming anything more than ornamental? Much of my own identity had rested in these ideals. But now I was coming to the view that the world would be a much more comfortable place if everyone wore running gear and hoodies.

When I'm wrapped up in weather-appropriate, multicoloured sportswear, having a beer after a race or a coffee in the middle of a bike ride, there is no fashion snobbery, no double gender standards and no parading of sexuality. Choice is based on practicality, warmth and aerodynamics. Women are judged not on their hair, labels and appearance but on their speed, strength and stamina. They are heroes for being fast and fit and determined, not for their sex appeal.

Come to think about it, in my new sporty milieu, I had rarely heard the sort of shallow judgemental comments we so often hear at the office or in rowdy groups. When there was a comment on physique it was to do with performance. Someone may observe that someone's muscular frame is why they're good at powering up hills on a bike, or that their lithe figure is good for endurance running. I didn't notice any posturing, sexism or hidden agendas. Perhaps it was because we'd found something more fulfilling than playing to the affections of the opposite sex.

Sport is the one platform where you can scientifically argue that men and women are *not* equal but, ironically, I have found the social scene in sport to be one of the least chauvinistic. Men will always perform better on speed and strength than women because they have a higher muscle-to-fat ratio, a higher capacity to process oxygen, narrower hips for better running economy and a higher red blood cell count. Yet in this environment interactions are based on nothing more complicated than shared interests. The same may not be said by women who do team sports like football, which is regularly criticised for its male dominance. But in my experience of the endurance sports community at least, I had not noticed the 'boys group, girls group' sort of separation that I'd witnessed in other areas of my social and professional life.

I looked back on my former self and cringed. To think that I used to wear hold-ups on a date, even in the winter! I've not exactly been a full-make-up kind of girl, but still, whenever I went anywhere sociable, dressing to my best, acting feminine, winning male approval felt the natural thing to do, as it does to many women. But now I was starting to see these priorities fall away and be replaced by getting fitter, stronger, faster and by the rewards of meeting new people.

I still wore make-up and took pride in my appearance, I still zipped up a dress when situation demanded, but I certainly wasn't going to go tottering round in heels and wearing dresses and 10-denier tights in winter any more just because some enforced aesthetic value says I'm more attractive for doing so.

But back to the flip-flops. For a week I couldn't do any training at all. Even the flexion of my foot through swimming hurt. My frustration soon turned to resignation and I decided this was perhaps a good chance for my body to rest. But after seven days the inflammation was calm enough to swim. And it didn't take me long to find a swimming challenge to turn my focus on.

CHAPTER 13

EAU DE THAMES

I heard about the Hampton Court Swim, a 2.4-mile race in the River Thames near Kingston in Surrey, from a girl at the track called Jess.

She had mentioned it a few weeks previously, when my foot was still well and good. My interest was piqued at the thought of another novel event to spend a weekend on. Now that I couldn't swim and couldn't run, it seemed just the ticket.

I had never swum further than 1 mile. But since when had I let inexperience stop me doing anything? I thrived on the challenge of an unprecedented distance. One thing I'd learned is that tenacity is at least 75 per cent of the effort.

I suggested the Hampton Court Swim to club friends from the French trip but no one else saw the appeal of getting into brown, murky, cold water first thing on a Sunday morning. So I entered on my own.

A few days before, I met a (non-sporty) friend for drinks in a riverside pub in Greenwich, where the river is wide and subject to tides. Sitting by the window, I looked out at the ferocious waves. In the dusky light it looked hostile and cold.

'I have to swim in that next week,' I said.

My friend shook her head despairingly. 'Well, you don't *have* to,' she said and poured me more wine.

This amused me, because I felt I did have to. I had to because I'd entered. I had to because I was dying to know how long it would take me to swim 2.4 miles. I had to because that was my plan for Saturday. That would be my reason for staying in on Friday. I had to because of the exhilaration and sense of achievement I would feel afterwards. I and 300 other entrants felt we had to.

The sanitary conditions in the Thames concerned me more than the distance or the currents though.

The day before the race, I visited a health food shop and asked if they had anything I could take as a precaution for swallowing dirty water.

'Like a purification tablet which works when it hits your stomach?' I asked.

The woman in the shop smiled. 'Are you going somewhere exotic? Is it a safari trip?'

'No, I'm swimming in the Thames.'

Her face dropped. 'Is it for charity?'

'No, for fun.'

Her face turned from surprise to confusion.

Why anyone would want to swim in what has previously been an outlet for London's sewers and chemical plants, for fun, was admittedly difficult to comprehend. She advised I take colloidal silver. I have no idea whether this is effective, but I didn't get one tummy rumble afterwards so I've since added a bottle of this magic potion to my kit list and now take a few drops before I do any open-water swim.

It was a damp, muggy July morning when I arrived at Hampton Court. I had an hour to wait and I sat on the dewy grass, nursing a coffee, in my wetsuit because it was warmer than the clothes I'd brought. I observed people around me, laughing as they struggled with wetsuits and taking group selfies. But there were also plenty of people on their own – challenge junkies like me who had a compulsion to spend well-earned free time pushing their bodies and minds through something unpleasant.

Entering alone meant I had no benchmark for my time. What was a good time and what was a bad time for this distance? In my gym pool I could swim 1 mile in around thirty minutes. But what would my time be in a river, with no kicks off the side and with a current, but with the benefits of a wetsuit (wetsuits make you swim faster because they give you buoyancy)?

We had to provide an estimated time on our entry forms, so that we could start with similarly paced swimmers. I gave 1 hour 45 minutes, which must have been very conservative, because I was in the second to last wave. In other words, with the novice, nervous swimmers.

As soon as I put my face in the water my goggles leaked. I'd had a whole hour to sit around and hadn't thought to check the tightness. Every race taught me a new lesson like this one.

I swam 20 metres, deluding myself that they'd stop leaking, before I had to pause and tread water while I adjusted them and watched powerlessly as everyone in my wave swam ahead. I let them. I was resigned to the fact that I could be one of the slowest here today. It wasn't that I had no faith in my swimming ability – it was more that, being new to the racing scene, I always presumed that everyone else did things like this all the time and they would by default be better and stronger than a newcomer like me.

But when I resumed swimming, with no particular effort I found myself gliding past swimmer after swimmer. I was delighted. I wasn't even trying! I even started to think that something was wrong. *Am I going too fast? Am I going to burn out? Is this longer than I have anticipated?* But I continued flowing effortlessly past blue hat after blue hat. I didn't have any breathing difficulties this time because the water was warmer. I passed more and more people. If I wasn't passing them, I was getting right up to their feet and was forced into breaststroke until the jam cleared.

Maybe I'm a born swimmer! Maybe I'll win! I thought these things, forgetting that I had started in one of the slowest waves, thanks to my stab in the dark at an estimated completion time. I passed everyone in my wave and then passed many from the wave in front. I knew this because they had green hats. Then I started to catch up with the wave before that, who had white hats.

The imprint on my memory from that swim is a dense block colour of brown, with flashing imagery of spectators on the riverbank. When swimming in open water, with your head continually submerged, all you see is brown, or dark blue if it is the sea. You can't see fish or plants or the interesting things people have dumped in there. There's nothing to listen to and nothing to occupy the mind. You have only the movement of arms and the rhythm of breathing to concentrate on. When you bring your head to alternate sides to breathe, you register a split second's worth of land vision. I got a flash of boats when I breathed to my right and spectators when I breathed on my left. But the flashes were so short they make you disorientated. You can either dread this experience as mind-numbingly boring or you can embrace it as a chance to enter a meditative zone.

Orange buoys marked each 500 metres and were a welcome break to the monotony. I tried to count them at first, using them as denominators for my creative fraction-counting. But I soon lost count.

I don't remember feeling tired and I don't remember feeling cold. I didn't find it hard, just uncomfortable because it was territory unknown and I was anxious that the river water would make me sick. When I saw the finish flags on the bank in my intermittent flashes of land, I was surprised they were there so soon. I didn't speed up because I was enjoying it and I wasn't in a race mindset. But when I handed in my chip to the timing desk I wished I had. One hour and one thirteenth of a second. 01:00:13. Had I been one fourteenth of a second quicker, my time would have been under one hour.

I spotted Jess, the girl from the track, near the finish. She was a serious triathlete and I had always been intrigued by her stories of races every weekend. She invited me to join her triathlete friends for brunch. We walked to a quaint deli and sat amid the well-groomed clientele of Kingston in our swimsuits, tracksuit bottoms and matted hair, with the whiff of eau de Thames. Everyone whipped out water purification tablets and dissolved them in cans of Coke. There is an old wives' tale that Coke settles upset stomachs so this was a preventative measure before 'the runs' got a chance to kick in. There were jokes about swimming over bodies and dead eels.

I found the innocence of this exchange comforting. 'Brunch' with friends used to be hungover affairs regaling debauched tales of nights out. This seemed so much more worthwhile and just as entertaining. It was a boost I needed. Being injured, I had missed the camaraderie and familiarity of run club activities. But it had also brought that niggly realisation to the surface again: that these cheerful post-race chit-chats were always fleeting. These people were part of a triathlon club in south London. I probably wouldn't see them again. I had enjoyed lots of flash encounters like these with different social groups from different sporty scenes. But it still remained that the most significant people in my life were my established friends, even though they'd never go anywhere near the Thames, unless it was on a boat with a bar.

My result put me in the top 20 per cent of females and I was astonished. I had only swum with others a handful of times but each time I was surprised at how I fared against more experienced swimmers. In the Les Stables pool I regularly found myself up against people's feet. In my first triathlon I ranked higher in the swim than in running or cycling. At one session at the West Reservoir, we practised 'drafting', which involves swimming close to someone's feet to derive the benefit of their slipstream, but I found that whoever I partnered with couldn't draft off me because I went too quickly.

This was a mystery since I have never had formal swim training. I put it down to years of gym use. As a skinny teenager, while most of my friends were trying to shed weight, I was trying to build upper body bulk through weight training. This may well have given me strength in the muscle groups relevant for swimming. Or maybe it was simply because of those hours and hours of catch-up drill in France?

Whatever the reason, I decided to cash in on this semblance of natural ability.

I started to go to a structured swim session hosted at my gym on Wednesday evenings. Yet another training group to add to my growing list.

It was basically one lane of the pool taken up by a load of alpha-male bankers from the nearby Canary Wharf offices. I was the only female ever to have joined.

'Is this swim club?' I asked, and I swear they all fell silent from their jokes and man talk.

'This is a speed session for strong swimmers,' said a discerning coach from poolside. He was Finnish, tall, muscular and good-looking.

'That's OK,' I said more confidently than I felt. 'If I can't keep up I'll stop.'

My first session was very much like my first track session: I hadn't got a clue what anyone was talking about.

'We're starting with one hundred easy, one hundred pull buoy, one hundred kick,' said the coach.

A 'pull buoy', I learned, is a float that goes between your legs so that you can concentrate on your upper body technique. 'Kick' is a drill where you hold on to a float so you can concentrate on your legs. 'Easy' was the only bit I understood – go easy.

There were other drills but they washed over me. Even now, I hate drills and I still haven't learned how to do half of them.

Each drill is designed to correct a certain aspect of your stroke but unless you know what your weaknesses are they can be in vain. When I was getting to grips with running and cycling, my approach had been 'kill yourself to keep up' and that's what had made me fitter and faster. So I couldn't derive any satisfaction from doing slow drills, concentrating on an aspect of body or arm movement. I needed to gasp for air and feel my heart thump against my chest and my nostrils flare, and slump on the side of the pool at the end of sets to feel like it was having any effect.

I muddled through the 15 minutes of drills and turned my focus on keeping up for the main sets. There were six of us in one lane and we set off at 10-second intervals. Scared of holding anyone up, I went last. While the others were thinking about pacing and 'ascending efforts', I kept my focus on one thing: keep on his feet. All I cared about was making sure the person ahead didn't get too far in front so I wouldn't be ridiculed.

'You did well,' said the Finnish instructor at the end, markedly warmer.

The second time I went to swim club, the alpha-male bankers acknowledged me. The third time, they even engaged me in conversation.

In much the same way as I had first approached track running, my first bike ride in France or that first-ever 10-mile run, I gave everything to keep up, to be accepted, to disguise my inexperience. To date, this remains my preferred and most effective method of training.

CHAPTER 14

CAN'T RUN, CAN CYCLE

As I was busy trying to get fast at swimming, I monitored the lump on the side of my leg with compulsion. It gave me no pain but it flared up the minute I did any exercise. The physio, on whom I had spent a small fortune, stuck pins in it every time I saw her. Something to do with releasing tension deep in the belly of the muscle. I was under strict instructions not to do any impact exercise like jumping or running. I mostly did as I was told, though I did occasionally jog to the swimming pool or slip a few jump squats into my strength routine. Each visit, she would look at me suspiciously and ask if I'd been resting. She knew my type.

Slowly, as the lump went down and my toes no longer hurt, she warmed to my suggestions to resume cycling. 'But if that lump goes up again, stop!' she warned. 'And still no running.'

Well, this was as good as a free pass to me. I tested out my peroneus lump with a couple of spin sessions. I was so paranoid about it that I became acutely aware of every sensation on my lower right calf. If a hair so much as blew in the wind I'd look down to see if the lump was back. Everything seemed OK.

Time then to start some proper cycling, like the long rides we did in France.

There were just two small issues: I didn't have anyone to cycle with and I didn't have a road bike.

I had stubbornly resisted investing in yet another bike. Not even the dubious looks at brick sessions at the Olympic Park from experienced triathletes on fancy bikes had swayed me. To me the purpose of cycling was to get fit. If I was doing it on a heavier and less efficient hybrid bike then surely that was better?

But when I heard about plans among the France group for weekend morning rides into Essex, I conceded I needed a faster road bike to be part of it. I bought the cheapest one on offer from a local bike shop. A mucky-green Trek Lexa with purple trimmings. The day I picked her up, I rode her home along the river and immediately felt superior to the leisure cyclists on 'normal' bikes. I was a real cyclist now. I was going to do triathlons on this baby.

I was lucky to find a cycling crowd who were more experienced than me but didn't take it so seriously that they couldn't accommodate a learner. Finding people to cycle with is one of the biggest obstacles for new cyclists because, unlike running, it's daunting to go out alone. I was still scared of cars for one thing; I didn't know any routes, nor have one of those satnav things for bikes; and I still didn't know how to change an inner tube should I get a dreaded puncture. Road cycling is so laden with customs and the potential for mechanical disasters that beginners need veterans to get them started.

Brenda, Cate, Philippa, Mick, Julian and Dave were just some of the friends I rode out with that summer. They were always patient and happy to go slower than I'm sure they were capable of. On every ride I got a new insight into cycling culture. Experienced riders can be unsympathetic to newbies who don't know about things like the importance of carrying food, not letting your front wheel get ahead of the rider-in-front's back wheel (dangerous), pumping tyres to the max (reduces the drag on the tarmac, reducing the energy-to-speed ratio) and hand signals to warn against potholes in the road. There is no way I could have built up the confidence, knowledge, speed and fitness without access to an experienced yet moderately paced group. It is far more common to find cycle cliques on an all-out, eyeball-popping mission to redline it on every ride.

Now, when I look back and try to remember what it was like for me as a beginner cyclist, I make an effort to pass on the kindness and patience that was extended to me.

Running-club cycle rides weren't an every-weekend fixture. They just happened occasionally, when someone emailed to suggest one. Not many people in running club were interested in long cycles – it was mostly the group who had been to the triathlon training camp in France that summer. Julian, a fiercely competitive cyclist, was one of them and it was he who got lumbered with me on my debut UK ride. It was a Wednesday during a scorching hot July spell. He had the day off, and I didn't exactly need persuading to do less work than I already did. I warned him that it was my first outing on a road bike since France, and the first on the new Trek. But he assured me that it didn't matter if I held him back.

If he did regret taking on a beginner for the day, he didn't show it. We got a train from Waterloo to Surrey. It was liberating to abandon work to train all day on a Wednesday. We took in Box Hill and Leith Hill, Surrey's most popular cycle routes. I had to stop at the top of Box Hill to take a work call. It felt rebellious to sit on the grass in the sun, covered in sweat and bike grease, speaking to someone who probably presumed I was sitting at a desk. Julian did another lap of Box Hill as I was on the phone.

I got a train home from nearby Dorking but he cycled the remaining 50k home. This was incomprehensible to me. The total distance I clocked up that day was just short of 100k but only if I add the bits to and from train stations. There were at least two tea stops so it was very much a staggered conquest. It took all day, leaving home at 9 a.m. and getting on a train at Dorking at 4.30 p.m. By then I was starving, thirsty, sticky, hot and grimy. My back ached, my legs were numb and I felt the return of another dizzy spell. Nevertheless 100k was a golden milestone. 100k is the typical distance of organised sportives (road races) and is the distance that most cycle or triathlon clubs set for their traditional Sunday 'long ride'.

I got as far as Clapham Junction on the train, where a guard told me I couldn't take my bike further in rush hour. In a huff, I carried it off and the chain fell off. I didn't even know chains could come off. I stood on the platform struggling to hook it back on, smearing oil all over my hands and legs, until the very guard who had thrown me off the train came to my aid and fixed it in about two seconds by pushing forward a springy lever on the back chainring.

If the train guard knows more about bike maintenance than me, I thought, *I really need to do something about this.* The following weekend, I booked myself on a half-day bike maintenance workshop and at long last I learned the theory of changing an inner tube.

Now that I had survived my first 100k ride, and still unable to run, I suggested bike rides constantly. One weekend, six of us cycled 95 kilometres to Brighton. It was my suggestion but I let the others manage the route. It was a cold, windy day, and as we descended the notoriously steep Ditchling Beacon my bike and I were nearly blown down sideways. When we reached Brighton after five hours of mostly country roads, we ate fish and chips on the beach and paddled in the raging sea.

Another time I ditched work again and did a mid-week ride with Dave. Despite a generation age gap, he was still the person I had most contact with at run club. Even after more than six months of club races, Thursday training, volunteering to marshal, a holiday and paying my washing-up dues in the bar, I still hadn't got anyone's phone number. I still didn't know anyone well enough to, say, invite to a birthday party. Sometimes I'd have a great one-on-one chat with someone but then I wouldn't see them for a few weeks if we didn't happen to go on the same Thursdays for a while. Dave was the one I had most continuity with and it was this which made it feel natural to form a friendship.

As I cycled to meet him on the canal at Broadway Market in Hackney, I was worried that our sojourn may be interpreted as something more by him, or by others. I didn't like him in that way, did I? Of course not. Then why did I always end up talking to him in the bar? And what was I doing arranging to meet him at 9 a.m. on a Wednesday to cycle out to the Essex coast for the day?

We cycled 50 miles (80 kilometres) to Maldon. I left the directions to Dave. I wouldn't have known how to devise a cycling route. He was quicker than me and had a better bike, so he ended up waiting for me at all the junctions. After 40 miles (65 kilometres), we had been going for almost three hours. I was counting down the journey. My body was still adapting to this many hours of exercise. It would take almost a year for my body to fully cope with a 100k ride. I didn't know then but I had a whole year of post-ride comatose afternoons ahead.

We hit the coast at Maldon and had cake in a tea room so quiet the staff could hear our every word. Then we took a walk and explored the harbour, wobbling in our cycle shoes because of the protruding plastic triangular cleats on the soles, before cycling another 10 miles inland to Chelmsford, where we got the train back to London.

Before we parted we stopped for an early dinner in a pub along the water in Wapping, equidistant to where we both lived. Tired, we tucked into fish and chips and cider.

It was turning to dusk when I rode home, weary, windswept and sweaty from a day in the saddle and a heavy meal. We parted company with nothing more than a thank-you and a friendly peck on the cheek. I rode along a stretch of the Highway which links Shadwell and Limehouse. This stretch of road is on the route of the Thursday club 10-mile run. As I cycled along it, I couldn't help thinking about that night nine months ago when I attempted it on my first visit.

Here I was returning home from a day and evening out with the very same person who had helped me get through that painful inaugural 10-mile run. Back then it was a cold, dark, drizzly, autumn night and I was lost. Not lost geographically. I knew perfectly well that I was near Shadwell Basin, bypassing the footpath through Wapping Woods where the path closes after dark. I was lost emotionally. Mourning the loss of a relationship and two friends who'd left my city; despondent with my career; wanting to be around people but desperately wanting to do different things than drinking. Bored. Agitated. In need of new direction.

Back then Dave was a stranger. Now he'd become a friend. Now it was summer. I was tanned, super fit, worry-free, riding a road bike, talking about things I didn't know about back then. I had felt so much anguish that night and now I was filled with contentment. If I hadn't done that run on that dark, wet night, if I hadn't ended my relationship even though there was nothing to replace it, I wouldn't be here now.

And if that much can change in nine months, I thought, there must be many more exciting things ahead.

There was a downside to so much cycling though. It allowed my running injury to heal but it did my lower back in. No sport is injury-proof sadly. It is a cruel irony that something so good for our bodies overall can be so damaging to isolated bits of it.

I'd never had a bad back before but from that day on, anyone who gives back pain as an excuse for inactivity receives my utmost sympathy. This was far worse than a bad foot. I couldn't even step into the shower or bend down to put my socks on without a struggle and great pain.

There was only one week to go before the London Triathlon and I was determined I would still compete. I searched 'cycling and back pain' every day and it seems it's not an uncommon ailment. I found blogs with tailored stretches and did them all. I went to yoga. I alternated ice packs with heat packs and had baths with Epsom salts. I rolled around with a tennis ball lodged in the small of my back and then lay flat on my stomach on my bed and tried to massage my own lower back (which nearly put my shoulder out because of the awkward twist).

Luckily, I hadn't done any lasting damage. The muscles around my spine had simply gone into acute spasm from being in such a contracted position for such a length of time. Hardly surprising given that I'd progressed straight from 45-minute spin classes to 5 hours on the road.

On the Friday before the London Triathlon, I lay face down on my physio's now-familiar couch having pins stuck into my lumbar spine. I asked for her verdict on Sunday's race. I so desperately, desperately wanted to compete. It would be my second triathlon and as it was based in the Docklands this was practically home soil.

'I wouldn't advise it,' she answered. 'But you seem like the sort of person who's going to do it anyway. So take loads of anti-inflammatories and, for goodness' sake, ice your back and that lump on your leg as soon as you finish.'

I was in.

CHAPTER 15

TWO HOURS TWENTY-NINE

Race nerves struck again that morning but this time there was a legitimate reason: I'd raised the bar for my performance. It was now August. When I entered, back in January on that entry-happy evening when my credit card got stopped, the standard Olympic-distance category had been full. The only remaining spaces were in an exclusive category for people who estimate to finish in sub 2'40". I wasn't exactly sure how supersonic that was, but I knew it would be good. It stated in bold red letters that competitors who were not done after 2 hours 45 minutes would be asked to stop.

I entered anyway. If I got chucked out of the race after 2 hours 45 minutes, that was still 2 hours 45 minutes of an experience that I would not have if I did not enter. But as the weeks approached, I became more serious about meeting the cut-off.

This would be almost thirty minutes quicker than my first triathlon. But it would be flatter, I had a better bike, and the water would be warmer so I was less likely to have a breathing problem and have to breaststroke for half the swim.

The day before the race, I was so excited I bought a new tri-suit and helmet to match my green bike. The night before, I dreamed that my legs couldn't move when I asked them to run.

It took me only 15 minutes to get to the ExCel Exhibition Centre. I was overwhelmed by the size of the venue. As I wheeled my bike through the vast exhibition space, it felt intimidatingly professional. The bike racking area was inside the exhibition hall. Being indoors made it more ominous. There were rows of stalls selling bike accessories, cycling holidays and energy bars. I kept eating the samples in the vain belief they would make me go faster, until I started to feel a bit sick.

I racked my bike in good time, diligently going through everything I would need. Helmet strap hooked over my handlebars so I could grab it easily. Race belt with number attached placed inside my helmet, also for grab-ability. Cycle shoes and run shoes neatly placed on the ground. The dried figs were inside a pouch on my bike this time (not in a polythene bag inside pockets of a faded fleece).

But my diligence couldn't overcome my nerves. Five minutes before my wave's briefing was about to begin, I realised that my goggles were no longer in my hand. I had no idea where I put them. Probably by one of the flapjack samples. I sprinted to the cloakroom, pushed my way to the front, flashed my race number marked on my arm (used in lieu of a cloakroom ticket), fished out my credit card from my bag, put the bag back in the cloakroom, ran upstairs, found the first stall selling goggles, bought a pair with a minute to spare before the race started and would have to do all three sports with my credit card tucked into the sports bra of my tri-suit.

Perhaps this sprint served as an effective warm-up because the race went better than I dared to expect. The swim ran along the exhibition hall in the Royal Victoria Dock. The water smelled of diesel but it was warmer than any open water I'd swum in and I swam the smoothest I had ever managed in open water.

I did go off course though. Swimming directly into the sun, I couldn't see the white buoys (even with my brand-new goggles!). When I realised I had swum too far over to one side and become separated from the pack, it only made me more determined. I swam extra hard to make up for the extra distance I'd covered in my detour.

When I got out of the water, mildly dizzy, I ran along the concrete path towards transition but was stopped by a marshal before I entered the indoor bike racking area. I was incensed. Why had I been stopped?

Apparently we had to strip off our wetsuits and put them in plastic bags before entering transition to limit the slipperiness on the concrete floor. Every race has individual rules like that. Had I not been buying goggles during the race briefing I would have known that.

I didn't apply sun cream in transition this time but I did take a mini tube on my bike to apply on the move. Using one hand, I tried to squeeze some out to smear on my cheeks but I dropped it on the road. For a moment I considered stopping to pick it up. It was precious stuff. For a moment there was a battle of wills between material Helen, who wanted to rescue the Decléor anti-ageing hypoallergenic SPF 50 face cream, and reformed Helen, who wanted to race. The latter won.

I pushed harder on the bike than in my first triathlon. Then I held back, unsure whether I needed to preserve energy. Now I knew what swimming 1,500 metres, cycling 40k and running 10k felt like. I knew that it was within my capabilities. Whenever I went up a hill or into the wind and felt my legs slowing, I imagined Mark, the coach from Les Stables, screaming: 'Increase cadence, increase cadence. Get them goddam legs spinning.'

The route headed east on closed roads from ExCel into Canary Wharf, through a tunnel called the Limehouse Link, which was super fast because it trapped the wind from the trail of cyclists ahead and propelled me through. Then it was along the Highway to Tower Bridge, on to the Embankment tracing the curve of the river to Westminster and Big Ben, where we turned around and came back the other way. I often ran along the Embankment and I felt sentimental racing on such familiar territory. To top it off the sun was scorching, just how I like it.

Then came the run. This was the bit I was worried about because my injury meant I had run very little for two months. But I felt strong. I sailed past people clearly struggling in the heat. I didn't feel a flinch from my bad foot and if I had lost fitness from not running for six weeks it didn't appear to slow me down.

Every inch of the three-lap course around the grounds was lined with spectators. There were a couple of vaguely familiar faces from the tri club open-water sessions I'd frequented over the summer. One of them, whose name I didn't even know, cheered me. There is nothing more singularly uplifting in a race than hearing someone shout your name when you think you are there alone. It's not necessarily the support – it's the camaraderie. I may not speak for all competitors but for me it reflects all the things I sought when I got involved in recreational sport in the first place.

When I struggled through the finish line, I had no idea whether I was within the crucial 2 hours 40 minutes. I only wore my watch for the run. When I was reunited with my bag from the cloakroom, I saw the automated text. It told me I had completed it in 2'29". I was bewildered. I had surpassed my expectations by far.

For the first time, I felt like I had truly raced to the best of my ability and fitness. It was a wonderful feeling and one I hadn't experienced before. There is nothing quite like the unique mix of satisfaction, exertion, achievement and delight when a race goes well. It whetted my appetite for serious competition.

When I got home I couldn't stop smiling. I met two (non-sporty) friends in Tower Bridge for lunch and as I got ready I kept saying out loud, 'Two hours twenty-nine!'

I should have been exhausted but I was bounding around. All that training, all that pain, all that coaxing myself through one more lap of the track, all those hill sessions and trying to keep up with the alpha-male banker swimmers had paid off. I had come eighth in my age category in one of the biggest triathlon events in the world. I was in great spirits but I tried not to bang on about it too much to my friends. They'd had normal Sundays – gone shopping, done yoga, texted dates – so they wouldn't quite understand the significance of 2 hours 29 minutes. They did, however, get much entertainment from me taking the Prosecco out of the ice bucket so that I could sit with my foot in it. 'Physio's orders,' I said.

For once, I was the one who wanted to drink more than them and stay out all evening. It was a Sunday but I didn't have any serious work the next day nor was I going to train again for a few days. I had been a much more reserved drinker over the last nine months and I worried that this positioned me as a boring friend. I worried that I would no longer be called on for a blow-out fun night but just for the minimal friend-maintenance catch-up. Now my old, carefree, party-chasing spirit resurfaced – it was always after a strong feeling of physical accomplishment when it did.

The London Triathlon was a turning point. I decided triathlons were 'my thing'. All the races with running club now seemed tame. Triathlons were bigger, longer, faster, required more skills and I appeared to be better at them.

So impressed was I that I compared my own time to an elite triathlete's (just out of curiosity!). At the 2014 Commonwealth Games in Glasgow, female triathlete Jodie Stimpson won it in the insane time of 1'58", which quickly put paid to any delusional dreams of becoming a late-life professional sportswoman. But, I decided, I would train to be the best triathlete I was capable of being.

Reading more into the sport, I learned about the levels of competition. Triathlon is one of the few sports where amateurs can compete at international level and earn a place on the GB team. It has more age categories than other popular sports. Larger competitions award prizes for every five-year age bracket. Organisers will introduce an 80–85 age category if there are competitors to fill it. In other words, triathlon lends itself to gung-ho competitive amateurs who want to play at being a pro.

The highest level of competition outside the elites is the so-called Age-Group Championships. There are two international competitions per year, World Championships and European Championships. Britain has 12 spaces for each five-year age group and qualification is open to all recreational triathletes, like me.

I found myself investigating how to qualify (just out of curiosity!). There are three qualifying races throughout the UK for both the European and World Championships. To get the grade you have to finish in the top four of your age group and within 115 per cent of the winning time.

Out of curiosity, I looked at the times of the top four females at one of last year's qualifying races: 2 hours 15 minutes. All I had to do, then, was shave 14 minutes off.

My approach to training felt different now that I had a goal. I hadn't had a specific goal before. Fitness was something I have always dabbled in for my health or physique, or more recently for a social life. 'Goal' is a buzzword in the fitness industry. Coaches, other athletes and personal trainers in the gym always ask what people's goals are. A common conversation opener at the club bar is: 'What are you training for?' I never had an answer.

But now, I had a goal: I would qualify for an international Age-Group Championship. Maybe not next year, nor the year after. To be honest, it didn't matter if I never actually qualified, as long as I had it to aim for. My livelihood did not depend on it. My ego wouldn't be too bruised. It's not as if I view athleticism as an inherent genetic talent that I desperately need to cultivate to save it going to waste. This would be my personal secret goal. If nothing else, it was nice to have one word to sum up my love of cycling, swimming, running and the lifestyle associated with it. That word: triathlon.

I set about my mission straight away. I subscribed to triathlon magazines and read books about training. Again, I recalled my teenage passion for horses. I remembered how I trained my barely broken, unruly mare all by myself, ignoring the doubtful comments from others. I trained her with diligence, day and night, rain or shine, and it paid off. Triathlon had reawakened the same focus, drive and connection with the outdoors. That teenage girl was back after years of suppressing that dauntless, primordial spirit which lives in us all somewhere.

CHAPTER 16
FOUR IN A ROOM

If my motivation for real work was slipping away before, now it fell off a cliff. Instead of researching article ideas to pitch or reading the news as I should do as a journalist, I'd find myself clicking on fitness articles, training blogs, adverts for races or more kit I didn't need. I was a marketeer's dream, opening and reading all the newsletters from race organisers. I was tuned in to every planned bike ride or running club trip. The books piled by my bedside featured training manuals, 'go-faster foods' and memoirs of ultrarunners.

My working day shrank as I fitted in a strength session or a swim in the morning, then wrapped up around five for whatever group evening training I decided to go to.

It wasn't just the training which took all my time but the stuff that goes with it. Namely, eating and washing. My appetite had become such that I could no longer afford to spend the day working from a cafe because I needed at least two lunches. My calorie intake was more than 4,000 a day. Going out to eat was becoming embarrassing. Some days I just ran out of ideas of what to eat next. I covered all my favourite food groups by lunch.

My orderly flat got overthrown by sporting paraphernalia. A decorative table in my hallway which used to display a vase and photo frame now housed a bowl with bike lights, cycle gloves, running glasses and reflector bands. A swimsuit was permanently draped on the back of a chair to dry; my heart-rate monitor lived on the draining board. The cultivated plants on my balcony were obscured by a bike, a track pump and a load of Allen keys.

My career ambition melted away and I found myself in a permanent state of unflappable Zen. Whereas I used to do a gym session or jog first thing in the morning to leave my day free for more important things, now I needed breakfast first because my training was more demanding. This new regime ate further into my day but I was very relaxed about it.

Normally, I am a rusher – always trying to maximise productivity, avoiding small talk and cutting corners wherever I can. But now I talked to everyone wherever I went. I started to attract new acquaintances like a magnet. I chatted to people everywhere, in no hurry to go anywhere. Fitness instructors saw me training hard and gave me free advice; strangers in cafes (when I actually made it to one to do some work) talked to me. I must have exuded an aura of openness.

I put this change down to my autumn of discontent. That brief spell when I felt isolated taught me the importance of making time for people. It is a shame we have to nearly lose something before we appreciate it.

There was another effect of my zealous fitness regime and that was on my love life. At first my increased fitness sent my libido soaring. I was full of energy and bursting with endorphins, which meant I became attuned to the appeal of sporty, rugged men with abs, like Philippe. But then as my training increased, the reverse happened. I lost all interest in men and romance. I could not have cared less. It was surprisingly liberating. I used to chase romantic encounters all the time just for the excitement, but in reality, they were unhealthily distracting, a roller coaster of highs when someone likes you and lows when someone never texts you back.

Now I had real activities to stimulate me. Training provided a clean adrenaline and endorphin kick. I could not think of anything I'd like to do less than dress up, send a million texts over where to meet and then waste some of my 14 units of permissible alcohol intake making small talk with a near stranger. Getting sleep, doing my stretches, reading about swim drills, and analysing my carb and protein intake were far more fascinating.

I got my hair cut short that summer. If there was a connection it certainly wasn't a conscious one. All I knew was that I was more content than I'd ever been with a low-maintenance hairdo, a practical wardrobe, less booze, more food, a broader muscly frame and no men in my life.

By the way, if you ever want to up the interest from the opposite sex, take this one singular piece of dating advice: pretend you're not bothered. As soon as I stopped being bothered about men or sex, I had interest from everywhere. Old lovers popped up and new interests appeared. I've used gyms for 15 years and never been asked out. That summer it happened twice. My greasy, sweaty, muddy, flushed, post-race photos on Facebook seemed to attract private messages from the opposite sex. Any occasional dates that were already lurking in the background got extra keen because I didn't text them back any more. But I let them all slip away. All I wanted to do was train and be with other people who wanted to train.

Then there was Philippe. A few weeks after the London Triathlon, I had my third and final one of the year, another Olympic-distance event, at Hever Castle in Kent. Philippe worked for the organisers, and months previously he had invited me to a hog roast on the eve of the race.

I didn't know much more information than that. I didn't know if said hog roast was for officials, for competitors, or the elite racing team which Philippe was part of. Whatever it was, it had seemed a grand idea when we were on the brink of a romance. Now that there was no romance, it seemed nothing other than awkward. But it did sort out my logistical problem as to how to get to Kent for an 8 a.m. race start on a Sunday.

The only reason I had entered Hever Castle Triathlon was because it said it was in Kent. Kent's pretty much London, I reasoned – there was bound to be a train. Except there wasn't. Not that early. So attending a hog roast with Philippe the night before was the perfect solution.

I asked him several times where we would be staying. Would it be a B&B? Camping?

He replied in a very vague and French way: 'Don't worry, Hélène. You will have a place to stay.'

I asked what time I should arrive and where I should meet him, and he simply replied, 'Come to Hever Castle and I will meet you.'

Should I take a sleeping bag? A towel? My own breakfast?

I got no answers, so I packed whatever I could fit in my ugly, orange backpack and set off, with bike, to Victoria train station at my leisure the afternoon before the race.

Ill fate struck immediately. The Circle Line was suspended, one of the few Tube lines on which bikes are allowed. I wouldn't cycle in London traffic on the best of days, let alone a Saturday afternoon with a bulging backpack that caught my helmet every time I turned my head. I spent the next half-hour searching for off-road cycle routes and the hour after that trying to navigate one. When I finally got on a train, I discovered a replacement bus service kicked in two-thirds into the journey.

There was no option but to cycle from whatever station I was turfed off at to Hever Castle. Typically, I had no data coverage on my phone so I couldn't load a map to see how far that would be. A steward enrolled to get passengers on to a replacement bus estimated it was about twelve miles away but no, he didn't know the way.

I cycled this way and that, backpack digging into my shoulders, asking in garages, stopping pedestrians, making my way however I could. I seemed to be going uphill a lot. Castles were, after all, built on hills.

I did all this, I forgot to mention, in flip-flops. My original plan had only involved a short cycle to the Tube, and another short cycle from a train station to Hever Castle. My cycling shoes were buried at the bottom of my bag.

By the time I approached the stately grounds of the thirteenth-century building, which was the childhood home of Anne Boleyn, it was pushing six o'clock. I wondered if Philippe had been trying to get hold of me. We had only ever communicated via the Facebook Messenger app so without data coverage I had no way of reaching him. I didn't even have his phone number.

When I got to the car park, there was no sign of a triathlon.

Frantically I turned my phone on and off, hoping it may connect to data.

Then a frazzled cyclist appeared. 'Are you here for registration?' he asked, his eyes bursting with urgency.

'No, I'm here to look for my friends,' I replied.

'They're closing registration in five minutes!' he cried.

This was news to me.

I decided to stick with him – wherever he was going, it sounded like that was where I should go. We entered the castle grounds. We had no idea where to head, but entering the grounds seemed a good start.

'You can't cycle through here,' a cross voice said and then went on to tell us that we were at the tourist entry to the castle. The triathlon 'village' was at the other side of the grounds.

We thanked him and promised we would walk our bikes through. As soon as we got around the corner, we mounted and pedalled to where we needed to go.

My new friend Matt was doing the middle-distance race – roughly twice the distance I was doing.

'We have to register tonight,' he said, which I hoped meant that for my distance, it would still be OK to register in the morning.

I told him about my eventful journey. '… And so I have no idea if my friend is even going to be there,' I finished.

'Well, if you're totally stuck, you can sleep in my tent,' he offered.

I was behind him so thankfully he didn't see the shock on my face.

At last, we saw the shapes of a marquee tent, flags and cars in the distance. When we approached there was very much the atmosphere of a festival winding down. People were dismantling speakers and picking up litter. Matt dashed to the registration tent. I wandered around aimlessly, hoping to spot Philippe's tall silhouette.

And then I saw him. Tall, sexy Philippe, towering above a cluster of four or five people.

'Hélène,' he bellowed, grasping my shoulder and shaking it hard. 'We have all been waiting.'

He kissed both cheeks demonstratively as a boy of about ten came up behind me and took my bike. I was so relieved to see Philippe I hardly noticed it being taken away from me. Before I could even turn around, he was riding it around the grass, his legs barely long enough to touch the pedals.

'This is a heavy bike,' the boy said, slamming on the brakes 2 inches from my feet.

'That is Brian's son,' said Philippe.

I had no idea who Brian was.

Then he introduced me to four people standing with him, who were all 'friends of Brian'. They were friendly but clearly tired – they'd been marshalling all day.

'When did you finish?' I asked.

'An hour ago, but we were waiting for you,' said a man called Simon. 'Philippe kept saying you'd be here any minute.'

I apologised but I was irritated with Philippe. Had he been clear about when and where I should be, instead of being deliberately mysterious, I would have made sure I was there. Had he told me where I was staying, I could have cycled there directly.

The 10-year-old boy wheeled my bike to the car park and then strapped it on to a bike rack attached to the back of a car. He had appointed himself in charge of it and I was perfectly happy with this arrangement. I'd been wheeling it around train stations all day.

I climbed into the rear seat and Brian's son sat next to me. 'Are you fast?' he asked assertively.

'I try to be,' I replied cheerfully.

'What's your best swim time?' he demanded, and did not seem impressed when I replied that I'd got 26 minutes 30 seconds at the London Triathlon.

'Have you ever won your age group?' he asked next.

I smiled and shook my head.

'I've won loads,' he replied.

I was still being grilled when we arrived at a house.

'This is Brian's house,' said the guy in the driver's seat.

I still had no idea who Brian was, and I didn't know who the driver was either.

'You can put your bike in the back garden with the others and your bags wherever you can find a space. It's quite cosy in there.'

Well, I thought, *at least this isn't a tent.*

Philippe arrived in another car behind us. We hadn't exchanged many words yet. Inside, the house was buzzing with people. Some were speaking French and some English. Some were in sportswear; some were in normal clothes.

Philippe walked in and got busy chatting in French. He made no effort at conversation other than the odd sigh of 'Hélène' whenever he was in my vicinity, accompanied by an affectionate shake of my shoulder.

Several people were in the kitchen preparing food. I put my bags down and offered to help and was promptly handed bowls of salad to transport to a big serving table in the garden.

'Whose house is this?' I whispered to a lady in the kitchen, hoping I could make an ally.

'Mine!'

'Oh, well, thank you,' I stuttered, 'for doing all this.' I gestured to all the food being prepared.

'I'm Brian's wife,' she offered.

I was still none the wiser as to who Brian was.

'Is the hog roast an annual tradition?' I asked, hoping the answer might lead to clues.

'Brian does it every year for all the volunteers. They work so hard,' she replied.

Brian, it transpired, was the founder of the Hever Castle Triathlon. Every year he provided a crash pad and food to the volunteer marshals, staff and any friends taking part in his race.

'Have you got a place to sleep yet?' asked Brian's wife. 'I'd go and bagsy a place if I were you.'

I disappeared from the kitchen into the hall, glad to escape and no longer feel like a spare part. I walked into a living room. It was covered in sleeping bags. When I say covered, I mean you couldn't see the carpet. Sleeping bags and pillows and backpacks took up every bit of floor space. I didn't have a sleeping bag. I had tried to fit it into my backpack but there was no way I could carry it on my bike.

'Some people are sleeping upstairs.' A girl with an American accent appeared in the doorway, as if reading my mind.

I ventured upstairs and met Philippe at the top, emerging from a bathroom door with just a towel around his very toned waist. I tried to keep eye contact.

'Where am I sleeping?' I asked. 'I don't have a sleeping bag.'

'Don't worry, Hélène,' he said. 'You will have a bed.'

'Can you tell me where, so I can take my bag to the room?'

'In the top bedroom.'

It was a small square room with a double bed. In the minimal floor space around the bed, there were already two sleeping bags.

'There is no room anywhere so we will have to share the bed,' said Philippe, walking into the room confidently, still naked other than his white towel.

Well, I thought, *there are worse things…*

It was a lively evening when the feast at last got under way. Some guests had raced that day in the sprint-distance event. Others were racing tomorrow in the Olympic distance, like me, or the longer middle-distance event. Others were marshalling, giving up their time in return for free race entry the following year.

One thing I'd learn about pre-triathlon parties is that you can guarantee they will wind down early. Most peeled away by 10.

Philippe was still chatting away in French, leaning back on his chair with a beer, when I announced I was going to bed.

'Hélène,' he sighed again, and said nothing else.

I queued for the bathroom. There was just one between about twenty people.

There were already two people asleep on the landing outside my room; another few in a dressing room, which I had to walk through to get to my room; and another two bodies in the sleeping bags either side of the double bed. I picked my way over them. Already I could detect the nascent sound of a snore.

Carefully, I changed into a T-shirt under the duvet in the dark. Just as I completed this mission, Philippe arrived. He eased himself in beside me and we both lay still, not daring to speak or touch.

All was still, and then the snoring crescendoed. It became so loud it was impossible to ignore. I heard a giggle from one of the sleeping bags at the foot of the bed. Snoring always starts off funny – ha-ha, someone's making pig noises and they don't know it – but it doesn't stay funny for long.

There was no let-up in the nasal trills. I was hot. I was wide awake. I needed the loo. I crept out of bed, climbed over bodies, went down a flight of stairs, found the bathroom, came back up and picked my way over bodies again. I tripped over one but whoever it was didn't stir.

Philippe put an arm around me and I allowed the comfort of it but nothing more. He had let me down that summer after all.

I must have got some sleep because I awoke in daylight and the space next to me was empty. One of the two sleeping bags on the floor was empty too. I looked at my watch. 6.20 a.m. I was sure I'd set the alarm for 6 a.m.

Twenty minutes later, I was being rushed on to my bike by Philippe and another French triathlete. They did not let me have breakfast – not enough time, they said, though I begged to differ. The race start was only a couple of miles away but with little sleep and no porridge in me the short journey felt as hard as the race itself. My porridge was pre-prepared in Tupperware in my bag, so I ate it raw and cold when I got there.

I have no objective way of knowing which event is the hardest thing I've ever done because the memory of pain is always the fastest thing to fade. At the time, everything feels like it's the most painful. This was particularly the case at Hever. It was mid-September so the water temperature had dropped. As I stood on the side of the lake with Philippe and the other competitors in our wave, I looked at the water with dread. Somehow it looked cold. Perhaps it was the darker autumn light.

'I'm so nervous,' I heard a competitor say beside me. I found it reassuring that others had the same sense of dread as me. Even though this was my third competition, I still presumed everyone else would be more experienced and gung-ho than me.

We dropped into the lake from a wooden pier and when the horn sounded and we started swimming, my cheeks smarted with the cold and my breathing irregularities returned. The lake narrowed into a funnel at one point and we became bunched together. I was forced on to someone's feet and though I hadn't planned to do so, I found myself drafting. A pair of feet just appeared near my fingertips. This was the perfect opportunity to put into practice what I'd learned at the triathlon club open-water sessions. Swimming near to someone's feet enables you to go faster because you capture the slipstream created by the swimmer ahead. It takes nerve because it feels like at any moment you could be kicked in the face. But that day I stuck to the feet and I felt my body propel through the water.

When I ran from the lake exit to transition, I looked at the number of bikes in my row – an indicator of how well placed you are. If there are lots of bikes, it means lots of people are still swimming. This was only my third triathlon but already I could spot a pattern. I was always one of the early females to get out of the water but then everyone passed me on the bike. It taunted me as they slipped by, one by one. After about ten had gone past, I vowed, *No more*! I would work so hard not to let anyone else pass. But they kept coming. Ten became 20. They overtook in droves on fancy bikes with noisy disc wheels. But on the run, I always overtook people again.

Triathlon results provide a breakdown of the swim, bike and run times and a ranking for each. I'd noticed how I was always in the top quartile for my age and gender in the swim and run, but in the bottom third for the bike. That is particularly unlucky, because in triathlon the bike leg is proportionally longer than the other two disciplines.

Aside from having a very basic bike, I believe the reason I fared so much better in the run part than the bike part is because I had become conditioned to pushing myself hard with running. Running is how my story began. Pushing myself to the point of nausea, shocking my body with cross-countries – that's what I did in the beginning as part of my plight to belong. Psychologically, it feels more normal to run at bursting point. I had not gone through the same pain barriers with cycling. Yet.

This bike course was full of hills, burning up all our energy before the run. I recognised some of the roads from where I had cycled the previous day with my backpack in flip-flops. Tauntingly, I passed the station which I should have arrived at, had the replacement buses not been in action. Knowing that the bike is my weakness, I tried to push harder, but still, competitor after competitor passed me. For every one that I overtook, about ten overtook me. This felt much harder than the London Triathlon because of the hills and the uneven, potholed roads. I lost my GPS watch on that cycle. I had it strapped to the handlebars instead of wearing it because I still didn't know if it was waterproof so I didn't risk wearing it in the water. I mustn't have threaded the strap through the loop properly and it probably slipped off the bars when I went over a pothole. I felt my heart sink. I wore that watch for every single run and cycle to record my times and distances.

The run was even harder. It was off-road with steep hills and jagged forest paths. Immediately after transition the course went up a hill. I felt truly spent. This worried me. I felt five times worse than I had in my previous two triathlons. *But this is hillier*, said my reassuring voice. *But I'm fitter so it should feel easier.*

At that point, Ben from run club ran past me, starting his second lap. That meant he was at least 20 minutes ahead of me.

That's a lot! But later, to my amazement, I passed Julian going at a snail's pace. He's usually a quicker runner than me so the hilly bike course must have exhausted him. This spurred me on because it confirmed that the hilly bike course had depleted everyone else as much as me.

I passed several more weary runners after that, probably all people who had whizzed past me on the bike. Now I was getting even with them on the run.

I ran without socks (to save time in transition) and two great big blisters were brewing on the inside arches of my feet, rubbing against the seam in my shoes.

I have never counted down a race so keenly. I finished in 2 hours 50 minutes. A whole 21 minutes slower than the London Triathlon. But I should not have been disappointed. I did not know enough about the sport then to understand that it is impossible to compare two triathlons – there are too many variables. Swim conditions are affected by currents and water temperature. Bike speed can vary due to wind or the number of bends or how well surfaced a road is. The run was on trail, which is much slower than road running. Also, unlike running races, the distances in triathlon are not exact. A 40-kilometre bike course could be 42 or 38 kilometres. The run can also be slightly shorter or longer than the advertised 10k. But still, the winning female completed that course in 2 hours 10 minutes. Admittedly she was a professional, but it did make my dream to qualify for an international Age-Group Championship seem ridiculous.

Philippe had already finished when I came in. So had Ben. The biggest highlight of a race is to see familiar faces at the finish line, everyone bursting to break the solace of the previous hours and share what they've been through. We chatted for a few minutes in the sun, enjoying the free buffet of fruit and cake (not every race is this generous!). But before any time at all, Philippe announced he and his French friends had a ferry to catch. Ben and Julian also got up to leave, keen to get to the comfort of their cars and back to London (cars which could unfortunately only carry one bike).

One minute, I was on a high from finishing my last race of the season, enjoying being surrounded by familiar faces. The next minute, I was all alone with my giant orange rucksack and mucky-green bike.

Sweaty, sticky and exhausted, I faced the ache of public transport. Could I remember where that train station was that I just passed on the course? I had no choice but to try. I hoisted my backpack on to tired shoulders and pedalled my weary legs out of the venue. I kept my eye out for my lost watch on the ground. It was probably lying on a grass verge somewhere along the course so it was worth a check however small the odds.

I found the train station, 3 miles away, which doesn't sound a lot but felt like the end of the earth. The engineering works were still on. The next station with a working train was 7 miles away. I set off, not allowing myself the luxury of emotion. *One pedal-push after another, I'll get there eventually. Just have patience*, I told myself, like in every other race I've had to will myself to the end of. But I was exhausted and negative thoughts crept in.

Wasn't the whole point of joining run club to avoid moments like these? Wasn't it for the promise of a thriving social scene and toasting the completion of a race in a pub? *So why am I here alone, a year on? What am I getting out of this?*

Joining a running club had been one of the best things I'd ever done, but moments like these forced me to admit that it had not provided a golden ticket to a fulfilling social life as I had optimistically imagined. It had enriched me in ways I had not expected but it had not plugged the gap for a lack of intimacy in my life – the thing which had spurred me there in the first place. Friendships take time and energy and consistency. I've always had a bit of a scattergun approach to friendships because I'd always relied on my popularity as a gregarious party lover and found acquaintances easily. But now that I had more authentic pleasures and a calmer lifestyle, I was learning that it's consistent, close friendships which are most the rewarding.

For the first time in many years, I started to think how nice it would be to have someone special here to share this arduous cycle. I'd always maintained that being single and independent allowed me to lead a fuller life, but perhaps that was because I didn't have a full life and was searching for something. Perhaps, I thought, the happier we are with our lives, the more we are open to the possibility of sharing them.

My last relationship had put me off the idea of sharing my life and weekends with someone. But on reflection, that was because we passed the time with things that didn't stimulate me. I felt I had to keep him at arm's length just so I could have a break from drinking and socialising all the time. Now that I had found a truer version of me – the nature-loving, wild spirit which I'd previously suppressed – I felt more settled.

More assured about the type of person I wanted to spend my time with. Confident that there are guys out there more like the true me.

I was still thinking these things when I arrived at the station. Snapping myself out of reflective mode and into a pragmatic one, I thought also that I should find more triathlon fans like me. Running club was brilliant but it was, unsurprisingly, mostly about running. I was realising that I got my biggest thrills from the more extreme stuff – like swimming in lakes and rivers, cycling for miles and triathlons. When my list of summer events ended, I would officially join the triathlon club, ready for next year.

CHAPTER 17

FELL HELL

It was almost seven in the evening when I finally got back from Hever and into the warm shower I'd been dreaming about for hours. I was so exhausted I went to bed an hour later. That meant I was wide awake by 5 a.m. I got out of bed to learn that my knees would not bend and I could only waddle like a penguin. I went to make breakfast only to find that I'd hoovered every readily available carbohydrate in my cupboards the previous evening, including the last dregs of porridge oats, which no doubt had lingered at the bottom of the glass jar for years, constantly topped up by replacement oats whenever they got low. My race number, 1,169, was still inked on the side of my calf where the stewards had marker-penned it at registration. When I tried to scrub it off it just faded into a greyish blotch. The kitchen sink was lined with slime where I'd soaked and then abandoned my wetsuit. The arches of my feet were inflamed with two blazing blisters, thanks to my experiment to run without socks. This was a proper triathlon hangover.

My enthusiasm showed its first falter. Race fatigue was finally catching up with me. I did not want to leave home that day and did not feel like training all week.

But the following weekend there was more. I had put myself down for a fell-running weekend on the Isle of Wight with a big group from running club. A fell, which I had to secretly research, is a hill on a moor or other natural landscape. That was enough to tell me that this would be tough.

I'd never been to any of the islands of Britain other than the mainland before. I hadn't seen much of Britain for that matter.

When I turned up at Waterloo for the train to Portsmouth Harbour, I was embarrassed to find that, yet again, my bag was the largest. But at least it was an appropriate backpack and not the Louis Vuitton wheelie which I'd sheepishly wheeled through the airport on the France trip. I sized up everyone else's luggage. How do you get two days of running kit, ample warm clothes, an outfit for the evening pub, toiletries, hairdryer and your breakfast into one shoulder bag?

Just three hours later, we arrived in the town of Ventnor, on the south side of the island. After a hearty pub meal, we split into our different rented houses for early bedtime, ready for our weekend of torture.

There were three races over two days. The first was just 4 kilometres: 2 kilometres up a sheer hill and 2 kilometres down. We began by the beach and it was up, up, up from there, winding up through the town centre that was lined with independent shops you'd never find in London, until we reached a stile leading to a footpath. Still going upwards, the path soon opened on to the Ventnor Downs, where it became so steep everyone was forced to scramble on hands and knees. The air was filled with the sound of gasping but there was no let-up on the gradient until the very top. From there we circled the top of the fell and then came straight back down the way we went up, which was as terrifying as going uphill was exhausting.

Fell running is a culture unto itself. Stoic fell runners consider their sport more hardy than road racing. Many of the meets are deeply rooted in tradition and history, and many rural clubs retain loyal members for decades – some of them have become communities. There is no talk of heart rates and GPS among true fell runners. Pace is insignificant in this wild sport because of the challenging terrain. To call an event a 'fell race' it has to meet strict criteria on the gradient of the ascents and they're classified accordingly. In other words, the hills have to be killers.

I was on bad form. I shared a bed that weekend with a club friend and, though it was no fault of hers, I couldn't sleep. But even if I had managed a good night's sleep, my body and mind would still have been tired. I had done some sort of race every other weekend or more for the whole summer and on top of that I had just developed a chesty cough.

Mentally I held back. I started to worry about aggravating my peroneal tendon again. I'd been running with no pain for the last few weeks and had even done two triathlons with no pain, but the words of my cautious physio played out in my mind: 'Never run with tired legs.' I couldn't shake the vision of tendons and ligaments beneath my skin getting inflamed and frayed and overstretched, as I'd seen in so many diagrams I'd googled.

We race as much with our minds as we do with our bodies, and niggling fears like these can act as a brake. The brain is our own inbuilt safety mechanism. If it believes there's a problem with the mechanics, it won't let you take off.

I finished way down the running order but there was no time to dwell on it because there were just three hours before the next race. We all marched to the beach and waded into the cool sea to soothe tired legs. Then we sat on the beach steps, eating a functional picnic of pasta salads, bagels, malt loaf, Battenberg and bananas. Food is fuel when it comes to races and eating was factored into our busy schedule as an essential activity, rather than a social nicety as it would be in any other situation.

I had never imagined a British beach could be so inviting. Previously being such a scaredy-cat with the cold, I'd always classed sea dipping as an activity to do abroad. But this beach was like a hot August day even though it was now the end of September. The sea was cold but I managed to stay in for a good quarter of an hour before it got to me. Afterwards I sat blissfully unselfconscious in a soaking wet sports bra and running shorts, salt-matted hair stuck against my face, letting the warm sun dry me. I'd missed out on so many of life's small pleasures like this, in favour of creature comforts and looking presentable.

The next race was 8 miles. By then my energy gauge was on zero. I would have liked to curl up in bed and sleep rather than go back to the start. Everyone who had taken part in this weekend before had enthused about how hard it was. Almost a marathon over two days, apparently. With the equivalent of a couple of mountains to traverse.

I told myself I would run slowly and enjoy the scenery. Another fake assurance I always kid myself with, to take away the trepidation of the pain to come. Normally when the race starts, competitive spirit takes over and I can't help striving to overtake people. But this time, I really did hold back. There are only so many times you can push yourself. Even elite athletes have to have easy days and months to keep them motivated. Every other weekend this summer I had found a new way to coax myself through the final miles or minutes of a race, training interval or mammoth bike ride. My willpower was tired.

Luckily the weather lent itself to taking things leisurely. The sky was spotlessly blue and the sun did not have a cloud to hide behind. The views on the clifftops made me want to stop and breathe them in. I remembered my first ever trail run – the Mercury Ten in Epping Forest in February. I remembered getting to the top of a small hill, seeing the views of London and articulating internally, *This is why I run*. Now, as I reached the peak of a fell, overlooking a glimmering navy-blue sea, those exact words came to mind again.

As usual, as soon as I finished the pain was forgotten. When we talked about the race in the pub that evening for dinner, there was no mention of the aches, the fatigue or the breathlessness, only the beauty on the course itself. I finished my dinner and ordered chips for dessert. I took no risks with dizzy spells these days and tomorrow I wanted to make sure I had enough carbs in my system for another 13-mile race.

There are two types of pain when it comes to exercise. There is cardio pain and there is muscular pain. On day one of our fell-running weekend, I had cardio pain. On the second day, the strain on my lungs paled into insignificance compared to the soreness in my legs. My quads were so stiff that when I got to the descents I was reduced to a sideways shuffle – that is one way of finding out which muscles are responsible for steadying us as we go downhill. My quads had clearly never been used so much. After 13 miles of hills they simply could not hold me any more. Any worry about exasperating my peroneal tendon had been totally superseded by the worry that I may not be able to walk at all for a month!

I was one of the last in my club to finish. The earlier finishers, and some club members who had skipped the last race, lined the finishing stretch to cheer the slower finishers. Even though we all had a rush to get back to our respective cottages and shower and pack before the bus, they still waited. It reminded me how much I appreciated the team spirit. I may not have made close, one-on-one friendships through being part of a club but I gained a lot from touching moments like that. And I learned too about the importance of generosity of spirit.

There was no time to dip into the sea this time. I just about made the bus only to miss the ferry, along with Brenda and Dave.

It was not entirely our fault. The bus dropped us at the ferry port with 5 minutes to spare before departure. Five minutes, that is, to get to the end of a pier that stretched as far as the eye could see. At first no one rushed because there looked to be little chance we would make it. But as we walked further along the pier the ferry still showed no sign of moving. One by one, our group started running. Me, Brenda and Dave stubbornly carried on walking. There were still 500 metres between us and the ferry and it was already 5 minutes past the time it should have departed, but the minutes ticked by and still the ferry remained in view. The ones who'd started to run first were now boarding and the rest were in short pursuit. Finally, Dave, Brenda and I broke into a reluctant hobble in a last-ditch attempt to make it in time. We reached the ferry barrier just as it closed.

'I couldn't hold it any longer,' said the guard, and the three of us watched in dismay from the port as the rest of the group waved from starboard and sailed away.

I felt sad. I wanted to be with the group sharing stories. But I was glad that it was two familiar faces with whom I was left behind. It was no hard feat to enjoy a gin and tonic from the port bar in the sunshine while we chatted and laughed at ourselves for an hour until the next ferry.

CHAPTER 18

PUNCHED AT SEA

Two weeks later, I was with Brenda and Dave again on another club trip. Ten of us were off to Greece to do the Spetses Mini Marathon, which actually isn't a marathon at all and nothing about it is mini. It's a two-day aquathlon. It involves a 5k swim across the sea from the island of Spetses to the mainland and back, and a 25-kilometre run (15 miles) around the mountainous island the next day.

To the others it was another weekend jolly. To me it was hugely symbolic. It was a year to the day since I first turned up at running club in my trendy gym gear and fleece, intimidated by what seemed like a room of stalwart adventurers. Now I was getting on a flight to Greece, with those very people, to swim and run a distance I could not have fathomed back then. To me this weekend was a private celebration. It signified the end of one full and happy year of achievements and also new beginnings. So, I decided to make a holiday of it and travelled there a few days early, to wander Athens and write in cafes. At least, that was the plan. But I didn't do any work at all. I had adventures.

An old friend, I remembered, has a holiday home outside Athens and it just so happened that he would be there when I was. 'Friend' is a little economical with the truth. He was a former flame, but still a friend. And so I spent most of my time in his beachside apartment on the outskirts of Athens.

He picked me up from the airport and we went straight to the beach. In the car, he showed a keen but coy interest in my upcoming 5k sea swim. He asked non-stop questions but quickly reined in any expression which may have suggested he was impressed. Being half Greek, he was brought up by the sea. If an English girl could rock up and swim to a neighbouring island for fun, he couldn't let on that it was a big deal. I was amused by his fake indifference. He no doubt remembered me more for dresses and heels and cosy, decorous drinking establishments. Now here I was, popping up on his home soil and casually mentioning a 5k swim across the open Aegean Sea.

We got to the beach and it was very windy. He was keen to see me swim. I fished out my bikini from the bottom of my suitcase. Pants and bras spilled out into the boot of his car. Then I had to find my goggles. In the process I lost my make-up bag. It fell on to the sandy road somewhere and I didn't notice. I went the rest of the five-day trip barefaced.

The sea was rough. I'd never swum in rough sea before. Not proper swimming anyway – paddling by the shore on beach holidays doesn't count. I tried not to show my trepidation. We went in without wetsuits and the cold triggered breathing problems again. Waves kept coming over my head so I couldn't breathe bilaterally (on both sides). But I couldn't show that I was struggling, not after I'd so confidently glossed over my 5k exploit in two days' time.

The waves got bigger as we moved across the shoreline but I struggled and spluttered through, trying desperately to keep ahead of him. Vanity is the most powerful driver when it comes to sporting performance.

We only swam for 15 minutes but it destroyed my confidence for the real thing. We had barely gone 500 metres in the choppy waters. I couldn't imagine doing that for another 4.5 kilometres.

Afterwards I could not warm up. There was nowhere to change so I threw on a dress over a wet bikini while we went for a drink and soon I was shivering. My thoughts turned to my warm, blue hoodie that I had lived in on the training holiday in France. One thing a year of outdoor sport had taught me is to take a hoodie wherever you go. Even to the Mediterranean. But had I brought it? Or did I look at the forecast daytime temperatures of 25°C and then throw in a load of beach dresses? Yes, the latter. I'd painted my toenails and got a wax, but I didn't bring a hoodie.

At sundown the temperature dropped dramatically and I hadn't accounted for wind, which makes official forecasted temperatures feel much cooler. This was a complete relapse to my old ways! I was very cross with myself.

My complexion was turning into blotchy hues of purple and my matted, salted hair clung to my face. For the next two days at his secluded villa, I thought longingly about my hoodie, willing it to miraculously appear and cursing myself repeatedly for putting fashion over warmth. This was a regression indeed.

The next day when I joined my running club friends at Athens port to sail to the island of Spetses, I couldn't help looking at everyone else boarding the ferry and noticing that they all had hoodies. All I had for warmth was a cream summer blazer to go over a dress. Cream. It was wrong on so many levels.

Three hours on a crowded ferry later, we arrived on the idyllic island of Spetses. The island restricts cars so horses and carriages are the main means of transport. We split into a convoy of carriages and wound around the narrow hilly streets to our hotel before going for a mezze feast at a restaurant by the sea. I sat with a blanket borrowed from the owner over my shoulders. Tomorrow I would buy a new hoodie.

Nerves were evident at breakfast the next morning. Few in our group had ever swum that far. I'd done 3 kilometres in the pool but that was without great big frothing waves.

'This could end in several ways,' said ever-cheerful Rob. 'We could end up in the hypothermia tent, we could get attacked by a shark, we could stray into a shipping lane, or we could finish and have the Greek banquet at the end.'

The sea was apparently rougher than it had ever been for this event. We learned later that the organisers had called an emergency meeting that morning to decide whether to cancel. The reason they went ahead was nothing to do with experts declaring it safe. It was because the ferry captains had kicked up such a fuss about the disruption to the shipping schedules that the organisers felt they had to go ahead. A reassuring insight into Greek health and safety.

We waded into the shallow water by the port, nervously waiting to start. The start was delayed by 30 minutes, which only made our anticipation grow. When we finally set off, my breathing problems struck again. More experienced now, I tried to console myself that it would pass, as it had done in other races. But 10 minutes went by, 20 minutes, half an hour, and still I was unnaturally out of breath. The sort of breathlessness I suffer in cold water feels different to the sort of breathlessness you get from exerting yourself. It's the sort you get from holding your breath rather than from dashing up a staircase.

I resorted to single-sided breathing because in the past that has solved the problem. Breathing every two strokes instead of three means you take in air more frequently. But this tactic did not work today. I must have been in a state of mild anxiety without realising it, unnerved by the aggressive swell of the sea and the uncertainty as to where the other competitors were. I have a theory that swimming events induce more anxiety than other sports because you cannot compare your position to anyone else's. With running or cycling, you can see how many people are ahead and can gauge the speed at which they pass. In open water you're blind to pace and disorientated as to your position. The only thing you have for guidance is a hysterical voice in your head screaming, *This is a race – get moving!* and sending your heart rate into the red.

I spluttered and gasped and fought the waves. I seemed to be getting nowhere. The coastline ahead looked no closer. The buoys, used for sighting so we could go in a straight line, kept disappearing beneath the swell. I'd never been this far out to sea without a boat – ever. On beach holidays I used to feel daring swimming 400 metres out from the shore. Now, just six months since getting to grips with front crawl properly, I was traversing a choppy sea to another island.

Thirty whole minutes went by before I stopped hyperventilating. By then, because I'd been breathing on one side only, my wetsuit had chafed one side of my neck. I became painstakingly aware of it as each metre went by. With nothing to look at but the dark blue haze of the deep sea and nothing to think about, my mind fixated on the rubbing and the stinging of saltwater. With every turn of my head to breathe, I envisaged the coarse edge of my wetsuit scraping against raw, pink skin. Then I started to think how much it would continue to hurt for the next three days.

Three weeks earlier at Hever Castle Triathlon, similar things had gone on in my head during the run when blisters were forming on my sockless feet. But there was a big psychological difference now: I did not have the option to stop.

I paused a few times to fold down the nape of my wetsuit to offer some relief but the pause in my rhythm only messed up my breathing again. Still the buoys disappeared under the undulating waves. I kept bringing my head up and straining to spot them but all I could see were imminent waves towering above me. All any of us could do was swim and hope it was in the right direction.

In my case it was not the right direction. I had veered quite dramatically off to the right. That is to say, into the line of swimmers on a shorter course coming back the other way. I only became aware of this two seconds before I smashed into one of them. I was focusing on my breathing rhythm: *One, two, breeeeathe. One, two, breeeeeeathe.* Every five or six strokes I would lift my head right out of the water to try to sight a buoy. It was on one of these sighting strokes when I saw them – a herd of red swim hats coming towards me.

I waved an arm helplessly in the air to alert them of my presence but it was too late. A red swimming hat hurtled straight into me. His arm, going over his head, punched me in the eye. My goggles fell off. I grabbed them and caught them before they sank.

The man who hit me was as shocked as I was, but not as hurt. My eye was smarting. He said something in Greek, which sounded polite, as if it were a token apology, and then he was off again. I stayed upright, treading water desperately, as my mind computed what had just happened.

'I've been punched. I've been punched!' I said out loud.

I was in shock. Breathing elevated again, my heart was racing. I felt incapacitated, stunned. Just as I would feel had I been punched in the eye on land, I expect!

'Focus,' I said to myself out loud. *Where is the shoreline? Where am I heading?* That's when I realised that in the act of being punched I'd lost a contact lens. I shut one eye and then the other. Then I tried lifting my eyelid away from my eye, while treading water with one arm, in case it had become lodged high in my socket. But no, it was definitely floating in the sea somewhere.

It's game over now, I thought. *There's no point even trying to get a decent time. At least I have a good excuse. If I come last, I can say it was because I got punched and lost a contact lens!*

I stayed still for another few moments, taking in what had happened and deciding what to do. Not that I exactly had a menu of options. As I regained my senses, I noticed (with my one working eye) that I was bang in the middle of two lanes of swimmers. One going one way, one going the other.

There were loads of them. Which meant… I wasn't last at all. The line of swimmers going in my direction were in the same start group as me. The ones going the other way were on a shorter course. I was still on track. I had to get moving!

Still shaken, I breaststroked, taking in my surroundings above the water before I felt brave enough to stick my head under again. *Go slowly*, I told myself, all sense of competitiveness gone. *One, two, breeeeeathe. One, two, breeeeeeathe.* A swimmer came up on my left and for a few moments we were swimming shoulder to shoulder, in harmony. This calmed me no end and so I decided I would stick with them, whoever he or she was. I tailed back so I could get directly behind his or her feet and draft off them to save energy, just like I'd been taught. Following their feet was so hypnotic I did not want to lift my head out of the water. For the last hour every time I had lifted my head to sight the buoys, I'd seen crashing waves and swimmers going in all directions. But by staying under the water focusing on a pair of feet I felt tranquil. I could forget the commotion above and leave the direction to them. *Just follow these feet and breathe*, said my inner voice, and I could have continued like that, burying my head in the water like an ostrich in sand, for hours.

Then I noticed there were three of us. Another swimmer appeared on my right. And so the three of us – strangers who couldn't see each other's faces – swam together in a triangle, like a pod of dolphins. I wondered if they found it as soothing as I did. I noticed that my breathing had now fully regulated for the first time since the start.

It would be easy now. Swimming isn't particularly taxing if you are calm so all I had to do was keep going – keep going until I'd swum 5k.

Then I decided to look up.

There were no other swimmers anywhere near us. Not one. Not for as far as my one eye could see. Why? Where were the buoys? I stopped and let my fellow mer-people slip ahead. I was disorientated again from being submerged in the water for so long. I shut one eye and squinted into the distance. I could just about see one of the yellow buoys. Then I looked behind to locate the previous one. The two buoys and I formed a perfect equilateral triangle, which meant we had swum exactly 45°C in the wrong direction. The other two swimmers were now 30 metres ahead. There was nothing I could do to alert them. They wouldn't hear me even if I shouted. And besides, they were probably Greek! Regretfully I watched them continue further out in the wrong direction. They'd realise eventually. I now had to get back to the correct course, alone.

Surely I must be at the back now. Such was my diagonal detour, not to mention the 5-minute stop when my goggles were punched off my face. But when I got back on course, near the buoys, there were still plenty more swimmers coming through. No doubt they had all had their own directional blunders.

Soon after that I reached the halfway point. A boat was anchored near the shore and two men in fluorescent bibs threw down bottles of energy drinks, saying something in Greek.

I did not know whether to feel exultant because I was halfway, or dismayed because I was only halfway. From here we had to turn around and swim all the way back.

The short break and the liquid in my stomach messed up my breathing, and I switched to breathing every two strokes again. Now that I was swimming the other way, it was easier to breathe on the opposite side because the waves were coming from the opposite direction. And so the other side of my neck started to chafe.

By the time I was halfway through the return leg, both sides of my neck were so raw from the chafing that they went numb. Instead my pain sensors turned to my nose, which was burning from the saltwater. My mind dwelled on the pain, feeling the salt-burn sweep through every single nostril hair.

With one-eyed vision I could not judge how far away the shore was. I could make out the flags of the finish in the distance but for ages they seemed to stay the same size. Then, all of a sudden, they got markedly clearer. Then I could make out spectators lining the port. I picked up speed. *Nearly there!* Soon my nose would stop burning. Soon I could put cream on my stinging neck. Soon I could be upright again.

At last I reached the pebble beach alongside the port. I scrambled out, stood up and immediately fell over, overcome with dizziness. I pulled myself up and fell over again. I had no control over my muscles and no way of telling whether I was upright, nearly upright or how much weight was on either leg. This was exactly what had happened in France when I got out of the freezing river.

Two medics came rushing over and forced me down to the ground, trying to make me lie still and flat. But somewhere in my disorientated haze I remembered the words of the race briefer at the beginning telling us that we had to walk over the finish line for our timing chips to register. I hadn't walked over this yet.

Gathering what little of my senses I could, I fixated on getting over the finish line. The medics spoke to me in Greek. I tried to fight them off and stand up.

'I haven't crossed the finish line yet,' I protested and pointed to an imaginary watch on my wrist.

But the bored medics seemed so pleased to actually have something to do that they wouldn't let me get up.

Regaining my strength, I wriggled away, stumbled over the line and then dropped down on the pebbles. The medics could pore over me as much as they liked now, but much to their disappointment I soon revived myself.

Brenda, Philippa from run club and her husband Declan had done the shorter distance and were waving on the pier.

'You're the first to finish,' they said, meaning the first to finish out of our group.

I was stunned. After my mishaps out at sea I was certain I'd be the one limping home last, but two got picked up by the rescue boat and the other two finished after me. This was an important lesson. We always assume when things get tough that they are directly affecting us, but of course I would not have been the only one who went off course and struggled with the waves and breathing in a rough sea. Everyone at sea that day had their own battles and navigation errors.

How you handle them is as much part of the contest as the swimming itself.

At the finish there was a banquet of local delicacies prepared by volunteers in the village. I loaded a plate with vine leaves and cured meats and pastries only to find that everything tasted of salt. Indeed everything continued to taste of salt for the next 24 hours. Even beer. I kept looking at the rim of my glass, wondering if it were some Greek custom to adorn a pint of lager with salt and lemon like a margarita cocktail.

Once refuelled, we found a bar in the heart of the town square to unwind in and tell stories about battling waves. I went to the toilet and unfortunately looked in the mirror. I had the beginnings of a shiner on my left eye, red chafe marks all over my neck and my nostrils looked like I'd been snorting crystal meth all morning.

The next day was the second part to the Spetses Mini Marathon – a 15-mile (25-kilometre) run around the perimeter of the island. Somehow I had another alarm fail. By the time I awoke I had 10 minutes to leave. There was no way I was missing breakfast ahead of running a distance I had only ever completed once before (the Orion Fifteen, back in March).

People were hurrying me but I told them to go ahead while I hoovered up whatever dregs of cereals and rolls were left at the breakfast bar. Without brushing my teeth, I grabbed a couple of boiled eggs and fruit for recovery snacks at the end. Then I half jogged and half walked to the harbour for the start. I arrived with 5 minutes to spare and an almighty stitch.

Having lost my running watch at the Hever Castle Triathlon, I had no idea of my pace or distance. After the first mile when the competitors were still bunched up, I heard a symphony of beeping watches. But after that I had no idea how far through I was. I paced myself the old-fashioned way – according to feel. This turned out to be a blessing. Without looking at my wrist every 5 minutes, I couldn't spend the whole time counting fractions and willing the miles away. Instead I could absorb the scenery and think nice thoughts. It felt less of a fight.

The time passed more quickly and smoothly. By running steadily and not caring about my pace, I ended up feeling stronger. Stronger than I had felt in any other event. After an hour, I started to overtake over-keen competitors who had gone off too quickly. This must have been what runners call 'pacing'.

We winded up and down mountainous roads in the blazing sun. Below us were views of a navy-blue sea dotted with islands (annoyingly much calmer than when we swam it). I remembered again that it was my one-year anniversary of joining a running club. To think that cold, wet, dark, torturous run along the Regent's Canal that night would lead me to some of the finest corners of the world 12 months later.

With 5k to go, I saw the first and only distance marker. I was stunned I had covered 20k (12 miles) already. Usually when I clock-watch, I'm surprised at how little I've covered.

To my astonishment I finished in the top 20 per cent of females for that run. To even more disbelief, I ended up being the third female in the swim (though there were only 10 women who finished the full 5k distance). And to my absolute jaw-dropping incredulity that meant I won the title for the combined events.

I had won something!

I tried to play down my elation and pretended I wasn't at all bothered about hanging around town all afternoon for the awards ceremony. Secretly, I couldn't wait to get on that podium.

But then an unforeseeable event robbed me of my moment of glory. During the awards ceremony, which we watched from the town square with beer that still tasted of salt, there was an almighty commotion. The mayor of Spetses burst on to the stage, chest puffed out, full of purpose, and cut into the compère's speech. It was all in Greek but it didn't sound courteous. The row got louder until the female compère burst into tears. I waited hopefully for it to blow over. But it went on. Other officials had now butted on to the stage. Bemused spectators lost interest and started to disperse. This did not look good for my medal.

I finished my beer disdainfully. The mayor ended his rant and stormed off, leaving an uneasy silence. Slowly, the stands were cleared away and items were packed into boxes. Somewhere in there was my first-place medal! The incident was the talk of the town and made the local papers. We later learned that there had been a dispute between the town officials and the organisers of the race over race entry money.

I never did get to stand on the podium, but perhaps this was a fitting reminder, on the anniversary of my love affair with outdoor sport, as to why I was here. My original incentives had been nothing to do with silverware and I was no less rich of experience for the lack of it.

CHAPTER 19
CYCLING IN THE RAIN

That was the last I saw of the sun until the following spring. When we got back to the UK, a damp, cold, dark autumn had set in and cross-country season had begun again.

I was dying to know how much quicker I would be compared to my debut races last year. So it was a huge disappointment to discover that there wasn't much difference at all. Thirty seconds or so over a 5-mile race at most. But what had improved dramatically was how I coped with it. I no longer felt sick and shaky afterwards or got so cold that I would shiver in the pub for hours. I no longer got home and stumbled around my flat as though I'd been hit with a rock. The prospect of a day out in the elements no longer seemed so hardcore because I knew what to expect. I knew I had survived it before and that gave me confidence even though it was just as cold and wet and muddy.

This time around I cycled to some of the cross-countries, which would have been incomprehensible last year. On one occasion I even cycled 10 miles in wellies. The venue's ground was waterlogged and I knew from experience the importance of having dry footwear to change into. I did it partly because I wanted to keep up my training volume and partly because it added to the survival challenge. If I could manage the logistics of packing cross-country kit to run in, dry warm clothes to drink in, more spare dry stuff to cycle home in, gloves for running, different gloves for cycling, waterproofs, bike lights, ear-warmers, food, the BB cream and mascara, then I could manage anything.

Cross-country races have sentimental value to me because they were the first races I ever did. Despite the mud and the cold, and their comparatively low-key status considering some of the more taxing feats I had done over the last year, cross-countries will always be special because they are symbolic of positive change. Every time I walk on to a cross-country field and see all the clubs' flags and tents, I remember how low and fraught I felt in those months of 2013 and how my life has transformed.

After the one-year anniversary of starting my journey, I kept looking back on annual milestones. The memory of that horrible strained period was still so vivid that I couldn't help saying to myself, 'This time last year...' every time I found myself at a fixture I had done before. I was more in love with running and outdoor challenges than ever. Not least because my body found it so much easier now. My zeal for joining in anything and everything out of opportunism had calmed though. I had settled into a happy medium of outdoorsy life and my old city-girl pleasures. This time last year I remember turning down a group of friends who'd set a Saturday lunch date because it clashed with a cross-country.

But this year I didn't feel compelled to do every single one. I was still as dedicated to my training, but I was happy to do it in my own time if a race would take too much out of my day.

Even though I felt a special relationship with cross-countries, I didn't take them anywhere near as seriously as triathlons. Yes, I went as fast as I could, but I didn't taper or anything scientific like that. For me their main purpose was still a Saturday out. Once I made triathlon 'my thing', my priorities lay in improving overall endurance, which was why I wanted to cycle to cross-country events and sometimes went to the gym for a strength session in the morning.

Now that I had my secret goal to qualify for Age-Group World Championships, my real focus that winter was getting miles in on the bike because that was by far my weakest discipline in triathlon. Optimistically I vowed that now the summer season was over, I would dedicate Sundays to cycling. Surely if you wear warmer clothes, cycling is just the same in cold weather as in the summer?

What a lot I had to learn…

My first problem with winter cycling was finding people to do it with. I wouldn't consider going out alone. The little cycling conglomerate from France, who I'd enjoyed summer rides with, were less than enthused at the prospect of riding in November. London Fields Triathlon Club, in which I was becoming more involved, did organise rides but it was all done via an email forum full of familiar banter. It all sounded a bit testosterone-heavy and I was nowhere near ready for that.

Dave, however, was on a similar mission to me. A knee injury meant he couldn't run and he announced he was going to get cycle-fit over the winter. And so began our cycling friendship.

Shortly after we returned from Greece, we mapped out a coastal ride through East Anglia with a stop in the seaside town of Wells-next-the-Sea. Leaving London and finding new territory seemed an exciting thing to do.

I prepared my bike the night before. I knew exactly what I needed now. Two water bottles – one with water, one with water and electrolytes; a nutrition pouch clipped on to my crossbar, which I filled with dried figs, nuts and an energy bar; a saddlebag under my seat with an inner tube, tyre levers, a multitool and a spare contact lens (still only one); in the pockets of my cycling jersey I carried money, a credit card, phone, banana, lip gloss (dual purpose because its moisturising properties simultaneously act as lip balm), house keys and a screwed-up, wafer-thin, waterproof jacket.

We got an early train to Norwich. The weather delivered a gloriously sunny, crisp autumn day. It was the first day of November and it was 17°C – warmer than when I had cycled to Brighton in August!

I left the map-reading to Dave. He still used the printed sort.

I struggled to stay behind his wheel – a gap kept opening up no matter how hard I tried. *Thank goodness I'm not cycling with the speed merchants in the tri club*, I thought, *because I'm having a tough enough time keeping up with Dave.*

This was my first autumnal cycle and, although it was a dry and clear day, I soon learned that off-season cycling was going to be a drizzly, muddy affair. In the damper weather, water from the road sprays everything. It gets into every groove of your bike, coats your chain, splatters your legs, shoes, face, sunglasses and sometimes gets inside the neck of your clothes and dribbles down your body. The pouch clipped underneath my saddle was coated in sludge.

Running produces a few small items of laundry: tights, running top, sports bra and socks. With cycling there is no end of garments: base layer, thermal socks, waterproof helmet cover, scarf (delightfully referred to as a 'buff'), overshoes – all of which get coated in road spray, oil, sweat and snot.

Snot, by the way, is an unavoidable fact of winter cycling. If you have ever wondered why your nose runs much more in winter weather it is because one of the jobs of our noses is to warm and humidify the air before it reaches our lungs. In the cold it has to increase moisture production to do this. Because we consume more oxygen when we exercise that increases moisture production further. The excess causes a runny nose.

There is only so long you can use the back of your cycling glove to wipe it before it becomes so annoying you have to turn your head to the side and give it a good blow into the air, which is fine if there is no wind. But on a breezy day don't be surprised if it backfires into your own eye or that of the person behind you.

I was also to learn that cycling does not stop you getting chilly like running does. Running is a constant effort. It's short and relatively intense and so you stay warm throughout. Cycling is a longer, steadier affair. Your heart rate doesn't go as high and your effort fluctuates as you go up and down hills or stop to deal with a mechanical.

It is inevitable that you'll stop to adjust something on a long ride. The chain falls off, the gears get stuck, the brakes need tightening or you get a dreaded P-word. All of these leave your hands and nails coated in black gunk, which you wipe on your shorts and then go on to eat flapjacks with. My stomach has become very strong thanks to cycling.

A 5-minute stop can send your temperature plummeting. Not only that, but with running, blood pumps into all corners of your body. With cycling, your arms, hands and much of your upper body don't move. You may as well wave them goodbye when the temperature goes below 10 degrees.

If this hasn't put you off, I'll tell you about some of the physiological side effects. Running makes you ache from using your muscles. Cycling makes you ache from not moving your muscles for hours. When I first started doing long rides, I ached between my shoulders, in my lower back, in my forearms from leaning on the handlebars, on my bum from the hard saddle and in my hips from being so compressed.

Cycling is also tedious and seemingly endless. The roads go on and on for mile after mile for hours. Sometimes they are straight, sometimes winding – I can never recall a route. I look at my watch and see another half-hour has gone by but I would not be able to tell you what I have been thinking about.

Yet I enjoy it. Well, I look back on a cycle and remember the scenery, the fresh air and the wind in my face, the relaxed conversation with whoever I've cycled with, and I always think how wonderful and refreshing it was. But at the time I don't know if I enjoy it or not.

We reached Wells-next-the-Sea and stopped to look at the coastal view. We tried to make our way to the edge of the shore. The tide was out and between us and the water was an expanse of marshland. To get near we would have to pedal along a sandy path. I prayed I wouldn't puncture.

After 2 miles we reached Holkham Beach. This was one of the most beautiful beaches I had ever seen, blending with the forest. Natural streams had formed in the sand winding through the plantation. Flocks of birds glided overhead. It looked more like Scandinavia than England.

Dave stood close to me. I stepped back, not wanting to confront the tacit semblance of attraction between us. Again I questioned whether I was attracted to him or just drawn in by a friendship that was based on more novel, wholesome and rewarding experiences than what I was used to.

We left Holkham and headed east. The plan was to drop down and pass through Sandringham and then on to King's Lynn, where we would get the train back. We turned off the main road and on to a country road, and then our day changed.

The sun had gradually been eclipsed by clouds. They got thicker through the morning and now the rain came. It came down like a sheet. We had just turned into a long, narrow, straight lane. The tarmac stretched out in front of us – a long, black, lifeless strip for as far as our eyes could see. It fell so hard we couldn't hear each other; we could barely see each other. I went ahead and cycled with my head and eyes pointing down against the torrent.

I'd never thought much about the holes in my helmet until now, presuming they were just part of the standard design. Now I could think of nothing else. I may as well not have had a helmet on. The water gushed in, cold against my scalp. Once it worked its way through my hair, it streamed down my face in wiggly lines. My waterproof was useless. The rain pelted down so hard it seeped up my arms from my wrists. It ran down the back of my neck. From there it ran down my forearms, it ran down to my bum and into the foam of my padded cycling tights, and I could feel a squelch whenever my buttocks shifted on the saddle.

After what seemed like half a day, the never-ending lane came to a junction and we stopped. Water was dripping from us. We laughed because there was no other form of expression.

From that point on, the rain hardly stopped. The only time we got a reprieve was when it switched from being torrential to steady.

Dave got out his paper map from a pocket and it disintegrated. Together we held up the soft pieces, trying to match up the grid and find a reference to where we were. We did this many times. Every time we stopped, he got out the map and we tried to jigsaw the soggy pieces together. Every time a little more fell away. The more we handled the map, the more it flaked until it became totally useless.

I got out my phone – Google Maps to the rescue again. But it was so wet it was dead. I had not yet learned the cyclists' custom of carrying a phone in a polythene sandwich bag. I sighed impassively, surrendering to the mishap. Temperance and tolerance are definitely attributes I had started to acquire through endurance sport. Shrugging off the fact that I'd just broken a £600 iPhone requires the same sort of philosophical approach as running the last lap of a track session when my body is screaming to stop, or cycling the final 10k of a 100k ride when I'm exhausted and starving, or trying to ignore neck chafing when I'm 2 kilometres out to sea. Such tests of character are the small prices we pay for the more valuable and lasting life lessons.

We paused, ignoring the rain for a few minutes to make a plan. We estimated we had another 25 miles (40 kilometres) and decided to stay off the recommended cycle route and country lanes and take the most direct roads. There was little point enjoying the scenic route in this. We headed in the direction of an A-road but, as we did, the steady rain became torrential again – even harder than before.

I've never witnessed raindrops so huge, not even in the tropics. It made a spectacular din. It was so heavy and wild it made me want to laugh out loud. The roads were flooded and the water was splashing up us, as well as raining down on us. We couldn't communicate. We rode in single file, enduring the lashing.

When we reached the main road it was immediately clear how dangerous this would be. The sheets of rain made us invisible to cars so we stopped, helplessly waiting for it to ease. Both of us were shivering and Dave grew impatient, suggesting we had no choice but to make our way cautiously along this fast road towards King's Lynn. I offered to go at the back because I was wearing a high-vis jacket, but when Dave went ahead of me, he immediately disappeared into the mist of the downpour.

I shouted to him that we had to stop. I was scared. If I couldn't see him, the cars behind me would not see me.

I saw a lane leading off the main road and suggested we take it. I didn't care where it went. I just wanted off this misty deathtrap. The lane, however, just did a big loop and we ended up back on the main road further along. Dave was not impressed. It was still raining hard.

We joined the road again for a mile or so but came off it as soon as we saw a smaller road leading off it. We zigzagged across the countryside with nothing more for directions than our noses. An hour later we passed Sandringham. And that's when Dave noticed I had a flat tyre. My first ever puncture! I wondered how long it had been like that for. I was so consumed with being cold and wet I hadn't noticed my bike feeling any different.

We stared at it for a minute, in denial. I was convinced that if I just pumped it up, it would hold for a bit – maybe long enough to reach a town where we could find a bike shop and pay to have it fixed? That was my contingency plan for punctures.

'I don't think that will work,' stated Dave quietly.

This was the moment I'd been dreading since becoming a cyclist.

We sheltered under a tree in someone's drive entrance and set about fixing it. I say 'we', but I left it to Dave. I managed to take the wheel off, which I thought was damn proficient, but then I couldn't even undo the cap on the valve because my hands were so numb. Neither could Dave. For 5 whole minutes we stood by the road rubbing our hands together to generate enough heat for enough sensation to undo the valve cap. Dave took off the tyre and removed the inner tube and then I stepped in.

'I need to learn to do this,' I announced boldly. I took the wheel from him and sat down in my squelching shorts on the wet gravel. 'But you can check I'm doing it right.'

Dave's face indicated he wasn't in the mood for giving a tutorial.

I put the muddy wheel on my knee, just like I'd been taught in my bike maintenance workshop. I ran my wrinkled fingers around the inside of the tyre to check for the incriminating thorn or stone. If you fail to remove debris from the tyre rim you might have to repeat the operation 10 minutes down the road. The rain started to pick up again. I tried to ignore it and carried on working my black fingers around the tyre, water dripping down my nose. I was smeared with gunk but this puncture would not fix itself. I began to shiver. Then I put in the tube. Dave guided me: 'Pump the tube up slightly before you begin. Start at the valve.' All the things that I'd forgotten.

The rain picked up even more and it became impossible to continue so we gathered everything up in a bundle and moved to a bus shelter, 100 metres down the road, where Dave took over.

Getting moving again was painful. Moving is always the fail-safe way to warm up with cycling, but the trouble is that for the first few minutes when you move the wind causes an extra chill factor so you feel even colder than you did while standing still. I wiggled my toes and feet and told myself that in just 10 minutes I'd be warm again. Any humour that we had previously prised out of each other had long been exhausted.

We were soaked from our hair to our toes. My hands, inside sodden gloves, were so cold I could no longer change gear.

It was going dark when we limped into King's Lynn. We didn't even have to confer now. We eagerly followed the signs for the station without a word. There was a 45-minute wait for the train and I was shivering uncontrollably. I couldn't take my helmet off because my hands could not squeeze the clip to undo it. Dave did it for me but I soon realised that the helmet offered a shred of warmth so I put it back on. My foam cycling pants squelched when I sat down. I remembered an assistant in a cycle shop once trying to upsell me a more expensive pair with padding made of gel, but I was having none of it. I'd be revising that decision after today.

When I got on the train I removed my soaking shoes and took it in turns tucking first my hands and then my feet under my legs to warm them, until Dave suggested I put my feet under his legs. In any other situation it would have felt uncomfortably intimate but I was so cold I didn't care. The train took two hours and we did not stop shivering but still, we managed to laugh about our day and talked about what new waterproof items of kit we would now buy. As we approached King's Cross, cruelly, we had to put our soggy shoes and gloves back on and cycle through London in the dark, shivering more than ever.

Both of us lived east so at least we could do half the journey together. I was glad to follow him. I was still scared of London traffic – and in the dark, on a Sunday night when traffic is busy, when we were wet, shivery and tired, it felt even more of an ordeal. Dave knew some backstreets to Liverpool Street and if it weren't for being so cold it would have been nice travelling through the still, quiet streets of London at night. He escorted me to Spitalfields Market, from where I knew how to get home, and we said goodbye politely, as if both of us wanted to draw a line in the closeness of our friendship.

CHAPTER 20

A MIDNIGHT GUEST

Cycling defined our friendship after that trip. With Dave's running injury and my dogged determination to improve my bike times in triathlon for the following season, we both had an incentive strong enough to defy British weather.

Over the cold winter months we organised rides almost every other weekend. Neither of us knew any routes nor had anything sophisticated like a Garmin GPS device to follow routes so we entered sportive events – organised rides with a marked route and feed stations – to make it a day out. Sportives aren't officially races but you do get a timing chip and a finish time. For me, cycling in numbers made the roads feel safer.

We encountered severe weather and found ourselves lost, stuck in the dark, frozen, and in all manner of scenarios to test our patience. Sometimes we drove each other mad and snapped but we built a solid friendship based on shared experiences and discoveries.

One time after cycling to a cross-country race, I left my bike locked up outside a pub in Bethnal Green for the post-race drinks and the front wheel was stolen. I was stranded 2 miles from home with a one-wheeled bike. This was the wheel of my dirty bashed-up hybrid bike, not the more valuable road bike. I'd never considered locking the wheels on this bike! Whoever pinched it would probably get no more than a fiver for it at a market.

I went back into the pub where some running club friends were still drinking and told them my sorry news calmly. This was the sort of thing my old self would have got terribly het up over. I would have let it consume my thoughts and I'd have banged on about the expense and inconvenience for hours. But I had noticed that I had become remarkably philosophical about misfortunes lately, including the mishap with the wet phone in Norfolk. I don't think it's a coincidence that this sense of composure seemed to develop alongside me getting involved in endurance sport. I think I had become so used to accepting discomfort, cold, exhaustion, dehydration and anything else thrown at me that my tolerance for life in general had expanded.

Dave came to my rescue. He left the pub and drove me and my one-wheeled bike home. If it weren't for him I would have had to carry the damn thing home. This turn of events left me questioning once more whether being so staunchly independent and single is such a good thing after all.

We usually did our long bike rides on Sundays, the day after cross-countries. Sometimes others from the club, like Ben, Mick and Brenda, joined and sometimes it was just us. Often we finished with a Sunday roast and cider in a pub with a fire. After one ride in Surrey, I remember a pub landlady taking one look at our blue faces and hurriedly ushering us to a table by a roaring fire where we were served the biggest roast potatoes I've ever seen in my life. I think she gave us extra because we looked like we needed them.

I had to learn all over again what kit I needed for winter riding, just as I had for summer riding. At first I wore way too many clothes and found myself dripping with sweat after 10 miles. That ends up making you even colder than if you wear too little because the damp sweat zaps your body heat. Winter cycling generally means you either wear just enough for on the move but freeze at the beginning of a ride and when you stop, or you wear enough to start out toasty warm but get boiling hot and soaking wet with sweat in the middle of the ride. This is why the cycling industry makes a fortune from rolling out new, improved, high-tech, moisture-zapping, intelligent-fabric base layers each year.

One luxury of cycling with Dave was that he had a car. I almost felt guilty for the indulgence. I had done so many events where I had to cart my bike on public transport while freezing cold, grimy or tired, that slumping in a heated car at the end of 100k felt like cheating.

Few of our rides went smoothly. One weekend we took part in the Gatwick Sportive, which starts near to the airport. I arranged to meet Dave there. I got the train to Gatwick but couldn't find my way out of the train station and found myself walking around the Gatwick departures hall in front of the check-in desks, wheeling my bike, in full cycling gear, looking for the exit.

That turned out to be a bad day for directions generally because later we got lost not once, but twice. How anyone can get lost on a signposted route baffles other cyclists when I tell them. What was supposed to be 50 miles became 65. Typically, both missed turns were right at the bottom of a hill so we had to climb all the way back up again when we finally realised our error and backtracked. Dave's bike then developed a gear problem and we had to stop every 10 minutes to adjust it. Each time we stopped, my body temperature dropped a little more. By the end I was shivering and counting every half-mile. We were the last people to cross the finish line.

On another ride, in Kent, I turned up straight from Sky News studios, after appearing on the morning paper reviews. Dave had picked up my bike the night before and drove it to the venue. I finished my early-morning TV appearance, changed from a dress into Lycra in the toilets, wiped off the war-paint make-up, picked up a bacon sandwich and got a taxi to a train station, where Dave met me at the other end. That took a lot of organising.

I remember that crisp winter morning. The contrast between the tense energy of a windowless newsroom and getting on a bike in the cold, still, damp air of the countryside felt surreal. It was only 10 a.m. and I'd been up for six hours already. I couldn't help thinking how thankful I was that I had discovered this side of life. My mind turned to past years, working long hours in newsrooms like the one I had just left, followed by an even more highly strung atmosphere of a bar to 'unwind'. I couldn't imagine not having what I had now: fresh air, open space, the elements, calm thoughts.

That ride was particularly precarious. Hedge cutters had been on a mission in the morning and thorny branches and twigs littered the road. The less-used narrow lanes were slippery with debris and decaying leaves. We passed rider after rider fixing punctures. Every 500 metres we saw an upside-down bike with the wheel removed. We looked at each other nervously. It wasn't the fixing of punctures I was afraid of – I'd done a few by now. It was the stopping when the weather was so cold in sweat-damp clothes. It was having to sit on wet ground while you handle muddy tyres with numb fingers.

Mercifully we finished the ride without one.

Crossing the line, a marshal asked, 'How many punctures did you get?'

'None.'

'None!' he replied. 'Congratulations – you're the first party to get zero between you. Some people got five.'

Five! I honestly do not know how I would have coped with that. I was relieved but I also knew that one day that would happen. The puncture fairies were looking down on both of us that day – probably that whole winter, actually. But punctures are a numbers game and I knew I ought to psychologically prepare myself for more tumultuous rides ahead.

In the middle of all this cycling, there were some weekend escapades with run club too. In January I went to Devon for a stunning half-marathon trail run along coastal paths. The Coastal Trail Series is known for its scenic routes near the seaside. There is always a 10k, a half-marathon, a full marathon and an 'ultra'. I joined Susan and David, the couple who took me for open-water swimming lessons at Stubbers Lake the previous year. They had use of a family cottage just a mile from the race start. Lots of people had planned to join the trip but, ever the devotee, I was the only one to take up the offer.

They arrived a day ahead of me. I planned to join them on Friday evening, before the race the following morning. Devon is a very long way from London and instead of getting the train, which would have been simpler and quicker, I opted to travel by minibus with a group from London Fields Triathlon Club, who also happened to be going to that event. Even though I was staying with friends from run club, I took advantage of the cheaper, and more sociable, transport option. But that meant I arrived late. Very late.

When I say 'arrived late', I mean I arrived in Devon late. I still had to find Susan and David's cottage. The minibus dropped me at the cottages the club triathletes were staying in. My bed was 4 miles away. I tried to book a cab but there was such poor signal when I called the taxi company I couldn't tell whether they registered my request or not before it cut out.

'You can always stay on the sofa here,' a girl from the minibus offered kindly, but I knew that would be a disaster.

I have had enough life experience to learn that me, sofas and sleep don't go well together. On a sofa I would be awake all night, worried about people coming in, worried that I was the surplus guest gatecrashing without paying my way, worried that I was going to get some awful skin rash or fleas from resting on a cushion without a pillowcase. Besides, my breakfast provisions were with Susan and David, and that was worth journeying on into the night for.

The cottages were secluded, tucked away down a fork of dirt tracks. Even if the taxi had registered my booking, they wouldn't know which dirt track I was at the end of. I decided to walk towards the main lane so I could flag it down, should it arrive. I waited earnestly for what seemed like an eternity. It was pitch-black. I didn't realise how dark our planet can get outside London.

Eventually I saw the faint lights of a car in the distance. *This is what it must feel like to see an angel*, I thought. Mercifully, it *was* my cab. I clambered in, dragging my wheelie case on to the seat beside me, and gushed about how pleased I was to see him. I recited the address of where I was supposed to be staying in a village called Beesands. The address was simply the name of the house and the village.

Blank face. The driver knew as much about the location of this house as I did. Half an hour later, we crawled through the village of Beesands for the third time, straining to read the house names on the quaint hand-painted gateposts. Beesands consists of one road, lined with cottages and a post office. For the third time we reached the last house on the road, turned around and came back the other way, reading the house names on the opposite side of the street. The meter was still going up.

I searched for an email and reread the instructions from Susan and David: 'Five-bar wooden gate, which is open. We've gone to bed but left the kitchen light on and back door open.'

Every single house we passed had a five-bar wooden gate and every single five-bar wooden gate was open.

Every time I saw a house with a kitchen light on, I'd cry 'That's it! That's it! No, wrong name.'

The taxi driver suggested we turn off the road and on to a dirt track. It was signposted for a farm, but we could see a few houses clustered together in the distance so it was worth trying to see if this track led to them. I saw a large five-bar wooden gate which was open, and there was a lit kitchen.

'That's it!' I cried again. I was convinced this time. My intuition told me so. There was no name on the house but we'd excluded every other bricks and mortar in the village.

I was so convinced I paid the cab driver, dragged out my wheelie case and watched him set off into the night, leaving me alone in the darkness with no phone signal. I walked to the house and tried the front door. It was locked. *Good. That's supposed to be locked.* I went to the back door. It was open. *Yep. Definitely it.*

I entered quietly and looked around. The kitchen looked curiously cluttered for a holiday cottage. There were coats hanging up, boots on the floor, pans in the sink (hadn't David and Susan said they had eaten out?). I froze, taking it all in.

Then I spotted a woman in an adjacent room, through an internal window, watching TV. As I saw her, she saw me. She turned white and my heart skipped three beats.

I went to the window and tried to do a friendly shrug which I hoped would convey: *Oops. Don't be scared – I'm not here to take your family heirlooms and tie you up in the pantry. I've got the wrong house because you left your back door open, but now that I'm here perhaps you can tell me where I'm supposed to be.*

I might have to work on my body language. Warily she got up and I waited just as nervously as she made her way from the room she was in to the room I was in. I hoped she didn't have a gun. This was the countryside after all.

'I'm so sorry!' I blurted when she appeared. 'I'm looking for a cottage. My friend said he'd leave the kitchen light on and the back door open.'

I've never seen so much relief pass over someone's face. Not even at the finish of that final fell race on the Isle of Wight.

I repeated the name of the cottage I was looking for.

Nope. She didn't know it. This was starting to look like a real disaster.

We stood in silence for a few moments.

Then suddenly she said, 'Oh! It could be that one.' She pointed out of the window to a house set at the bottom of a slope.

I wasted no time. I thanked her, apologised again and dragged my Louis Vuitton bumping along behind me, through her garden, which I didn't know was her garden because it was so dark, and towards the cottage she had pointed to.

Between me and the cottage was a stone wall. It was so dark I could see no other way to get to it – by now I was so eager that I became fixated on the most direct route possible. I threw my case over the wall then clambered over myself, my small backpack strapped snugly on my back. Dangling from my small backpack was a sleeping bag (this would be the first time I had used it since university), which I'd forgotten about.

As I attempted to drop down the other side of the wall, the sleeping bag got caught on the top of the wall, breaking my descent but slamming me against the stones. I was hanging by the straps of my sleeping bag, my wriggling legs suspended above the ground.

'Oh shit!' I cried out loud.

I detangled myself and eased myself down to where my case had landed below. The Louis Vuitton was filthy, the sleeping-bag case ripped and my knuckles grazed. But no matter. There, on the wall in front of me, was the name of the cottage I was looking for. I let myself in quietly. On the worktop were two race numbers and timing chips. *Definitely it.*

I tried to creep upstairs but still woke David and Susan. It was now past two in the morning. I apologised for what seemed like the fifteenth time that evening and went to bed. We had to be up in 4.5 hours.

In the clear light of morning I looked up at the house which I'd intruded upon the night before, and saw that I could have walked directly from there to this cottage by road, instead of ploughing through her garden and almost hanging myself on a stone wall. It had looked so much more complicated in the dark.

The weather was dry for the race but freezing cold and fiercely windy. We huddled under a marquee for the briefing. Much was said about the 'mandatory kit list', which included a whistle, a foil blanket, a windbreaker (whatever that is), plasters, a first-aid kit, a water bottle and a mobile phone. I didn't have any of this, except for the phone. I was used to club cross-country races where no one wears anything more than shorts and a vest, no matter what the weather.

As for the water bottle, I had never run with one. Everything I had picked up about running was from running club friends mostly concerned with short, fast road races. No one ever took water with them. But today was an altogether different breed of running, with every possibility of falling down a cliff face, hence the need for whistles and emergency things like that. I hadn't had a clue where to even buy a whistle so I'd ignored that too.

I did, however, remember to pack my own essentials, namely tissues, dried figs and Elizabeth Arden Eight Hour cream to smear on my cheeks to protect against the biting coastal wind.

The race official told us sternly that there would be spot checks of our mandatory kit list at the end. Those who didn't have the stuff on the list would be disqualified (or DQ'd, as it's referred to). That didn't bother me too much. As long as I got disqualified after I'd finished and not before I set off, it didn't really matter. I wasn't exactly chasing a podium place.

The run reminded me of the Isle of Wight, only it was longer, rougher, hillier and even more beautiful. It was more beautiful than any I'd done before. It started with the sea in vision and wound along a coastal path and over stiles.

I started out steadily, appreciating the ocean air and taking in the view whenever the footing would allow my gaze to divert from the ground. There was no pressure to perform well today. A completion time on a trail run means nothing because the terrain is so variable. And anyway, there were only three of us here from run club so no one would really know how good or bad our times were. I decided I would just run steadily and enjoy it.

After a couple of miles, the marked path became impossible to run because of rocks and steps and it was so narrow that there was a backlog of runners. I am always secretly pleased when this happens because it is a chance to walk without guilt or shame.

At the end of that rocky stretch we reached a lighthouse at the peak of a cliff. The wind was ferocious. We ran straight into it. I put my arms out to the side, letting the wind take my weight as much as possible, and it very nearly lifted me off my feet. I could feel it whipping my cheeks and commended myself for remembering the Elizabeth Arden Eight Hour cream.

After the lighthouse we dropped down to near sea level again. The wind eased but the path became perilously narrow and there were several places where there was a sheer drop to the side. Now I understood why they wanted us to bring a whistle and a foil blanket – it was in case we fell down a cliff and no one could find us.

For 7 miles the route traced the coast, ascending and descending, on tracks, through fields and across heather. Just after halfway we went inland and through woods. The only water station was here and I stopped to refill my water bag – a 250-millilitre pouch which clipped on to my bumbag. The mandatory kit list had specified we carry 500 millilitres minimum. A water pouch was a very rudimentary way of carrying water. Most competitors had proper 'water packs' strapped to their back with a tube they can occasionally suck to get water.

I'd stopped to eat figs from my bumbag, which had all congealed, when David appeared. I waited as he filled his water so we could run together.

'I'm flagging. You go on,' he said, and on I went at my pleasantly unstrained pace.

Now that we were inland, the ground had changed and we went through thick mud on footpaths and bridleways. Several competitors were running with dogs, which I'd never come across before. One canine came bounding past me, dragging an apologetic owner who'd clearly lost control. It cut in front of me, almost tripping me over and splashing mud straight into my face.

After 10 miles I started to flag. *Only another three to go. That's 5k. The equivalent of running from run club down the canal to Limehouse.* There went my persuasive inner monologue again.

The end came, as it always does.

The marshals were doing spot checks of the mandatory kit list. I avoided eye contact with the marshal and tried to slip inconspicuously through the roped-off finish funnel to where the water and medals were being dished out. They didn't stop me. Phew.

Knowing David wasn't too far behind, I waited. I recognised some of the triathletes from the minibus the day before and chatted with them. I had only dabbled in a few triathlon club sessions – the Monday bricks and the Sunday open-water swims during summer – so I knew a couple but not well.

David finished 15 minutes after me and Susan soon after that. By then I was shivering, but it was another 20 minutes before we headed to the pub as we gathered bags and dissected the race. I had put on warm clothes but the strong wind cut through every layer and I was going blue with cold. I started to feel my old symptoms of dizziness return. It appeared that almost every other competitor found the same pub as us. It was full of sweaty, exhausted, hungry runners and the faint smell of damp kit was evident. We had to wait to get a table, in which time I thirstily drank a pint of cider and it went straight to my head. When we spotted enough space on a bench by a table for the three of us to squeeze on to, we all ordered fish and chips and were served what looked like battered whales. I ate every bit of mine but two hours later I was hungry again.

We sat and chatted and watched other runners trickle in. The fastest of the marathon runners would finish an hour or so after us, then when the marathoners were done, in came the first of the ultrarun finishers, who had completed 34 miles. I watched the looks of relief on their faces as they entered the warm, some with supportive partners, some with friends, some alone. I knew the feelings behind those facial expressions. There was once a time when I would have felt these people were out of my league – superhumans who couldn't possibly have normal lives if they spent their weekends running over Devon cliffs in gale-force winds. Now I considered these sorts of outdoor challenges an essential part of being human.

CHAPTER 21

WINTER WHEELS

Dave and I continued cycling every other weekend until a fall at the beginning of January stalled it for a few weeks. I was on my way to hill training in Greenwich with friends from the running track. I saw ice on rooftops when I drew my blinds that morning – the first frost of the season – but I didn't let it deter me. I'd never cycled in frost before so I did not know the danger. As I rounded a corner on the river path on the Isle of Dogs, my front tyre skidded beneath me. Before I could blink I was on the ground. I felt the side of my head – inside a helmet, thank God – hit the pavement with a thud.

I shook myself off and carried on. Other than a bruised hip and some shakiness I was fine. It wasn't until the next day that the damage kicked in. I couldn't lift my neck off my pillow. Whiplash.

I went to A&E following the advice of NHS Direct. I made my sorry way there looking like Queen Victoria in a self-made neck brace made out of shredded cardboard. I waited in a chair for three hours only to be prodded and told to go home and rest. I should have stayed at home and done exactly that instead of struggling to hold my neck up in an uncomfortable waiting-room chair for three hours. Another thing I was learning as an athlete is that for most injuries or loss of form the prognosis is usually rest.

Being unable to train during the most miserable month of the year had a silver lining. When I had to forego the club cross-country race the following Saturday, I looked out of the window at the horizontal sheets of rain and was positively relieved to have an excuse to stay in the warm and dry. I always enjoyed activities when I actually did them, but there was always trepidation before I started, especially in the cold. I have no doubt that part of the drive to do all this tough stuff was proving to myself that I could put myself through hardship. I'd already had a year of proving that so taking a couple of weekends off now and again didn't bother me as much as it would have a year earlier.

I didn't let myself get too comfortable though. I was back in the saddle and out in the drizzly weather again three weeks later. I have many fond memories of winter cycle rides with Dave – counting down the long miles to the feed stations, excited by what free food there would be, stopping to look at maps when we went wrong, getting cold, getting splashed in the face by road spray. I associate my formative days of cycling with these rides.

I was tempted a few times to join the rides with the triathlon club but I always found an excuse not to. It was more comfortable cycling with Dave. He didn't mind waiting for me if I couldn't keep up and would help me change the inner if I got a puncture.

He was tolerant in other ways too. Being freelance, my work was never confined to Monday to Friday. There was one Sunday ride where I had a story due to go to print the next day and I kept having to stop to take work calls. I was asked by a typically demanding news desk to get an extra quote from an interviewee and so I did a power-interview at the side of the road and wrote my quote on a cafe receipt as howling wind blew around me.

Sometimes we bickered. No matter how many times I reminded him to take fuel on the ride, Dave turned up with nothing. Fuelling is deeply ingrained in cycling culture. Well-informed cyclists wouldn't dream of leaving home without pockets of flapjacks, bananas or sugary energy gels. Everyone takes exactly what they need for the distance, so asking to share is big. Dave didn't bother with any of that. He relied on the feed stations, which were often empty because we were so slow or we were on our own rides with no free food. I was highly protective of my fruit and nut mixes because my digestive system can't tolerate the junk food that most feed stations provide. If the flapjacks have butter in them, I'm screwed. So I started buying him his own bag of dried apricots every time we went on a ride.

He got frustrated with me for not signalling to turn right early enough. I got frustrated with him for suddenly stopping without signalling. Then there were times when he would disappear ahead of me and not realise for miles. I would always start out full of energy and vow to stay right behind his wheel, but before long my energy would dissipate and he'd slowly pull away. Once he went almost an hour without realising I was no longer behind him.

For months it seemed like I didn't improve at all. The only people we ever overtook were families on mountain bikes. I couldn't understand how all these other riders – some of them quite rotund, if I dare say so – could possibly be fitter than me. I trained five days a week, sometimes twice a day, mixing running, swimming, gym stuff and cycling. My training routine this year was less running focused and all triathlon focused. I couldn't wait for the summer triathlon season to begin so that I could see how I had improved and perhaps see how far off my times were to qualify for World Champs. Last season was just experimenting, I thought – next season I meant business.

Yet long rides felt like such a slog. On a sportive the first feed station would usually be around 20 miles in, and I remember being desperate to get there for a rest. It takes much longer to build up endurance fitness than speed. It can take years for the body to fully develop its oxygen processing capacity and to become efficient at burning body fat for fuel, instead of burning up its sparse reserves of glycogen. I knew very little about sports science then and simply could not understand why all my training didn't translate into improved long-distance cycling.

I blamed my bike, conceding that everyone else must have fancy carbon ones. Someone suggested that instead of getting a new bike, I invest in a professional bike fitting. A proper bike fitting involves assessing the whole body for muscle weaknesses and experimenting with different positions to see which generates maximum power output.

I got this done and the following weekend went for a 100-kilometre ride. Twenty kilometres in, my lower back was in agony. The new position had me leaning further forward and the muscles in my back had not had time to adapt. I spent 15 minutes lying on the side of the road trying to stretch out the spasms so I could carry on. And it still made no difference to my speed!

I may not have been getting faster but I was getting more resilient and confident. Confident enough to one day dare a club ride with the alpha types at the triathlon club.

It was typical that the club ride I picked as my first happened to be the most challenging group cycle event on their calendar. There was a group trip to an infamous sportive called the Hell of the Ashdown in Kent. I didn't even look up what it involved. I just saw emails about it and it seemed a good way to get to know more members of the club.

I felt strangely disloyal planning a ride without Dave. But it was something I felt I needed to do. I loved our days out but I'd started to crave the dynamics of group riding, like the previous summer when six of us cycled to Brighton. My summer cycling friends – Brenda, Philippa, Cate and Mick – went out occasionally, but not regularly. I was comfortably able to keep up with Dave now and I wanted to push myself again. By making plans to go out with a new group, a younger group, with banter and the promise of new beginnings, it felt like I was making a statement that I wanted to step back from our friendship.

The Hell of the Ashdown takes place on the last weekend in February and historically it nearly always snows or is icy. The clue to how challenging this ride is, is in the name. The 115-kilometre (70-mile) route is designed to take in as many of Kent's hills as it can.

It turned out to be one of the coldest weekends of the year so far. The evening before the event I walked along the South Bank in central London to meet friends and felt the chill go right through my winter clothes. I was filled with trepidation for the next day. I'd be cycling all day in this! Alternatively, I could do a spin class at the gym in the morning in the warm and dry. I started to convince myself. A spin class would be safer. Skidding on ice is what gave me whiplash a few weeks ago. I wouldn't have to get up so early and I could do with the sleep…

But then I checked myself. I'd never get to make new cycling friends if I didn't go. I would dress appropriately and I would get through it. My determination, as ever, was fuelled by the prospect of ingratiating myself with new friends and using my weekend to the max.

Once more I found myself peeling away early from my night out. My friends carried on. I felt I'd sated my desire to catch up. The night was just on that tipping point – when people start to drink more and become not merry but nonsensical. One of the downsides of not drinking as much as I used to was that my drunk radar became hard to ignore. I could detect incoherence and ethanol-infused breath from word two. I was glad to leave but I couldn't help getting a niggling feeling that by opting out early, before things got raucous, I was creating a distance between me (Helen, the sensible one going home so she could cycle tomorrow) and them.

But cycle tomorrow was what I wanted to do. I didn't want to languish in bed – I wanted to flourish in the open air, even though that open air was going to be Baltic.

The following morning I duly got up with my 6 a.m. alarm. I looked across at the roof of the building opposite and, sure enough, it was laced with ice again. The last time I saw ice on that rooftop and then got on my bike, I ended up with whiplash. Still, I was up now, so I willed myself to continue with my plan.

The plan was to meet at London Bridge. For a train, I presumed. I pedalled fast, conscious that I was the new kid and couldn't be late. When I arrived I spotted only two cyclists. The weather was so horrendous that out of the 10 on the list, only the two most hardcore had actually turned up. Plus me.

A kind and helpful guy called John, the club team captain, was one of them. I'd met him at swim sessions before and I was relieved to see a familiar face.

'The others have seen sense and backed out,' he said. 'We'll take it easy to the start – we should be there for nine.'

I computed the words in my head. *Does that mean what I think it means? That we're cycling to the start?* That was another 15 miles. The course itself was an unprecedented distance for me and now there would be more.

'Yeah, fine,' I sang, trying to sound casual.

The other guy didn't even introduce himself and barely said two words for the entire journey. This may have been something to do with my attire. I was wearing a high-vis hard-shell jacket

– good for winter commuting, not passable for slick and fast aerodynamic road cyclists. And, I was carrying a backpack. This was to leave at the race HQ, not to cycle the route with. I had extra layers in there and freshening-up necessities, should there be a visit to the pub afterwards. I didn't exactly exude the aura of a competent cyclist and many cyclists get snooty at that.

The terror began as soon as we set off. It became quickly apparent that John's 'taking it easy' pace was significantly faster than what I was capable of cycling – ever.

We dropped down to the Elephant and Castle roundabout, where I said a small prayer. I had never attempted (and would never normally attempt) such a junction on two wheels. I followed their tracks exactly and emerged unscathed. We pressed on to Denmark Hill. Until that point there were enough traffic lights to break the pace so I stayed with them. But as soon as we were out of the city, they powered ahead effortlessly, leaving me puffing and fighting to keep up, weighed down by my unseemly backpack and sweating underneath my non-breathable jacket.

John was patient and waited for me at every junction, asking if I was OK each time. It was blatant that we would miss our 9 a.m. start time but he didn't once express any urgency or irritation. The same could not be said for No Name, who remained facing forward at every stop and zoomed off as soon as I breathlessly caught up.

An hour into the journey, we hit a long, gradual hill where I lost them entirely. They got so far ahead I didn't know if they would wait or not. I pushed on, expecting to see them around every bend, but they were nowhere to be seen. On I went for another 15 minutes, not knowing if I should turn off anywhere. *Another 5 minutes*, I thought, *then I'll stop to look at a map and make my own way there.*

After 4 minutes I saw them. Waiting. I vowed that I'd keep with them from there on, but because of a wrong turn earlier there were still another 7 miles to go. The stop-wait-start continued. I was now boiling. I could feel the sweat saturated under my backpack. I desperately wanted to take the stupid jacket off but I didn't dare ask them to stop again.

At long last we passed Biggin Hill airport and I knew we were close – I remembered from the map. Now I kept expecting the start to appear on every corner, but no such luck. There were still another 3 miles, uphill. When we reached a schoolhouse on a narrow lane where the Hell of the Ashdown was to begin, I was drenched in sweat, exhausted and starving hungry. It had been 20 miles from London Bridge and we hadn't even begun the course.

John and No Name went straight to the start. They didn't need to adjust anything, nor even go to the loo. I, meanwhile, had a whole checklist: use toilet, drink coffee, eat a couple of bananas, take off layers, put backpack in cloakroom, refill water bottle, look at route, take a photo for Facebook, reapply moisturiser for wind protection...

'You guys go ahead without me,' I insisted. 'I'll go at my own pace and I'll see you at the end.'

'You won't be that far behind us,' said John kindly, which was obviously not true at all, but a nice gesture.

I was going to be way, way, way behind them, and I'm sure they were mightily relieved when I announced I would ride alone.

I went inside the schoolhouse, where there was a canteen serving breakfast. I got a hot black coffee and sat down to compose myself, hoping some of the sweat from my clothes would evaporate, leaving me with half a chance to retain body heat for the 70 miles of hell ahead. I drew this process out for as long as possible. The canteen was emptying. The last set-off time was 10 a.m. and it was nearly that now. I willed myself back outside to the cold, damp air and on to my frozen saddle.

Almost everyone had set off by now, except for a handful of procrastinators like me. I wasn't going to have company but at least I wouldn't be demoralised by everyone overtaking me. My next thought: *What if the feed stations run out of food?* That got me going.

Within minutes I found myself at the foot of a precipitous hill. I had to press down with all my might on each pedal. Just as I was building momentum, the hill crossed a junction, forcing me to stop. When I tried to start again, I wobbled. *Please let the pedal go round, please let the pedal go round*, I willed, but I couldn't get the bike going and I had to walk with it until the hill flattened out slightly.

At the top came the blood-curdling descent. The winter roads were wet, muddy, icy and thorny. Soon after, I caught up with a girl also riding alone, which was a welcome sight after my bruising ordeal with the fast boys this morning. I slowed to ride alongside her for a while and we commented on the killer hill we'd just survived. She told me she'd recently joined a tri club and she knew hardly anyone and they'd all gone ahead of her.

'Me too!' I replied, buoyed that I had found a kindred spirit in this merciless sport. We rode together for 15 minutes and I nearly suggested that we stick together for the ride but I wasn't sure if she would welcome company or not.

My dilemma was solved on the next descent because I soon sailed ahead. Many inexperienced cyclists are overcautious going downhill, especially on wet, greasy roads like today. But descending hills was something I'd learned how to do at Les Stables: the trick is not to look down at the road but look ahead. That way the tarmac doesn't look like it's moving so fast. Stick your inside knee out on corners for extra balance and don't use the brakes on a bend, only before.

I slowed at the end of the descent and looked back. There was no sign of her, so I decided we probably weren't ideal riding buddies after all and pressed on.

The route was mercifully flat for the next 15 minutes but we were exposed to icy wind. It bit into my cheeks and lips. Ice glistened on the road. I proceeded with astute concentration, poised to control any sudden skid.

I ploughed on into the cold air, switching my mind off to the bracing sensation on my cheeks. The hills came thick and fast. Hills in all shapes and sizes. Hills on narrow, windy lanes; hills on main roads; vertical hills; gradual, deceptive hills; slippery hills; straight, tedious hills. I overtook riders fixing punctures on the side of the road and, as usual, asked God to spare me. There was no Dave this time to finish off the bits I couldn't do.

My extremities were so frozen they smarted. My entire torso was wet with sweat. I was using a running watch (a replacement for the one I'd lost at Hever) to record the miles and I kept looking at it. I'd now done 40 miles since leaving home, 20 of which were getting to the start.

As I was doing the maths to establish how many more miles of this hell I had to withstand, it started to hail. *Just ride*, I said to myself.

Another hill. I tilted my head against the wind and the oncoming hailstones.

I pushed one numb foot down after the other, breathing heavily through my numb lips. Suddenly my rear wheel locked, sending my bike to a jerking halt, and I was thrown forward off the saddle. I reacted quickly, steered, unclipped from my pedals and managed a controlled topple on to the verge without hurting myself.

Wedged on the top of my wheel was my clip-on mudguard. It had come undone and slid down the seat post to land on the wheel, acting as a brake. I'd only got a damn mudguard because someone at run club told me that in winter it was etiquette to use one to stop road spray going all over your fellow riders' faces. Fat lot of good that is when you're always the one at the back!

I got out my Allen key multitool from my saddlebag. Despite everything, for a brief moment I felt like a worldly explorer again, doing a roadside fix in a hailstorm. Until I realised I couldn't fix it. Every time I thought I'd secured the strap to my seat post, I rode 1 metre and it fell straight back down again. My fingers numbed in seconds whenever they were out of my thick gloves and I was shivering now that I'd stopped moving. I gave up, unclipped the mudguard completely and abandoned the wretched thing by the side of the road.

It dawned on me that I hadn't seen a yellow arrow for a long time. I couldn't think where I might have gone wrong so I carried on. I hit a junction. No yellow arrow. *Definitely gone wrong somewhere*. I should have gone back then to retrace my tracks but the very thought of cycling back up a hill I'd just come down, looking over my shoulder for missed signage, knowing that almost every other rider would have got ahead, was too much for my frozen body to cope with.

'Fuck it,' I said out loud. I was now on 45 miles since leaving home. Another 15, I reasoned, and it would be perfectly acceptable to get a train home. Sixty-two miles (100 kilometres) is the magic distance for a 'long ride' in cycling circles. There had been two goals today: get to know some tri club members and get miles on the bike. Well, it was blatantly obvious there was not going to be a jolly in the pub after this ride, so bang went goal number one. As for goal number two, I could simply cycle around random lanes until my watch told me I'd done 60 miles. Then, I could find a train station. This was Kent – there were bound to be loads of lines leading to London. I was so cold that I was fully prepared to abandon my bag left at race HQ.

Spurred by the prospect of an early reprieve, I picked up my pace. When I got to a junction I took whatever road looked interesting. My hands wouldn't have been able to operate my phone even if I'd tried to look at a map. Up this lane, down that lane. I came to a dead end but I didn't care. I just wanted to make up miles, tick off another long ride and go home to central heating.

The hail stopped but the biting-cold air was just as cold and biting as when we began. Then I came to a main road which looked strangely familiar. It was the same road I cycled in flip-flops heading to Hever Castle Triathlon to meet Philippe all those months ago (when I was similarly lost). Hever Castle would do! That was a nice route. I turned off into a small street which I remembered from that day. It did mean another hill but I had long resigned myself to this being a day of hills.

I went past the castle entrance and I recalled that late summer's day, five months ago, when I and another triathlete sneaked through the gardens on our bikes to reach the other side before registration closed and he offered me a space in his tent because I couldn't find Philippe. It seemed so long ago and so different to this frosty, damp day. I also recalled from that day that there was a train station 7 miles away, which could get me to London Bridge in 45 minutes. I'd done 50 miles now. Add another three at the other end to get from London Bridge to home and it made it perfectly acceptable to stop now.

Seven miles. That's all. I was almost singing the words in my head. I rounded a bend and a T-junction lay ahead. I remembered the station being to the right. Or was it left? Just then, a pack of cyclists with numbers pinned to the front of their handlebars whooshed past from the right. Then more behind them. And more.

I'd inadvertently stumbled across the route! Not only had I managed to lose and then find the route, but I'd managed to find it significantly further along to where I'd lost it. I knew this because of the sheer numbers of them. This was the main pack of riders, who had set off much earlier than me.

This was too fortuitous to pass by. I decided to rejoin the ride, at least for a little bit. I turned left, the opposite way from the station.

'How much further to go?' I asked someone as he rode alongside me.

'Twenty-five.'

'Kilometres or miles?' I called after him, but he'd gone.

Should I finish it, or turn around and go to the train station after all? As I pondered, I became swept along by the stream of cyclists and the decision was made for me. But almost immediately came another epic climb and I regretted my decision. *I could still turn back*, I thought, but made no moves to do so.

I tucked in behind someone's wheel, getting all I could from his draft. He detected my presence from my loud panting. 'There's a feed station at the top of here,' he encouraged.

That comment was my deciding factor. A feed station meant a stop, meant flapjacks, meant temporary warmth, and real tissues to blow my nose with instead of wiping it on my soggy glove again. I was going to finish this.

After 4 minutes of mad pedalling behind a stranger's wheel, we reached a community hall with a welcome yellow temporary sign saying, *Feed stations*. Community halls, schoolhouses and church halls are commonly used as feed stations in cycling events. I was delighted to find malt loaf was on offer – dairy-free options at feed stations are often limited. I sat on my sticky hands to warm them, watching vivacious groups talk and joke. I heard someone say there were just 20 kilometres (12 miles) to go. The words sounded magical. No need to abandon my backpack in the cloakroom back at base. I could get through 20 kilometres.

What no one mentioned was that those last 20 kilometres were 20 kilometres of climbing. Nor that it would start to rain. It was light at first then the shower turned into huge, heavy raindrops. Not as hard as it had rained in Norfolk, but hard enough to get down my neck and up my sleeves.

For another 30 minutes I endured a succession of Kent hills. Then I spotted a sign telling us there were 15 kilometres to go. I felt cheated. It was supposed to be 15 kilometres, 5 kilometres ago. By now I'd cycled further than I'd ever cycled before. After another 20 minutes, the outside of my right knee started to click and hurt. I had never felt that before and I started to worry I was giving myself an injury.

I stopped by the side of the road to massage it. A support car pulled up and asked if I was OK. I never got that when I was stuck at the back and my mudguard kept slipping down and jamming my wheel, did I?!

'Bad knee,' I said. 'How much further is it?'

'It's just fifteen k.'

Still 15k! It had been 5 kilometres since the 15-kilometre sign, which had been another 10 kilometres since someone promised there were only 20 kilometres! I didn't care about finishing now. If I saw a train station, I'd take it. There was no one to finish with or for. I was totally depleted. I wanted to be at home. In my doom I convinced myself that I'd be ill next week from spending the last eight hours damp and cold.

But there was no train station and so I made the finish line as the rain still poured. I had done 75 miles since leaving home.

By complete fluke this was round about the distance I was supposed to have done, had I done the correct route. I managed to shave off pretty much the same amount of distance as I'd had to cycle to get there. I propped my bike against a wall and left it in the rain while I went inside. I found the canteen. It smelled of wet human bodies. I ate a baked potato with beans, staring blankly into space. I was traumatised.

As I slowly regained awareness, I felt disheartened. Wasn't the whole point of leaving my friends last night, getting up at six and forcing myself out into the morning frost to meet new people? Not to sit in a school canteen watching other groups chatter, having got soaked, lost, mentally broken and fallen off my bike. I could have gone on a bike ride with Dave.

I waited another 30 minutes in case John and No Name came in.

I told a marshal that my registered time would be deceptively speedy because I'd managed to cut out a quarter of the course.

He typed a few things into a computer, looked up and said, 'Don't worry, I don't think you're going to get a ban for that.'

What that meant was that I was so far down the list anyway, even with my 20-mile shortcut, that it wouldn't make the slightest difference to anyone.

I was getting colder in my wet clothes as I waited for John and No Name and there was no guarantee they'd come into the canteen anyway, or even finish at all, so I gathered my wet accessories and headed outside to my mucky but loyal steed.

Now the final hurdle: find a train station. There was no damn way I was cycling home the way we came. It was 5 miles to Hayes, where there was a station, according to Google.

It was raining hard again and I had to stop every few minutes to check the map. That meant taking off my gloves and reaching underneath my waterproof jacket to get my phone out of a pocket. Each time I stopped my hands got colder. Eventually they got so cold that the touchscreen didn't register them. I got irritated. *The technology exists to make touchscreens which work with gloves, so why don't phone manufacturers use it?!*

If all my pain and cold first manifested itself as frustration, soon it turned to tearfulness. I could feel that familiar tension building in the back of my eyes as everything just gets too much. Exhausted, aching, cold, wet, dirty, alone and paranoid that I was causing irreparable damage to my right knee.

I stopped some poor pedestrians in the pouring rain for directions to the station. Human helpfulness prevailed and eventually I arrived at the familiar red logo of National Rail. There was a 20-minute wait for a train to Lewisham. From Lewisham, the DLR (Docklands Light Railway) to Limehouse. The whole process took an hour and a half. I perched on the end of a seat on the train, hugging my knees to my chest and shivering, my muddy bike leaning against my legs. I was beyond thoughts. All I could focus on was the countdown to getting home.

When I got home, I dumped everything in my doorway – mud-splattered water bottles, mud-splattered saddlebag, mud-splattered lights, pump, cycle tights, shoes, socks, thick gloves that had failed to preserve any circulation. I grabbed a slice of rye bread, smeared it with almond butter and took it into the shower. No time to waste! I turned the water as hot as it would go and got in (yes, as I was eating my sandwich). I didn't want to get out. Even the two seconds between turning the shower off and reaching for the towel were unbearably freezing. Too cold to moisturise my dried chapped skin, I wrapped up in two dressing gowns, pulled on woolly slippers, my feet still numb, and blasted the hairdryer on the hottest setting until my hair was almost singed.

Later, I stared blankly at the TV. I was so tired I couldn't even understand *Casualty*. Nothing was registering. The imagery of rainy hills and lethal lanes whirred around my mind's eye. Everything hurt. No matter how many layers I put on, I couldn't feel warm. No matter what I ate, I was immediately hungry. Before this day I did not know that it is physically possible to feel full and hungry at the same time. It took five days to regain full feeling in my fingers and toes.

What had I been thinking, going on such a ride in those conditions? Why couldn't I say no sometimes? In the back of my mind was my goal to become a decent triathlete and that meant going through the same pain with cycling as I had with running. But there was more to it than that. I was ever trying to prove that I could survive hardship. Last winter, when cross-countries felt comfortable, I took up triathlon. When long cycles with Dave got too easy, I broke away in search of a more aggressive group, which had an added challenge of penetrating a group of strangers. I can only think that it was through lack of challenges in other areas of my life or of the conventional life-grounders of people my age, like a husband or kids or a managerial work responsibility, that made me want to pedal through hail and ice for 70-plus miles. Maybe training and racing were just filling a gap?

But then, aren't we all just filling gaps all the time? Isn't that why most people start families at a certain age? Maybe that's why entrepreneurs continue to be driven even after they've made their fortune. Maybe that's why people just never stop rushing around, filling time with stuff that makes us feel like we are achieving.

Despite the state of me, I still glowed with satisfaction. I'd surpassed another distance today. Providing my clicking knee recovered, this surely had to make me a stronger cyclist. Surely it would get me closer to qualification level for World Champs?

CHAPTER 22

HELL BEGINS IN DERBYSHIRE

The Hell of the Ashdown put paid to me attempting to cycle with the triathlon club again for a while. But as winter drew to a long-awaited end, as the traumatic memory faded and I got braver, I started to make enquiries into other triathlon club rides. I was relieved to discover that the club rides weren't just made up of speedy guys after all. The girls had their own cycle group, which seemed tamer and friendlier. So one Saturday I joined a few of them for an 80-kilometre ride out to Essex.

I concentrated hard to keep up and to my delight I found I could – just! It pushed me just the fractional amount required for improvement. When I got home and looked at our speed (which I still recorded using a running watch), I was surprised to find it was several miles per hour faster than when I rode with Dave. Yet I always felt I was going as fast as I could with Dave.

There was only one explanation: I can incentivise myself so much more when I'm trying to avoid the social shame of being left behind. That is how I started running and it is still my most effective training tool. To properly train, I need someone to impress.

Strangely though, I found that I missed Dave when I rode with my new buddies. I missed his familiarity, the fact we always conferred on the route and stopped often to adjust clothing, have a drink or swap figs and apricots. On larger club rides, there was no stopping. If you needed to take off a layer you learned to do it on the move. I missed getting into a warm car after we stopped and, most of all, I missed our ritual of a country pub with lunch and cider afterwards.

In May we did our last and toughest ride together. It was the Tour of the Peaks. The name still makes me tremble. One hundred and twelve miles around the Peak District. In case you've never been to the Peak District, imagine a giant roller coaster. Now replace the tracks with roads. Then picture miles and miles and miles of bleak, brown land where nothing grows. Add dark clouds to the background, a ferocious wind – always headlong, never a tailwind – and there you have the Peak District. We cycled in this for no less than nine hours.

Our journey through hell began in the picturesque village of Bakewell in Derbyshire, from where we headed immediately uphill.

'Please can we take this very easy?' I requested, as Dave pedalled purposefully ahead.

I was happy to let all the fancy carbon bikes go past – we had 112 miles to get through. Not forgetting that my very average road bike would be significantly heavier than any of these hyperactive MAMILS (Middle-Aged Men In Lycra) careering past us on designer carbon.

Out of the entire 112 miles, only five of them were flat. That part was a valley. The rest can be summed up by hyperventilating up an endless spiralling vertiginous mountain, headlong into a 20-miles-per-hour wind, and then descending perilously steep roads, around hairpin bends with butt cheeks clenched, teeth gritted and hands clinging to the brake levers in pure terror. And repeat. And repeat. For nine hours. If hell were a place on earth, this ride would be the road into it.

The inevitable puncture happened right at the top of a peak, as we were the most exposed to the wind as we possibly could be. It took 15 minutes to fix and just as we got the last bit of the tyre around the rim of the wheel, we heard the sound that every cyclist dreads – hissing air. I had accidentally caught the inner tube in the rim of the tyre and pinched it. I, or rather we, had to start all over again.

If we were near the back before, the double puncture sent us to the very back. When we got to feed station number two, the officials were clearing up and all that was left were sweets. I'd eaten everything I was carrying and could feel one of my old dizzy spells coming on. I had radically underestimated my fuelling needs. This was probably quadruple the effort of a typical long ride – twice the distance and three times the ascent. A few crusts littered on paper plates revealed that there had been sandwiches.

'Do you have any bread left?' I asked.

A marshal disappeared to a van and came back with a bag of stale, white, cotton-wool-like bread rolls. 'These are a bit old,' he said. 'But if you're desperate…'

269

We gobbled two each and stuffed another two in our pockets. We must have looked like we were off to feed ducks. Then I had a black coffee. I shot up the next hill, standing in my saddle the whole way, breathing noisily and leaving Dave far behind. 'You're strong!' he exclaimed when he got to the top, but I knew it was purely down to a carb and caffeine rush. I'd come crashing back down soon.

At 62 miles (100 kilometres), I rode alongside Dave. 'Do you want the good news or the bad news?' I chirped. 'The good news is that we've just completed what normally constitutes a Sunday ride. The bad news is that we have the same to go again.'

'No way,' retorted Dave sternly. His tone told me he wasn't feeling as humorous as me. 'There is no way I can do that again.'

We'd been going for more than six hours and I was inclined to agree.

Twenty miles later, which took almost three hours because of the severity of the climbs, we came to the penultimate feed station. It was also out of food except for a few mushy bananas.

'I'm afraid I've got to advise you to stop,' said a purposeful marshal with a strong Yorkshire accent. 'You can continue but it will be at your own risk. We can no longer offer race vehicle support.'

We had missed the cut-off point hours ago.

Dave took less than a millisecond to respond: 'Can we get a lift back with you then?' He didn't even contemplate conferring with me. I would have at least liked to assess options – perhaps we could have carried on for a little way but cut it short by taking a more direct route to the finish? But Dave was on homing instinct. He was already wheeling his bike to the 'sweeper van' – a bus towing a trailer of bike racks to transport the failed riders home.

I didn't say a word. Many times when we'd cycled in treacherous weather or been exhausted, Dave had gone along with my diehard determination to max out every ride. But this time he was not to be reckoned with.

We crammed on to the bus with five burly men, their faces as white as sheets. As soon as I sat down, I realised what a good idea it was to stop. I'd been so focused on getting through the ordeal I had blocked out how cold, achy, hungry and dizzy I was. The sweeper van drove the remainder of the route, bike trailer in tow, looking for defeated riders to pluck off the moors.

Our first casualty appeared 2 miles after we set off. He was sitting on the grass verge in front of a stone wall, sheltering from the wind, hugging himself. He was clearly delirious. There was nothing wrong with his bike. He had simply succumbed to exhaustion. He had tried to carry on until he quite literally fell over. He was helped on to the bus and he slumped on the back seat, mumbling incoherent nonsense for the next 20 minutes while we fed him Jelly Babies.

We picked up another man who had pulled a calf muscle and could no longer carry on. He had been waiting patiently for a support vehicle for nearly an hour.

'Look at this!' exclaimed Dave, pointing out of the window as we drove up a monster of a hill. 'There is no way we could have finished this. No way!'

And a dulcet symphony of 'no ways' echoed across the minibus in agreement.

By the time we got back to the event base, I was shivering and so dizzy I couldn't focus. But we had to get back on our bikes and cycle back to our hotel. It was only 2 miles but we could manage no more than 5 miles per hour. My dizziness was so intense it took every bit of concentration to follow Dave through the cycle paths back to the village. I've never fainted in my life but this was probably the closest I've ever been.

I needed three days' rest after the Tour of the Peaks but that event proved to be the single biggest transformational contribution to my fitness so far. When I emerged after three days of sitting down a lot, the change in my fitness blew me away. I joined the Thursday 10-mile run and felt so strong and fresh, I could have run and run. It had (only!) taken me a year and a half but I was finally learning the importance of rest and recovery for fitness.

That event may sound torturous, but with every event so far the post-race exhilaration outweighed the hardship. Extreme pursuits had become a quest. Finding new ones was so much part of my life now that I couldn't contemplate not doing them. I wanted to maintain all that strength, fitness and mental diligence I had acquired. It was still partly a way to fill a weekend with something sociable. But the greater drive stemmed from something more visceral – an instinct to use my body, feel exertion and assure myself that even though I live in a cosy, westernised society where it's tempting to spend all our free time sitting around in decorous surroundings enjoying the finer things in life, I could do more if I wanted. It felt, and still feels, like I had to keep this side of me alive.

The following bank holiday weekend, I did the Tour of Wessex – a whole three days of cycling with London Fields Triathlon Club – and I could not believe the difference in my power. The famous sportive covers 220 miles over three days, and that's just the short option. In the weeks leading up to it, I had yet another inferiority complex that I would be the least experienced, and the slowest. At one point it looked like it might be just me and nine super-speedy alpha males, so I was most relieved when three girls signed up too. I could not have wished for a nicer group of triathletes to spend my first club weekend away with.

Once more, I found myself in another stunning part of Britain I had never seen and, once more, was struck with gratitude for discovering this new sideline to my life. Wessex includes the four counties of Dorset, Somerset, Hampshire and Wiltshire, two of which I had not visited before. Each of the three days took in a different route from the same start point. The Cheddar Gorge featured on day one, Britain's biggest gorge (I had to look that up – it's a valley between rocks), with dramatic views of limestone cliffs and caves.

I had done many big organised sportives with Dave but since I was always holding us back, or we set off late, I did not often get to ride with the main pack and this one felt festive in comparison. We hung around at feed stations to chat and take pictures. Mercifully, the girls seemed as unconcerned about clocking a good time as I was. We never went more than a mile without encountering another group.

Riding with three more experienced girls, I learned even more cycling etiquette. I considered myself an advanced-level student now. Beyond the yells of 'clear' and 'left!', there were still some mystery gestures I hadn't yet found anyone to ask about. These girls taught me that a hand twisting behind a rider's back, for example, means they are veering out into the road (to avoid a parked car or something) but not actually turning. And, I noticed, everyone wore caps under their helmets. I don't know why exactly, but it seemed to be the done thing. I bought one at one of the stands and immediately felt fit for the part.

It was a total delight during those three days to discover I was stronger and more energised than I'd ever been on a bike. The previous weekend's epic feat through the peaks of Derbyshire, Yorkshire and Cheshire seemed to have changed my physiology. The hundreds of winter miles suddenly seemed to come to fruition that weekend. It must have been the combination of the extreme stress of that moors ride, followed by rest. Whatever it was, I will always remember the Tour of the Peaks as my coming of age as a cyclist and the preceding winter's stormy rides as my indestructible foundation.

CHAPTER 23

THE DAMBUSTER

Over the spring months, with cross-country season over, I spent less time with running club and more time with triathlon club. The greater variety of events appealed to me more than simply running. I adopted the same yes-woman attitude to weekend fixtures as I had in the early days of joining the Harriers.

Many of the races I did with them first were small, local aquathlons, duathlons and sprint-distance triathlons. This was the beginning of my second season of triathlon and I felt 10 times more confident than last year.

In June there was one race I earmarked for myself, without the club. It was an Olympic-distance qualifier for the Age-group World Championships. This was what I had quietly set my heart on late last year. I didn't realistically expect to qualify so early on in my triathlon journey. I entered because I wanted to see where I lay in the field – or, I should say, to see how much work I had to do.

I might have transformed my triathlon skills over the previous year, but I still had not improved my organisational skills when it came to race logistics. I entered my fourth triathlon yet again without checking how I could get there on race morning. One thing triathlons have in common is that they start early. It is usually so that lakes and rivers can resume their normal business of sailing boats once the crazy cold-water swimmers have done their thing. This is highly discriminatory to those of us who don't own cars, if you ask me.

Ben and Julian, who seemed to do all the same races as me, had also entered. But neither could fit a second bike in their car. So I would have to hire a car and get up at 3.30 a.m. to drive to Leicestershire ready for a 6 a.m. registration.

To add to my complications, I also had a hire bike. My gears had developed a problem for some reason. It could be fixed, but not in time for the Dambuster Triathlon. So the shop loaned me one, which I was supposed to pick up at exactly the same time as picking up the hire car at the opposite end of London the afternoon before the race.

Everything about this mission smacked of impending disaster. As I coordinated hire cars and hire bikes and prepared porridge in portable Tupperware, I considered ditching the whole thing. *Why*, I thought, *am I hiring a car on my own, getting up before dawn, driving 200 miles, using a borrowed bike which I haven't even tested, for a World Championship qualifying race in which I have not got a hope in hell of qualifying?* I felt the familiar pang of disappointment that I was going on another adventure alone.

The forecast was cold. The lake was going to be freezing. If I didn't do it, no one would even care.

Yet I found myself going through the motions on the Friday afternoon – picking up a bike and a car, printing out directions, laying out my kit, reading the race info.

'Which model did you order?' asked the receptionist in the hire car company.

'One where the rear seats go forward' was my response. I could name all the makes of cars I knew on one hand. I just needed one that fits a bike in the boot.

I hadn't driven a car for almost four years. In the time since I last started an ignition, modern cars appeared to have implemented a safety feature which requires you to depress the clutch and the brake simultaneously before the ignition will start. I did not know this and I soon marched back into the office insisting the engine wouldn't start.

To add to my complications, once I got the car home ready for my morning escapade, I had plans to go out that evening.

Poignantly timed, one of the two friends who had moved abroad and played a part in spurring this whole lifestyle change in the first place was back for a visit. We met in a restaurant in the West End and tucked into good food and water. This was far removed to how we used to spend our nights, which would start with a bottle of wine before we'd even ordered food. But this suited both of us. She too had lots to do that weekend on her flying visit. She too had become 'more sensible', she told me, and had found new friends who did more wholesome things than drink and party. Both of us had evolved. I noticed how natural it now felt to tuck into juicy conversation without an alcoholic lubricant. I no longer felt I had to justify not drinking and I no longer felt chatting was any less intimate or fun without.

I found I didn't talk about my new sporty antics that much. Our conversation featured exactly the same mutual favourites as we had always talked about – men, careers, family, friendships, how we're feeling generally about life. Despite everything I'd been through, the things which connected me to my closest friends were the same as ever.

Drink or no drink, I still did not fall sleep easily. I was still awake at midnight, knowing my alarm would sound in just a few hours. As I lay awake, I thought that if I didn't fall asleep I couldn't possibly go to the race. More excuses. Why was I so nervous? Was it because it was a qualifying race? Or was it because I didn't want to face the disappointment of going to another race alone?

The next thing I knew, my alarm went off, so I must have got some sleep. That meant no excuses.

Three hours later, I was queuing for registration in a chilly tent near the banks of Rutland Water in Leicestershire.

I bumped into Mark, our instructor from Les Stables in France. He seemed surprised to see me. When he met me over a year ago, I couldn't clip and unclip cycling cleats into pedals, I got signs of early hypothermia after my first open-water swim and he teased me for wearing sparkly gold flip-flops down to the riverbank. But now here I was at six in the morning, having driven from London on my own to take part in one of the most competitive races in the country – a World Champs qualifier.

Twenty minutes before start time, I had my signature pre-race drama. This time my faux pas was that I hadn't put the stickers on my bike. At registration, competitors are handed an envelope containing a timing chip, race number and two stickers with your race number for your helmet and for your bike. I had put my timing chip around my ankle but left the envelope with the stickers in the car, which was a significant distance away. My bike and helmet were already racked in transition. The race briefing was already under way. *Skip that.* I sprinted to the car for my stickers and pleaded my way back into transition because it was now closed. Again, I arrived at the start line to my fourth Olympic-distance triathlon with 3 minutes to go, flustered, but well warmed up.

I've done enough races now to spot that it is nerves which make me so hare-brained. At most races there is an hour between registration and starting. Other than racking your bike, helmet and shoes in transition, there really isn't much else to do. But I find a million things to do. I need to stretch; I need to go to the loo; I need to put on wetsuit lube (for chafing), apply sun cream, warm up; I decide I need to have one last banana and drink a coffee.

But despite my fluster, despite my sleepless night, despite the fact I was on my period, despite the fact that I nearly chose not to come at all, I was on flying form that day.

The water was fresh but I was prepared. The previous weekend I had dragged myself out of bed to join the early open-water swim at the West Reservoir so that my body could curtail the shock of the cold today. The previous week I'd had breathing trouble again when I first got in. But today my body was ready for it. I relaxed and slowed down. I breathed every two strokes instead of three, to get more air, and within minutes I got into a smooth, effortless rhythm. Whenever I got close to a pair of feet, I drafted off them, letting go of all fear of being kicked. I focused hard on gaining as many seconds as I could. I glanced at my watch when I got out. The time started with a 25. I'd never done 1,500 metres in less than 26 minutes.

Transition was not so slick. I couldn't get my helmet off my bike handlebars because my hands were too cold to undo the clip. I lost at least 20 seconds while I rubbed my hands back to life.

Then it was on to the hire bike. I hadn't even had time to test it since picking it up from the shop yesterday so a surprise was in store. This baby was a couple of kilos lighter than my own bike and its gear system was a grade up. Those small changes were metamorphic.

I actually overtook people, something I never did on the bike leg in triathlon. I kept looking at my speed on my watch in delight. 28 kph. 33 kph. 35 kph. Every pedal seemed to propel me twice as far as my own bike. *I'm going to burn out*, I thought. *I can't possibly keep going this fast the whole way.* But I didn't burn out. I even overtook men on fancy time-trial bikes with their thick-rimmed wheels for wind resistance.

My hands and feet still didn't warm up from the cold water though. I went into the run with numb feet, a disorientating sensation if you've never experienced it because you don't know how hard you're pounding the ground.

I ran solidly, pushing myself just the right amount to ensure I used everything I had without burning out before the 10 kilometres was up. One by one, I overtook people. The run at the end of a triathlon is the real test of fitness. The body's aerobic energy system will be drained by then so it's all down to how well trained you are for endurance. Time and time again,

I find that the people who whizz past me on fancy, expensive, time-trial bikes will later be plodding and panting on the run. Gliding past them on two legs feels like justice. Running is one of the fairest sports because it has nothing at all to do with accessories and everything to do with your own engine.

I was stunned at how strong I felt on this run. I kept a constant pace of just over 7-minute miles, which brought me in at 43.5 minutes. Only one female overtook me, though of course there were many more ahead of me. To this day, I've never run a 10k at the end of a triathlon so fast.

When I inputted my number into a computer at the end I learned that I finished eighth in my age category. My first reaction was disappointment. I had felt so strong and had been so impressed with my pace in all three disciplines. Surely I should have come higher?

Then I saw Ben and when I told him my time and position he was ecstatic.

'Eighth is brilliant at a race like this!' he enthused. 'You've almost certainly qualified with that time.'

Qualification places for World Championship races automatically go to the top four in each age category. But if any of those four have not registered their intent to qualify it will pass to the next placed athlete, providing that they finished within 110 per cent of the winner's time. In other words, if four people ahead of me had not applied to qualify, I was in.

I went from disappointment to immense pride. Cheerful now, I hung around chatting to Ben, his wife Michelle and their friends.

'The bike course was really fast and flat, wasn't it?' I said.

There was a brief silence and a few looks of disbelief.

'That was *not* flat,' said Ben.

I tried to picture the course. I suppose it wasn't. It must have been the hire bike. A better bike model had made it feel flat compared to what a slog everything felt like on my usual bike. I was starting to build a good case for an expensive new purchase.

I wouldn't know that day if I had qualified. Organisers have to check times and compare them to the names of those who have registered intent to qualify.

We stayed to watch the later waves finish and soon after I put on my hoodie over my damp tri-suit and got into the hire car, eager to get home for a hot shower and sleep. I had become accustomed to putting all personal hygiene standards on hold after triathlons. No matter how fussy you are (and I am), there is no choice but to sit out the homeward journey covered in a mix of live bacteria from whichever lake you have swum in, sweat, trickles of sticky energy gels, residue of pee from the inevitable reaction inside your wetsuit when you get into cold water and any bladder leakages from running at maximum effort at the end of a two-hour race with no loo breaks. Plus – no apologies to squeamish men, because the following is an unavoidable fact of female life – period leakage. Which brings me to mention that no one has yet invented anything to accommodate for the female triathlete at this time of the month. There is no tampon in the world that can survive swimming in a lake for 25 minutes and race organisers don't usually put toilets on the course for Olympic-distance races, only for longer courses. Women have no choice but to ignore it and put up with the mess.

I was already imagining my shower and what I'd eat when I got home, when I saw the car behind flash their lights. I hadn't got a clue what they wanted and continued on. Two minutes later, another car did the same. The driver pulled up beside me at a junction and wound her window down. 'Your rear tyre is flat as a pancake,' she said, and drove off.

The irony! All the prayers I'd said about not getting a puncture on my bike and now it was the car wheel I had to worry about. No matter how nifty my inner-tube-changing skills had become, I doubted they'd apply here.

I pulled over, called the emergency number on the paperwork that I had (luckily) remembered to bring, waited 45 minutes for an answer and another hour for roadside rescue to arrive – during which time I had to pee in someone's garden because there was absolutely nowhere else to go. The high from my race performance negated any frustration. I took it all in my stride and waited patiently.

I was not the most attractive damsel in distress – in a hoodie and a tri-suit with period stains, with hair matted and stuck to my head, stinking of sweat, eyes puffy with goggle marks.

Another 20 minutes and it was fixed but they only had the resources to fit a small, temporary wheel, with a 50-mile-per-hour speed limit, so that added another hour to my journey. By the time I got back to London, the hire car branch had closed and I had nowhere to return the car to.

What followed was a comedy of errors which turned my World Champs qualification attempt into a grand expense. There is no metered parking where I live. Even on Sundays. I called Europcar to see if I could drop my ill-fated vehicle off at a different branch with later opening hours. But I could not get through. I tried Twitter. I tried publicly appealing to them on Facebook. I posted a photo of where it was illegally parked but no one would respond. So I left it where it was and went to bed.

Next morning, parking ticket. I called the company telling them I would return the car a day late because I got a flat, only to be told I wasn't allowed to drive it because my insurance would have expired the previous day. The only way I could get into the driver's seat legally was to pay for another 24 hours' hire. Not only that, but I had to pay to replace the flat tyre too. What should have been £45 to hire a car for a day turned into £350. But amazingly I was still in a good mood – because I'd just had the race of my life.

CHAPTER 24

LIVING LIKE AN ATHLETE

Days later, I got the text: *Congratulations – you qualified!*

It wasn't an official text. It was from Ben, who had seen the list of athletes online. I hadn't looked because I hadn't imagined I'd qualified. I was with colleagues at the time and so it wasn't appropriate to share it, but I felt like I would explode with excitement. I could think of nothing else.

The 2015 Age-Group World Championships would take place in September in Chicago. That was only three months away. Despite the high, I also felt some reluctance. This had been a super-goal and I had achieved it far sooner than I expected. When I'd fantasised about this, I'd imagined that if I did qualify for the highest level of competition for amateur triathletes, it would be a year from now at least. I'd thought I would have a better bike by then, would be earning more money by then and perhaps could invest in a coach. Often the more distant our dreams, the more elaborate we make them. When they surprise us by suddenly coming true, the high expectations can be daunting.

I considered not going and trying to qualify the following year, when I would be more experienced and could perfect my training. But that went against everything about my approach so far. I had faced every sporting conquest to date with fearless enthusiasm. Why should this be any different? What was the point of all those soggy, winter miles on the bike and those frigid open-water swims at seven in the morning if I didn't seize the results?

So I resolved that the next three months would be dedicated to World Championships prep. World Championships! Those two words seemed incongruous to my non-sporty heritage. I had never associated myself with athletic prowess. There was not enough time to effect any dramatic changes in my performance so I did the only thing I knew had worked before: train as hard as I possibly could within the time and physical restraints available.

This was stage two of my experiment to see what my body was capable of. I resolved to do everything I could to optimise it, like not drink alcohol, consume the right foods and supplements, get proper sleep, get sports massages, apply consistency to my training and resting instead of randomly joining in whatever sessions or races maximised my social life with run club and triathlon club.

There was no one who I could confer with on a training plan. Both the running club and triathlon club have great, informative, group sessions designed for improving speed and skills but when it comes to specific race training it's down to the individual. Even when I did ask coaches or club members for suggestions, I found that they didn't quite get the magnitude of my devotion to the cause. I was ready to push things to the max. I had the time and dedication to train twice a day – no club coach had a plan up their sleeve to fit with that. To think that in 18 months I'd gone from wincing at running through a puddle on a cross-country course to a maverick who wouldn't get on a bike for less than 100 kilometres.

So, I made up my own training plan. It had no input from experts but it did fit with the bits I'd picked up from triathlon magazines and books. Thus my weekly training quota consisted of: long bike ride (100–120 kilometres); short, stationary bike session of speed intervals; long open-water swim (2–3 kilometres); short pool swim of speed intervals; long easy run (around 10 miles); short tempo run (4–6 miles) or the hill-running session; track-running session of speed intervals; gym session.

That was the menu anyway. I rarely fitted it all in but it gave me a quota and therefore an aim. Each of these sessions was classified in my head as speed (short and fast intervals) or endurance (long and slow). I could mix it up accordingly and make sure I was getting an equal combo of both types of training.

My work, imaginably, suffered more. Dreaming of how I would perform at World Champs was a form of escapism from career worries. When I did sit down at my desk and apply myself, I didn't seem to reap any rewards. Training gave me unfailing results and no end of stimulation. I threw myself into my experiment with reckless abandon. I was reconciled with this summer being an exercise in living like an elite athlete.

It wasn't just about training. I got my swimming stroke and my running gait analysed – there was no time to change my technique to have any noticeable effect but it was all part of the experimental appeal. I had blood tests to identify vitamin

287

and hormone deficiencies and thyroid functions. I took a VO_2 max test to establish accurate heart rate zones. Not that I knew much about how to utilise the data to maximum effect, but I knew that training at 'threshold heart rate' makes you able to withstand high efforts for longer so it was bound to help somehow, I thought. Finding out new things about my body, inside and out, was part of the exciting journey.

Shortly after the Dambuster, I returned to Les Stables in France with a similar group to the previous year. Dave was there too. We were still good friends but because our cycles had come to an end, we only really saw each other at the club now, amid the hustle and bustle of group gatherings. It was great returning to France with much of the old crowd. Instead of the nervous newcomer smuggling in a hairdryer, this time I was the zealot suggesting extra bike rides and extra swims. I even went into the river without a wetsuit a few times to prepare for the possibility of a non-wetsuit swim in Chicago.

Under triathlon rules, if the water is above 22°C wetsuits are not allowed. A wetsuit gives you extra buoyancy and therefore is an advantage, so practising open-water swimming without one occasionally is a good idea in case this is the race situation. We weren't supposed to go swimming in the river alone, but I couldn't always find someone who wasn't flat out with exhaustion to join me, so some afternoons I sneaked down to the river for 30 minutes for a quick 1,500 metres, much to the chagrin of the conservative members of the group.

We repeated the breakfast swim, which the previous year had floored me. It was significantly warmer this visit but even so the experience was entirely different from the previous year. While most of the group walked back to base from the cafe after the swim, Ben, Julian and I swam back, against the current, and I killed myself to beat them.

I joined the fast group on the cycles – not by accident this time. I was in a faster bike group than Dave, which put my improvement in perspective. One afternoon, after a 10-mile run in the morning, I persuaded Julian to squeeze in a 70k ride. He was the one who had to wait for me time and time again in the Surrey Hills a year earlier when I did my first 100k ride. Now I cycled at his side leisurely.

Some friends became concerned I was doing too much. Chris, who I jokingly referred to as my 'running nemesis' because our PBs in every main distance were exactly the same, warned me kindly that I might 'burn out'. But I was not to be deterred. I knew my body better than anyone. When I was tired, I rested.

As race date loomed, there was GB team kit to buy, flights to book, hotels to investigate, other athletes to make contact with. And there was a bike upgrade to do.

The mucky-green Trek Lexa had to go. With his heavy aluminium frame and scant number of gears (compared to more sophisticated models), he had trained me well. He'd taken me through storms and near-Arctic expeditions, but for a world-class competition, loyalty alone wasn't enough. I needed something better than a £500 bike.

I spent the good part of a month trying out magnificent machines I longed to afford, usually in daytime hours instead of doing any work. The one I fell in love with most was a Bianchi, not least because of its snazzy blue-and-black colour scheme. This Italian make is a designer brand in the bike world, with a cult following and several Bianchi owner cycle clubs.

After diligent research, hard work and a bit of fortuity, three weeks before I was due to leave for Chicago, Bianchi agreed to lend me a bike because I was taking part in a World Championship race. I got my very own Bianchi Oltre XR2, who I fell in love with immediately and named Bluey, because of his celeste blue colour.

Riding Bluey felt like a different sport. The week after I took him home, I dared for the first time to go cycling with the speedy boys' group from my triathlon club, who I'd never dared ride with before. I managed to nearly keep up.

My three months of living like an athlete felt carefree as far as work was concerned but there was a downside. I found that a stricter training regime ruled out impromptu social rides or low-key fun events. My running club, for instance, hosted relay races in the park one Thursday for fun, and, another week, a 5k 'mob match' with a rival running club. But because I was sticking to my quota of different speed and endurance sessions, I couldn't take part.

I cancelled some of my other race plans too. I had a half-ironman distance planned in August and a 100-mile cycle in September in my home town while visiting my mum. But these longer events would counter my training. The race in Chicago was an Olympic-distance event, which requires both speed and endurance. Too much endurance takes away speed and vice versa. It was ironic that something I started as a means to be more sociable had now got to such a level that it was becoming an insular experience.

CHAPTER 25

WORLD CHAMPS

It was the afternoon before flying to Chicago in September 2015. I was plonked on the floor of my balcony, Allen key in hand, bike upside down, bubble wrap flapping around, laptop beside me blasting out a YouTube clip explaining how to disassemble and pack a bike into a bike box. I had been here for some time.

For thirty quid the local bike shop would have done it for me, but there was extra gratification in doing it myself. This could well be the worst idea I have ever had. Once I started there was no going back. The moment I took the first pedal off (which took the best part of an hour), the option of cycling it to the shop was off the menu.

The bike box was borrowed from tri club. The pedal spanner was new. The bubble wrap was rescued from recycling bins. The YouTube clip featured a dashing, young, sculpted, American college kid with gleaming white teeth effortlessly removing pedals, wheels and saddles in an orderly workshop, with all the right tools appearing magically by his side when he needed them. My reality was very different.

Three hours in, when I'd finally removed the relevant parts, I had the task of arranging the frame, handlebars, seat post and wheels into the half-octagon-shaped box in such a way that the lid would close. I was covered in oil and surrounded by screws, none of which I knew belonged to which hole. Most cyclists would draw up a detailed diagram of their bike before taking it apart, measuring the angles and heights of all the adjustable parts so that they could put it back together at the other end in exactly the same way. I've never been much of an artist so I drew a stick diagram of a bike on the back of a ripped envelope with an arrow pointing to the seat post and its height.

The rest of my packing, however, was easier than for any other trip I've ever been on. So proud was I of my GB kit that I took no other clothes. I would wear my GB tracksuit with *GBR Croydon* embroidered on the back everywhere, other than during the race itself.

I wore it to travel in, imagining walking tall through Heathrow airport like an Olympian. But this image was soon dashed when I had to wheel the bike box on public transport. Wheels on bike boxes don't go around corners. Walking with it requires a continuous zigzagging of straight lines. I had to stop every five steps to lift the front end of the box and re-angle it in the direction of travel. I couldn't help thinking that the ordeal was a bit like playing pool. I would aim the bike box in what I thought was a dead straight line along a corridor or Tube platform, only to find that my aim led me straight into a wall after five steps.

The flight was full of GB team athletes in the same tracksuit as me. But none, I noticed, were travelling alone. Most were with partners or companions who looked like club friends. I sat next to a man on the plane competing in the 50–55 age category – he was with his wife. From the airport to the hotel I shared a cab with a girl in my age category – she was with her boyfriend as her supporter.

That evening it was the race briefing and once I'd wrestled the bike box to my room, I tagged along with a girl I spotted in a GB T-shirt for the short walk along South Michigan Avenue to the official team hotel. She was not only with her boyfriend, but two friends too. Friends and a boyfriend who had all presumably used up holiday allowance and paid for flights to be here to support her.

This should have been an evening of excitement. I had arrived in the bright lights of America's third largest city for the race of my life. But every time I spoke with someone I couldn't help feeling deflated. I felt shut out, although I didn't entirely know from what.

When we arrived at the GB team hotel for the briefing, I spotted Ben and his wife Michelle near the back row. The sight of two familiar faces was heartening. They had arrived two days earlier. I sat down beside them and we chatted and compared hotel notes. So far mine did not look like it was harbouring much international team spirit, despite me picking accommodation where I knew plenty of other GB athletes were staying.

There were more than 300 British age-group triathletes in that room that evening, competing in either the sprint- or Olympic-distance triathlons or the aquathlon. As usual, I eagerly listened out for plans for drinks in the hotel bar after the briefing. But there were none. None that were officially open to all anyway. I watched from afar as people headed to the bar in their private groups, or in couples. Ben and Michelle were for early nights as the next day was Ben's race – the sprint distance. I still had three days to acclimatise before mine. So I walked back alone to my hotel, where I fell asleep immediately, only to be wide awake at four in the morning with jet lag.

The next morning my pensive mood gave way to excitement again as I joined Michelle to cheer on Ben in his big race. It was a scorcher of a day. We wore GB T-shirts and rushed between different parts of the course to catch Ben as many times as we could, waving Union Jacks furiously at every athlete we saw in GB kit. My heart fluttered when I watched competitors getting into Lake Michigan for the swim start. *This will be me in two days' time…*

Afterwards we had lunch in the sunshine and I listened to Ben as he shared some useful race insights. The run out of the water to the bike racks is uphill so go easy. The run between the bike racks and the mount line is long so consider clipping shoes to pedals in advance and running barefoot instead of in cleats. The run course is long (a few hundred metres longer than the official 10 kilometres) so pace accordingly. I took it all in, but in reality I knew that when it came to race strategy, I wouldn't get too technical. I'd use my inner pacing mechanism to go as fast as I could possibly sustain over roughly two and a half hours.

Ben and Michelle invited me to join them for dinner most nights and I was grateful of the company and the chance to get to know them more, but I was aware of intruding on what was a holiday for them. I had envisaged a party atmosphere among the GB athletes and it left me disappointed that there wasn't one. There was no shortage of friendly GB team faces and they were easy to spot in the blue and red uniform, but I never managed to penetrate any groups beyond a few minutes of small talk about race prep. A niggling feeling of loneliness lingered at the back of my mind, which I didn't want to face because I wanted to concentrate on my race.

My feelings surprised me. I've always loved and protected my independence. I have always viewed being single as a choice, not a consequence. In fact, I've mostly fought to stay single, eschewing the constraints of a long-term relationship for the liberty of being able to do what I want, when I want. Yet, quite unexpectedly, here in Chicago, it hit me how much of a minority I am in with my chosen status.

At any other club event or trip, there's always a buzzy crowd and it is irrelevant if the people I'm with are single or not or whether they turned up on their own because people are there to mix with others. It's all about light-hearted companionship. The atmosphere is a random collection of personalities and it doesn't matter if you have special friends in it or are on the periphery. I had not considered that World Championships would be any different. But this was more serious. World Championships was clearly considered poignant enough to include one's nearest and dearest; too important to rely on cursory club mates for support.

That unsettling thought was creeping in again. Over the last two years I had avidly filled my weekends with every club holiday, group bike ride or race going. I'd joined not just one sports club but two. But it had occurred to me several times that these activities were a temporary reprieve. Perhaps that's one of the reasons I had to do more and more of it. Maybe I had spent too much effort chasing fun group dynamics at the expense of intimate friendships? Perhaps this is why I had never fully resolved those feelings of emptiness from two years ago.

The afternoon before my race, I set off for a gentle bike ride along a cycle path on the shore of Lake Michigan with three others from my hotel. Three others whose names I now can't even recall, which was telling perhaps of these unfolding home truths.

Goodness knows what my fellow competitors thought of me. Almost immediately after setting off, my handlebars started to slide downwards and I found my upper half going lower and lower. I had attempted to put my bike together myself in my hotel room. One of the others was carrying an Allen key and tightened it as best he could, and when we finished our ride I immediately went to find the GB team mechanic, who fixed the handlebars and told me my back wheel and my pedals were also loose.

The night before race-day, we racked our bikes and left our bits in transition. I was surprised at the strict rules. We were only allowed to leave the essentials: run shoes, bike shoes, helmet, sunglasses and race number. So no sun cream even if I'd wanted to use it! No towels either because these are seen as an aid to help you recognise your bike. One of the lesser-known skills of triathlon is being able to remember where your bike is among the long line of bike racks when you're dizzy and disorientated after a cold-water swim, and a bright red towel, for instance, can help you do that. In every other race I'd done, transition would be littered with towels, bananas, energy gels, talc and arm-warmers. Not here.

Because the racking was done the night before, there was even more time for flappable nerves to take hold on the morning of the race. For the fifteenth time, I checked I had everything before setting off in good time along South Michigan Avenue towards Millennium Park by the lakefront, where the race would start at midday. I had ages before then.

I stopped in Starbucks for my habitual pre-race coffee. Caffeine is a performance enhancer so I always have one if it's a race I care about but avoid it before training so that I don't get too reliant on it – that way I maximise its effects before a race. I even asked for an extra shot for my normal double shot, ignoring that old adage 'never try anything different on race-day'. As I stood in line, in my skimpy tri-suit, wetsuit over my arm, I attracted the attention of a fellow competitor in Team New Zealand kit.

'What time is your wave?' he asked.

We chatted for a while and as I was about to leave he pointed to my ankle. 'You have got your timing chip, right?'

I felt my heart somersault, my face go white and the extra shot of caffeine send blood surging through my veins. 'Oh. Fuck!'

I downed the rest of the triple-shot coconut-milk skinny cappuccino and sprinted – in my tri-suit and flip-flops, wetsuit clutched under my arm, goggles around my neck banging me on the chin – back to my hotel.

If that person, whoever and wherever they may be now, had not had the foresight to look at my ankle, I am certain I would have done the entire World Championships with no timing chip, thereby automatically disqualifying myself.

Before reaching the start, I had to go via the bag-drop to leave my flip-flops and any other necessities I could not race with, like phone, hotel key and non-racing sunglasses. The bag-drop was a good half a mile from the start and the pavements were scorching. Caffeine and adrenaline were still firing through my veins and suddenly I got very, very angry.

Hadn't race officials thought about people who have no friends, partners or family with whom to leave shoes at the race start? I had to walk on a blisteringly hot pavement in bare feet for half a damn mile, squinting into the dazzling sunshine because no one had considered that the singletons, here alone, might need somewhere to leave their stuff near the start line.

I was incensed. Nerves, adrenaline and repressed melancholy from the last three days erupted into a fireball of anger. I've been similarly frustrated at races or cycle events in the UK when organisers don't include instructions as to how to get to the venue by train. It irritates me that they assume everyone has a car, or a person to take them in a car. What about those who have neither? I thought about this now too, an irrational rage of victimhood flaring through my veins.

I reached the start pen on the verge of tears. One by one the different age categories set off in 5-minute intervals. Supporters wished their loved ones good luck, took photos for Facebook and took their flip-flops from them.

Here I was, at the culmination of months of preparation and excitement and happy daydreams, and yet I felt irrationally angry. Of course, the real reason I felt angry was not because some race planner hadn't thought of people's feet getting burned. It was rooted in the more sombre soul-searching of the last few days.

It is hardly surprising then that I hyperventilated again on the swim. Someone swam over me in the scramble at the start and I emerged from the water, panting, coughing and bewildered. I could not regulate my breathing no matter how much I tried to be calm. Today it felt worse than it had ever been.

I tried the breathing-on-every-stroke trick. But I couldn't even do that. Breaststroke was all I could manage. *World Champs and I'm breaststroking!* This desperate, chastising inner dialogue just made me panic all the more.

People glided past me and my soul sank. All those tedious speed intervals in the pool. All those weekends getting up at 6 a.m. to cycle to the reservoir. All destroyed by a few nerves and too much caffeine.

I can't remember how or when my breathing returned to normal but eventually I could swim again. I tried to make up ground, urgently passing any swimmer in my way. As I approached a buoy to round a corner, there was someone on my left. I surged ahead of them, determined to pip one more, to feel less bad about the time I'd lost. That proved to be a mistake because after I rounded the buoy, I veered off in the wrong direction. In the distance I heard a whistle. I didn't register it for a while and then I heard it again and looked up. I had turned too much. There was another buoy to go around.

Had I been gracious and let the other swimmer go around the buoy first, I would have followed them and not gone wrong. I had to swim back, adding another 30 seconds.

Was there any point in even trying now? It felt like I had lost so much time. *Why do I always make mistakes like this? Why don't I pay attention in the race briefing? Why don't I look at maps? Because I'm always late for race starts!*

But I snapped myself out of such negative talk. The rest of the swim was a straight line to the other end of the bay. All I had to do was go straight and fast. My goggles had fogged but I ignored that. There was such a dense stream of swimmers that it was easy to see where I should be heading. I didn't need to sight any buoys.

I stumbled getting out of the water and the uphill run to transition felt intense. Breathing is always more difficult after a cold-water swim so the short run felt like an all-out sprint.

One thing I had done well was plan my transition. For the first time ever I had actually walked the path from the swim to the bike, and the bike to the mount line, and had mentally run through my movements: put on sunglasses, helmet, bike shoes, in that order. It was the quickest transition I'd ever done so, if nothing else, at least I would go home with an expensive lesson in managing transition.

I came alive on the bike. My doubts, panic and anger had dissipated and I was in race mode. The route, three laps on closed roads, weaved through a maze of underground tunnels and flyovers. I felt like I was steering through a computer game. I usually find the bike to be the most tedious part of a triathlon but I was not bored for a minute of this.

It was my first race on Bluey and I felt exhilarated by his easy speed. I wasn't anywhere near as out of breath as I used to be on my old bike. Not to mention how much slicker I felt on my new racing machine. At the end of the bike course, I tried to slip my feet out of my cycling shoes while still on the bike so I could run barefoot instead of in my cleats to transition, but I could only get one foot out so I hobbled the 400 metres with one shoe on and one shoe off.

Then it was on to the most painful part – the run. For whatever reason, I could not reach the speed I was aiming for. My goal was to run the 10 kilometres at a pace of 7-minute miles. But I couldn't hit it. It was hot. I was tired – jetlag maybe? Whatever the physiological reason, I pushed to the very edge of my limits but I was slower than previous performances. The human body is unpredictable like that.

By my third and final lap I was gasping for air, but the crowds spurred me on. 'Come on, GB! Come on, Croydon!' they cried, picking up on my surname printed above my bum.

Random people cheering for me, cheering for their country. It was touching to hear. Cheering for one's own is an integral part of humanity. In almost every culture a sense of shared nationality brings people together and in times of shrinking communities and autonomous lifestyles, I always find it heartening.

I panted loudly through the final 100 metres along a blue carpet in front of a grandstand full of spectators. It was the set-up of a world-class elite event – there was music, a computerised time screen over the finish line, a commentator announcing the names of finishers as they came in. I heard mine vaguely.

I went over the finish line in a time of 2'23" and almost collapsed.

A marshal said, 'Well done', and someone threw a medal over me.

'Where's the water?' I gasped. I had no breath for pleases or thank yous and no composure to smile.

There are usually marshals thrusting bottles of water in your hand at a finish line but I couldn't see any. I drink very little in races because you have to slow to swallow, but today was especially hot. All my focus now turned to quenching a raging thirst.

I found the water stash just beyond the finish line, by a photo stage. The stage had a blue board as a backdrop with the Chicago World Championship logo and the names and flags of all the countries in it.

Athletes from different nations queued up with their medals for that all-important finish-line picture with a professional photographer. A group from the Mexican team went up together. Then one from Canada. Then some Germans. The queue went down as groups of four, five and six stepped up together, posing against the backdrop, puckering biceps, lifting each other up, laughing and posturing for the camera.

Then it was my turn.

I got up on the stand and that's when it hit me.

I held it together enough to smile for the camera – a fake smile, hiding the tears welling up behind my sunglasses. I walked away with my head down. I made my way past the hoards of triumphant triathletes hugging each other, sharing moments of the race. I was out of the enclosed finish area now and into the public meeting place. I squeezed my way through the crowds, desperate to get away while I could still hold it together. I looked around, just in case, but there was no one I recognised. I'd just done the race of my life and there was no one here to say 'well done'.

I just about managed to pick up my bag. I dared not speak to the baggage attendant for fear of my voice breaking. Then I rounded a corner into a public garden and the tears came. I sat on the grass and let myself cry and cry.

I had willed that finish line to appear but now I wished it hadn't because now it was all over. Not just the race but my journey. My project. My goal. My running Facebook commentary about GB tracksuits and packing Bluey in a box and wheeling him around airports!

The finish line marked the culmination of everything I'd pushed myself through, not just over the last 2 hours 23 minutes, but over the last two years. All the aching legs; the cold, dark evenings cycling to run club when everyone was a stranger; the times I'd reluctantly headed out to training on icy, wet, dark nights; the never-ending cycle rides in atrocious weather; the dreaded track sessions; the Saturday hill sessions, which left everyone on their hands and knees with exhaustion; all the effort to mix with new groups in the hope of finding intimate friendships. I'd maintained stalwart faith that it was all worth it. It was all leading me somewhere. And it was. It had led me here. A blue-carpet finish line with TV cameras and *GBR Croydon* above my bum. But there was nothing lasting about this experience.

It felt good to cry. I made no attempt to stop. I was exhausted. Dehydrated. Disappointed with my swim. Disappointed with my run. Disappointed that such a promising experience ended up making me so sad.

I rummaged for my phone. If there were a text or a Facebook message from someone to ask how it went, or a 'good luck' from a few hours ago, it might have made everything OK. But there was nothing. There had of course been lots of public good luck messages on my Facebook posts. Many, many friends and acquaintances had wished me well on there. But it was the lack of any personalised missive which struck a chord. It highlighted the lack of intimacy in my life.

I called my sister – £2 a minute from America but that was the least of my worries. She listened to my sorry tale of all the other athletes being with their families and told me what a great achievement it was to be here. And then told me to make sure I enjoy the after-party and have a few beers. My six-year-old nephew took the phone at one point and, hearing his aunty upset, told me he loved me, which just made me cry more.

When I had calmed down and my overheated body had cooled, I walked my jelly-like legs to pick up my bike from transition. There was a long, snaking queue because of tight security checks. It looked like this line could easily be three hours. I recognised some guys near the front from my flight. We had talked in the airport so I walked straight over to them, jumping the queue brazenly. I couldn't face standing alone and waiting for three hours right then.

They let me push in and we talked about the race. 'That bike course was a bit windy,' said one.

'The run was long,' said another. He wasn't speaking metaphorically – what he meant was that the course was slightly above the official 10k, which means competitors' run times could be a couple of minutes above their typical 10k time. He wasn't complaining about it but some athletes get very upset about 'long run courses' because results go online and they assume that others look and make judgements about performance. A bit obsessive, if you ask me.

'I missed out a buoy in the swim and had to go back,' I said, hoping someone else may have done the same, and therefore make me feel better.

'Losing thirty seconds in the swim won't make much difference,' offered one of them.

It was probably insignificant small talk to them but in that moment it was a saviour to me. Three near-strangers sharing an experience made me feel connected again. Being with people then made the whole trip feel worthwhile again.

But it was temporary relief. I was aware that it was this sort of shallow connection which I'd relied on continually over the last two years to give me some sort of fulfilment. When I first threw myself into running culture, busying every single weekend with races and trips, I'd been filling emptiness with chatter, hoping it would make my problems go away. That sort of social interaction definitely has a place. But we need deeper and personal relationships as well and, as this turn of events was showing me, I hadn't taken any time to rebuild those.

Later, when I returned to the hotel with my bike and kit from transition, I went through my normal post-race motions – protein shake, stretch, upload my times to Strava (Strava, in case you don't know, is a social media platform for running and cycling geeks). My mood was neutral; my emotions burned out. I stayed that way for the remaining two days of my Chicago trip.

I joined Ben and Michelle in the grandstand later that afternoon to watch the elite men's race and a cut-throat contest between Jonathan Brownlee and Javier Gómez, but I didn't take much of it in. On the final night the three of us attended the closing ceremony. I was really grateful to have familiar company and to talk about normal things as well as our races. I integrated cheerfully with as many other people at the party as I could, but I was subdued.

When I returned home from Chicago, I felt surprisingly upbeat. It was as if my emotional outburst had given me clarity. That end-of-race epiphany set off several weeks of honest reflection in which I came to understand what I'd really been craving over these last two years: intimacy and strong, lasting friendships. These things were far more important to me than I had realised. Just like in my pre-sporty life, I'd once more chased fun and activity, gracing the periphery of numerous social circles instead of trying to build meaningful connections with just a few.

I even admitted, for the first time ever, that it wasn't activity I was craving, but love and closeness. As a staunch, self-confessed commitment-phobe it was quite radical for me to admit, even if I did only verbalise it internally, that yes, I would like to have someone to share these wonderful experiences of cycling, running and swimming with.

The seed to this admission had been planted when I endured that lonely cycle to a train station after the Hever Castle Triathlon and had grown a little every time I found myself doing something alone. It now seemed quite simple: in my old life where my hobbies were basically drinking, buying shoes, dating and social butterflying, I didn't want to have a person to do it all with because those things weren't truly what I wanted to be doing. Being tied to someone else with those habits and values would mean I would do them more, when deep down I knew there was more to life than that. I was basically a healthy person trapped in a party person's body. To think that I went through all those pain barriers over two years just to realise that!

I decided, after returning from Chicago, that I would not do another competition on that level – not unless it was with a group of real friends or a special person with whom to enjoy the experience.

I did not start running (and then cycling and swimming) for medals or admiration. I fell in love with these activities because something about them sang to my inner craving for adventure. A sense of adventure that I had previously channelled into decadent but uninspiring thrills, glamorous but shallow accolades. I fell in love with this world because it was so refreshing to break away from the routine and convenience of urban living.

I'm not a bad athlete, but I'll never be a podium athlete. I don't have the genes for that. The thing that gives me pleasure is knowing that I've pushed my body to the limits of its capability. That isn't measured by race results. My most enriching transformations over the last two years have not been my race times, my VO_2 max or my lactate threshold. It has been the personal barriers I have overcome, the lessons, the people, the genuine conversations and my newfound durability.

The reason that my experience in Chicago was so disappointing was because I did it for the wrong goal. A flawless performance, a world ranking and a field of competitors who don't even allow themselves a beer over a three-day holiday is not what stimulates me about this lifestyle. It is the variety, the authenticity, the way it allows us to see through the artificial constraints of civilisation and connects us back to our primitive selves, even if it's just for a little while. Those are the things I love.

When I turned up at Victoria Park Harriers on my maroon shopping bike two years previously, I was looking for an easy answer to replacing lost friends. It was a fluke that I found something so much more enriching. It enlightened me to the joy of the outdoors and gave me confidence in what my body can do and what my mind can coax me through.

I'd imagined that starting a new hobby would be like walking into an episode of *Friends*. I had been chasing more social stimulation, more buddies, more activities to mask a void of meaningful relationships in my life. By filling my time with every event going, I had almost fallen into the same trap as I always had – relying on the bustle of group dynamics for my sense of social belonging. That's why that feeling of emptiness that had led me there in the first place was the very thing which I still felt at the end. Many of us fill our time with activities, spreading ourselves thinly and widely among vast social networks, chasing success, making ourselves feel important so we never have to confront our flaws. This is what I had done.

When we're young perhaps we get away with maintaining friendships on this basis because close bonds form so easily.

But I'd realised that when you get older you can't build them on a few beers in a clubhouse bar.

The reason no one was waiting for me at the finish line in Chicago was because I had never invited that level of closeness in. The reason I had never invited that in is because I had never been fully reconciled with the lifestyle I led and the person I was. Until now.

EPILOGUE
SEPTEMBER 2017

Two years after that World Championship race and I am still a race junkie. I still avidly fill my weekends with outdoorsy fitness stuff. The more challenging, the better. I am still a member of both the Victoria Park Harriers and London Fields Triathlon Club and have cemented strong friendships which I hope will last for years to come. I still get myself thoroughly freezing cold, dirty and dizzy with fatigue. But I'm probably not as fast, and certainly not as obsessive.

The joy I get from challenging myself, defying the elements and using my body to its full potential is no less. But I like to think I've restored the balance of my newfound pleasures with those of the past. Old friends are relieved to see that party Helen occasionally reappears. I still love five-hour cycles on a Saturday, but I also occasionally enjoy five hours of dancing with reckless abandon. That isn't to say I've gone back to my old ways. Those two years helped me discover a new side of life – not a new life. My experiences did not change who I am, but added dimensions to who I am. They have given me resilience, confidence, serenity and a lot more ideas for a day out.

When I had my meltdown at the end of my big race in Chicago it was the things that I'd neglected that summer which I felt the loss of: friends, fun, love, balance and beer! There are many ingredients to being happy, many facets of life to experience, many aspects of our personalities to express and many activities to enjoy. The fitness lifestyle and all that involves – cross-countries on rainy afternoons, cycling weekends staying in a hostel bunk bed, floodlit track sessions on freezing, wet nights – have become an integral part of who I am. But to reject all elements of my previous lifestyle would make life as one-dimensional as it had been before.

What a privilege it was to compete at international level. What a luxury it was to dedicate a summer to getting to know my body and its capabilities. What a freedom it was to downgrade priorities like work to train twice a day, sleep lots and spend all my money on sports massages, blood tests, DNA tests and supplements. But I am happy to leave it as a once-in-a-lifetime experiment.

In the year following that World Championship event I got even fitter, but not down to any focus or sacrifices. It was simply down to my old mantra of entering everything which looks like fun or which my club mates are doing when I happen to have nothing else to do on a weekend.

In the month of May I ran the Milton Keynes Marathon. Three weeks later I did a half-ironman-distance race with tri club mates. Two days later I flew to Mallorca on a club holiday for a week of intense cycling (and some swimming) in the mountains. From there I flew to Wales for the Gran Fondo Bianchi – 112 miles cycling over the rolling Brecon Beacons. I was invited as an honorary Bianchi owner – yes, I even got to keep Bluey! That August I did my most epic feat yet. A swim-run event in Norway consisting of 52 kilometres (30 miles) of running over cliffs and rocks and trails and 9 kilometres (6 miles) of swimming through fjords, lakes and cold seas. We swam in our trainers and ran in our wetsuits and carried all our kit. I couldn't walk for two days afterwards.

I had no A-races marked in my calendar. (Coaches recommend athletes label the races they care about as 'A-races' so they can taper. B- or C-races are to be treated as training.) But performance is not my driver any more, as it was not in the beginning of my journey either. That's why I don't use a training programme. I train because I want the permanent rewards. Burning energy and feeling my body come alive are visceral drives for me, like eating or sleeping.

Later that summer (the one after Chicago), Ben suggested a spontaneous plan to cycle to Paris the following week. I didn't need to give it thought. I didn't need to do extra training. My core level of fitness allowed me to shrug and say, 'Why not?' Four of us set off on the Thursday, arrived by Friday afternoon, had beers by the Champs-Élysées and got the Eurostar back that same evening. Then I slept all day Saturday, did an Olympic-distance triathlon on the Sunday and came fifth in my age group. Who knows, if I hadn't cycled to Paris maybe I would have come fourth? But then I wouldn't have cycled to Paris!

This epitomises what drives me to stay fit and able. I would like to always have the capacity to cycle to a new city at a moment's notice. I might not be at the front, but I'll finish. It isn't just the physical ability I relish but the mental grit too. In my former life, I would have needed to know where we would sleep, whether I'd get to wash my hair and what the deal was on carrying a change of clothes. Now I just say to myself, 'It's twenty-eight hours. I can deal with anything for twenty-eight hours.'

Sometimes club friends, seeing my zeal to push myself further and harder and in all weathers, say things like: 'Imagine how good you would be if you applied some science to your training.' But times and positions were not why I was drawn to running or triathlon in the first place. I did succumb to competitiveness when I qualified for that big Chicago race but an age-group world ranking didn't do it for me. I train so I can cycle, run and swim with different people, see new places, use my body and eat cake afterwards.

One of the things I value most about becoming an outdoor-sport enthusiast is the overall efficacy I've acquired. Three years ago, I reckon if I had been dropped from a helicopter in a remote place with no food or water (you just never know!) and had to find my way back to civilisation, I don't know if I would have survived. Now I know I would.

The resilience I've acquired through endurance sport is transferable to all areas of life. Put it this way: if you can talk yourself through a 5k swim in choppy waters with one contact lens and a red raw neck, having been punched and being unable to breathe, the most tedious of board meetings or the longest of train delays passes like a flash of lightning. I have become more patient because I've reprogrammed my mind to think that all unpleasantries eventually come to an end – it's just a case of counting fractions.

To date, every long aching run, every breathless interval session, every mind-numbingly repetitive pool length, every lung-lacerating hill session, every freezing soggy cycle in the pouring rain, every shivery train journey in wet clothes, every wait in a hire car for roadside recovery while covered in sweat, lake algae and period blood has eventually come to an end. All these scenarios have ended with me delivering myself safely home to a hot shower, food and a warm bed. No race has ever turned into an eternal inferno of hell. No coach or instructor has ever said I have to stay on the track or in the pool for evermore.

One of the most wonderful discoveries has been unearthing the capabilities of my body. Witnessing the miracle of our self-repairing engine of our bodies come to life when we use it. As the former skinny schoolgirl who was scoffed at because I was scared of catching the netball, who was always cold, totally clumsy, never picked for teams, every event I do is a triumph. I never believed I was tough or sporty. I saw myself as delicate and sensitive, and I focused on looking good indoors instead of outdoors.

I still don't believe it sometimes when I overtake a succession of people on the run at the end of a triathlon. I still feel like a gallant warrior when I get into a lake, river or sea and swim. I still feel cool when I fix a puncture on my own. I still get surprised by the reflection of my body because the defined muscles, broader shoulders and solid thighs are uncharacteristic of how I've always seen myself.

Philippe once said to me, 'When I first saw you I thought you would be weak. But you are not weak – you keep up.'

This stuck with me because it went right to the heart of my self-limiting beliefs. His comments proved that I could outdo others' expectations and my own. We all can.

Before I discovered all these new, rugged, outdoor endeavours, I wouldn't say I was unhappy but my life felt unexplored somehow. I had fun but it was one type of fun – drunken giggles or destructive indulgences. It was these limitations which caused a restless search for new things, new people, new stimulation while never actually finding anything or anyone different.

It was this limited lifestyle which made me unhappy in a relationship and in ones before that. Now I have found things I truly enjoy and which give me fulfilment. We can never be open to sharing our life if we are not happy with it ourselves.

That summer after Chicago, I did meet someone special. I have no doubt that this is because I opened myself up through sport to new possibilities and attitudes – and that means the prospect of sharing my self. When we met I was still absorbed in triathlon training. Even though I had eased off significantly since Chicago the previous year, it probably was still a dominant conversation topic. He, however, was going through a more hedonistic phase. His priorities and focus were friends to get him through a bad time after the breakdown of his marriage. Seeing the rewards he derived from nurturing close friendships and making time for fun made me miss those bits of my old life. He helped me reconnect with the things I'd neglected when I became so absorbed in my World Champs race. In turn I reawakened in him a former drive for outdoor activity and adventure, and soon he was trying to beat me at cycling and running.

I no longer feel a relationship is holding me back from discovering new things because I have discovered the things which make me feel alive. Likewise I have stopped being such a social butterfly and now spend more time and effort nurturing the friendships I value.

Finding love isn't the ultimate happy ending. It is just one of many rewards and awakenings since I opened myself up to new activities, new people and new values. Love can't be guaranteed to last for ever, nor can my fitness or physical health. But the life lessons from the last two years will. Every time I ventured out of my comfort zone, every time I visited a new place or environment, every time I got cold, every time I faced the world without my heels and lip gloss; every person who taught me something, let me ride with them, fixed my punctures for me, cheered me on, or was just there contributing to this previously unexplored world of outdoor adventure – all played a part in the things I learned and the person I grew to be.

ACKNOWLEDGEMENTS

My biggest thanks go to all the people who give the world of endurance sport its strong sense of community spirit.

I would never have had a positive story to tell – or any story to tell – if it weren't for the many volunteers who marshal races, coach running sessions, organise trips, load bikes onto vans, drive minibuses, welcome newcomers and wash up after club events. I've never come across a culture with more enthusiasm and positive energy than the one I continually find at the heart of recreational sports clubs.

Particular thanks go to my own clubs, Victoria Park Harriers and London Fields Triathlon Club, for the opportunities and hours and days of fun they've provided for me and all other members.

Individual thanks are owed to anyone who's fixed my punctures, lent me warm clothing, tools, bike lights, shoes, goggles and even wheels (once!). Also, to those who've given me lifts, slowed down for me on group bike rides, answered stupid questions and given heartfelt advice.

Appreciation goes to my non-sporty friends for cheering me on with my new lifestyle and entertaining my torrent of lycra-clad social-media posts from every single bike ride I ever did in my early enthusiastic days of cycling. To Tim for listening to me talk of nothing else in the last weeks of writing.

There is only one person I've ever shown early drafts of writing to. Suki Bains has read the first chapters of all three of my titles and she's the only one I trust to give honest and valuable feedback, so thank you for that and I hope your job isn't done yet.

Huge thanks to my editor Debbie Chapman at Summersdale for her energy, enthusiasm and insightfulness. Having a memoir edited is a little like therapy because someone tells you when you're dwelling on the meaningless too much or when you've glossed over something quite telling. Thanks also to the rest of the Summersdale team for their support and to Madeleine Stevens for her role in the later edit phase.

And finally thanks to my family. At last, I have written a book about a wholesome subject of which they can be proud. My first book, a dating memoir, must have been a hard one to pass off as a proud parent or sibling. So thank you for always being supportive of a colourful media career, no matter where it's taken me.

YOUR PACE OR MINE?

What Running Taught Me About Life, Laughter and Coming Last

Lisa Jackson

ISBN: 978-1-84953-827-5
Paperback
£9.99

Reading Lisa's entertaining book will encourage even more people to join the ever-growing running community. I promise you won't regret it.

Nell McAndrew, marathon runner

Your Pace Or Mine? *proves that you don't have to be fast to find running fun.*

Jo Pavey, four-time Olympian

Lisa Jackson is a surprising cheerleader for the joys of running. Formerly a committed fitness-phobe, she became a marathon runner at 31, and ran her first ultramarathon aged 41. And she's not afraid to finish last.

But this isn't just Lisa's story, it's also that of the extraordinary people she's met along the way – tutu-clad fun-runners, octogenarians, 250-mile ultrarunners – whose tales of loss and laughter will inspire you. This book is for anyone who longs to experience the sense of connection and achievement that running has to offer, whether you're a nervous novice or a seasoned marathoner dreaming of doing an ultra, and proves that running isn't about the time you do, but the time you have!

Have you enjoyed this book?

If so, why not write a review on your favourite website?
If you're interested in finding out more about our books, find
us on Facebook at **Summersdale Publishers** and follow us on
Twitter at **@Summersdale**.

Thanks very much for buying this Summersdale book.

www.summersdale.com